Wakefield Press

SOUTHWORDS

T0358162

SOUTHWORDS

Essays on South Australian Writing

edited by Philip Butterss

Wakefield Press

Publication of this book was assisted by the
Commonwealth Government through the
Australia Council, its arts funding and advisory body.

 Promotion of this book was assisted by the
South Australian government through the
Department for the Arts and Cultural Development.

Wakefield Press
Box 2266
Kent Town
South Australia 5071

First published 1995

Illustrated and designed by Kerry Argent, Adelaide
Typeset by Clinton Ellicott, Adelaide
Printed and bound by Hyde Park Press, Adelaide

National Library of Australia
Cataloguing-in-publication entry
Southwords: essays on South Australian writing.
ISBN 1 86254 354 2.
1. Australian literature – South Australia – History and
criticism. I. Butterss, Philip.

A820.999423

CONTENTS

EDITOR'S NOTE

I would like to thank all the contributors for their enthusiasm and patience in putting this collection together. In particular I would like to thank Mandy Dyson for research assistance; Cally Guerin for editorial assistance; Michael Bollen and Wakefield Press for support and suggestions; and Jane Copeland, Bruce Bennett, Shirley Bowbridge, and the librarians at the Barr Smith, Mitchell and Mortlock libraries for their help.

PREFACE

Philip Butterss

As global media networks make increasing inroads into our lives, the boundaries between nations – not to mention states within nations – are rapidly being broken down. Why, then, at a time when spiralling numbers of Australians are opening their homes and offices to the rest of the world via the internet and pay television, this collection of essays on South Australian writing? The trend towards globalisation is itself, in part, responsible for continuing assertions of the importance of the regional and the local. Literary criticism has devoted increasing attention to the question of regionalism in Australian literature over the past decade. In fact Hal Porter, a writer who spent a few years in South Australia, suggested that 'most writers in Australia are regional writers. The place is so big. No one can encompass all of it' (Kinross-Smith 326). Similarly, Bruce Bennett has argued that it is important to reconceive Australian writing to give proper acknowledgment to the diverse experiences depicted in that writing:

> A common assumption has existed in Australia that a 'Sydney or the bush' division best describes our physical and cultural inheritance. Those of us who live neither in Sydney nor in the bush know that this is a distortion of the real physical differences between places in Australia and imposes a false uniformity upon an actually quite various and imaginatively diverse nation. My contention . . . is that the study of actual places and regions, writers' relations with them, and depictions of them, should be inserted into our national consciousness to correct these over-simplifications. (16–17)

It is now possible to say that the Sydney/bush opposition has been well and truly dismantled, but there remains a considerable focus on the east coast in the various ways that 'Australian literature' is constructed.

Overlapping with this focus on regionalism is postmodernism's interest in the local, as a counterpoint to the forces of globalisation. One area touched by this debate is the Australian film industry. Those, such as Liz Jacka, who would argue for an increased emphasis on the local in Australian film, suggest that the problem is not necessarily that American media are swamping Australian products. Jacka points out that 'the local is suppressed almost as much in American culture as it is in Australian . . . the local is recognisable as applying to a particular and specific set of circumstances and forces that operate at any given time and place, be they signs of place, accent and idiom, or more diffuse but no less vivid ways of hooking into the social unconscious or social "imaginary" of a particular subculture' (117). This collection of essays, then, arises partly from these related movements.

One of the questions frequently raised in discussions of regional literatures is that of distinctiveness – is it possible to identify any aspects of life in South Australia as distinctively South Australian? Some point to physical qualities – the light, the predominance of particular types of vegetation, the dryness, the prominence of certain styles of architecture or certain building materials. Certainly there are linguistic differences: terms such as 'fritz', 'yakka', 'trombone', 'stobie pole'; the use of the long 'a' in a few words by a wider range of socio-economic groups; perhaps even an Adelaide girls' private school accent. But these supposedly distinctive features are either open to dispute, or minor, or apply only to parts of South Australia or to particular groups within South Australia.

Some people point to historical factors supposedly peculiar to South Australia, such as the fact that no convicts were transported to the colony, or the emphasis on the fair treatment of the Aborigines in Governor Hindmarsh's proclamation speech, or the importance of dissenters among the early colonists. On the other hand, convicts and their descendants frequently moved here; one could not argue that Aboriginal people have been treated well in this state; and the relevance of the dissenting tradition to the lives of most contemporary South Australians is far from clear. There is a widespread view of South Australia as a centre of high culture – car registration plates identify this as 'The

Festival State', restaurants and cafés abound, and the South Australian Department for the Arts and Cultural Development fosters a wide range of creative activities, including local writing. But this is by no means the only state where café society flourishes, or where the arts are funded.

On a less celebratory note, Salman Rushdie is well-known for his suggestion that beneath the sleepy, conservative exterior of Adelaide is an Amityville of 'exorcisms, omens, shinings, poltergeists'. As Rushdie's essay on his experiences at the Adelaide Festival of Arts makes clear, this impression was as much an elegant summary of the views of some of the residents he met while here as his own considered assessment. Barbara Hanrahan is one who had previously explored the double-sided nature of the city in considerable detail in her fiction. In fact it was also a view of Adelaide held in the nineteenth century, and expressed, perhaps with more clichés, by Caroline Leane (writing as 'Agnes Neale'), whose *Sunbeams and Shadows* (1890) includes these lines:

> O Adelaide! we who gaze on thee,
>   Entranced at thy loveliness stand;
> O beautiful, beautiful city!
>   Fair pearl of our bright southern land.
> But when night in her dark cloak enfolds thee,
>   And the stars burn in glory on high,
> There cometh a moan from thy bosom
>   That quivereth up to the sky –

Yet in spite of this common enough assertion of Adelaide's unique flavour, the 'weird' is hardly part of the experience of most of its residents, and still less of most South Australians. As with all essentialising, any attempt to find what is distinctive in South Australia will necessarily ignore difference – ignore the variety in physical characteristics from the South East to the West Coast, the diverse cultures and subcultures that thrive here, and the variations *within* those cultures and subcultures, not to mention class difference and gender difference. On a personal level, we all feel the distinctiveness of place – South Australia will have a particular set of associations, experiences, memories for each of us. But there are an infinite number of possible South Australias.

If it is not possible to identify, with any certainty, characteristics that are uniquely or distinctively South Australian, is it possible to identify such features in 'South Australian writing'? Although there have been important periods when groups of local writers banded together around particular issues, personalities or venues – for example the Jindyworobak movement discussed by Robert Sellick or the Friendly Street poets discussed by Andrew Taylor – it is clear that there has not been anything approaching a school of South Australian writers, and it is not often possible to determine strong lines of influence between different South Australian writers. Those who have edited anthologies of South Australian writing agree that there does not seem to be a distinctive set of concerns running through the writing produced in the state. In the introduction to *Unsettled Areas* (1986), a collection of short fiction, Andrew Taylor suggests that writers in South Australia feel less isolated than some of their colleagues in other regions of Australia, and more comfortable with seeing their work alongside that produced in other parts of Australia.

Even if there are many South Australias, there is, to use Benedict Anderson's phrase, an 'imagined community' of South Australians. For a significant number of people who live in this state, being 'South Australian' – having horizontal bonds with other South Australians – is an important part of their personal and social identity. Examining the creative work produced by other 'South Australians', including writing not set in South Australia, may well contribute to those readers' sense of themselves, and understanding of themselves. The work of Barbara Hanrahan evokes a distinctive and profound vision of Adelaide, and for generations of younger and not so young readers Colin Thiele has provided vivid representations of lives lived in South Australian landscapes.

While this collection contains essays discussing a number of writers who deal directly with South Australian experiences in their work, there are also essays on writers whose chief concerns are not specific to this region, and whose work is set in far-flung places. A by-product of the focus on the regional and the local can be to accord a higher importance to writing that falls into those categories, and in Australian literary criticism there has at times been a tendency to value writing because of its preoccupation with place or, more generally, with identity. The essays in this book demonstrate that South Australian writing has much broader interests than merely the lived experiences of South Australians.

Another reason for the collection is that South Australian writing has received less than its fair share of literary criticism. There are, of course, some notable exceptions to this general tendency, and, in any case, it is only a question of degree. Nevertheless, it is probably true that South Australian writing has not achieved the visibility it deserves in the nation's literary culture. Part of this, of course, is for structural reasons – the size of the market for writing in South Australia is such that it has been difficult to publish critical work of book length solely devoted to writing by South Australians.

Just as South Australian writing has, to some extent, been margin-alised, there are two particular areas of marginalised literature – writing for children and crime fiction – where South Australia's contribution has been particularly significant, and essays dealing with these areas begin and end this collection. In the opening chapter, Barbara Wall examines the rich field of writing for children, from *Who Killed Cockatoo?*, published in the mid-1860s and probably the first Australian picture book for children, to the more recent work of writers such as Colin Thiele, Max Fatchen, Gillian Rubinstein, Eleanor Nilsson and Mem Fox.

South Australia has also been prominent as a producer of crime fiction, as Michael Tolley's essay, which concludes this volume, amply demonstrates. The essay surveys a body of crime fiction substantial enough to fill a lifetime of sleepless nights. Charlotte Jay's *Beat Not the Bones*, the first of only two Australian books to win the coveted Edgar Allan Poe Award from Mystery Writers of America for best crime novel, is examined in detail in David Smith's essay, where its 'haunting and often provocative interaction' with *Heart of Darkness* is elucidated. Smith argues that *Beat Not the Bones* rewrites a number of aspects of Conrad's novel (in a similar fashion to the reworking of Charlotte Brontë's *Jane Eyre* in Jean Rhys's *Wide Sargasso Sea*), and concludes that Jay's novel allows one of *Heart of Darkness*'s most intriguing characters a voice long denied her.

If the conventional view of nineteenth-century Australian literature is as a male-dominated field, four essays in this collection prove that such an opinion is based on a very selective reading of the writing produced during that period. My chapter on Fidelia Hill, the first woman and first South Australian to publish a volume of verse, describes the life and work of a determined woman and an able poet. Susan Magarey discusses the several careers of Catherine Helen Spence, the best-known of South Australia's early novelists. Spence has been seen as 'the founder of a genre of realist fiction in Australia', as the originator of 'a feminine (though not feminist) tradition', and as inaugurating 'the line of middle-class novels of society developed later by Rosa Praed, "Tasma", Henry Handel Richardson and Norman Lindsay'. Both Spence and her younger friend, Catherine Martin – whose novel, *An Australian Girl* (1890), is discussed by Margaret Allen – dealt with a broader range of social, political and intellectual questions than much of the writing produced by men during this period. *An Australian Girl* opens with a wonderful description of a hot December day in Adelaide in the late nineteenth century, and moves on to provide a detailed sketch of colonial South Australian society, and to address deep philosophical, religious and moral issues.

The fourth of the nineteenth-century women writers examined in detail in this book is Ellen Liston. In his essay Rick Hosking examines Liston's short story, 'Doctor', recognisably a precursor to stories such as Henry Lawson's 'The Drover's Wife' and Barbara Baynton's 'The Chosen Vessel'. Hosking draws on impressive historical research to argue that this confronting tale of violence between European colonists and Aborigines in the 'contact zone' has close links with the Elliston massacre of 1848.

Where 'Doctor', in effect, offers a justification of European violence towards Aborigines, the subjects of two other essays – David Unaipon and the Jindyworobaks – represent a desire, problematic though that may be, that Aboriginal and European culture might live together in a more constructive way. In her essay Sue Hosking shows how David Unaipon, long claimed as the first Aboriginal writer to publish fiction in Australia, often attempts to reconcile Western belief systems with Aboriginal belief systems. The Jindyworobaks's interest in reconciliation is apparent in the name Rex Ingamells chose for the movement – he glossed 'jindyworobak' as 'an aboriginal word meaning "to annex, to join"'. Robert Sellick shows that, although often misguided, the search of the Jindyworobaks for an 'Aboriginality' can be seen as a forerunner to potentially more fruitful attempts at reconciliation.

As well as having a distinguished writing history, South Australia has a rich contemporary literary scene, and four essays in this collection examine the more recent directions taken by writers with a close connection to this state. Andrew Taylor's chapter on recent South Australian poetry charts the past decade and a half of poetry, showing the strength and diversity of poetic output, and particularly the energy associated with the Friendly Street readings, regular events since 1975. Barbara Hanrahan, whose recent death prematurely ended the career of an extraordinary writer and artist, is the subject of Kerryn Goldsworthy's chapter, which sets out the complex ways that Adelaide shaped Hanrahan herself, and is in turn shaped in her fiction. Lyn Jacobs surveys the work of Nicholas Jose, whose fiction is set in South Australia and in other locations around the world, and whose concerns range through the personal, the historic, and the political. And finally Brian Matthews, himself a creative writer of considerable note, offers a particularly creative essay that moves between the private life and the fiction and poetry of Peter Goldsworthy, probably South Australia's best-known contemporary writer.

In a collection such as this one there are inevitably many omissions. It has not been possible to examine popular figures from earlier periods such as Adam Lindsay Gordon, C.J. Dennis and John Shaw Neilson. In his essay on recent South Australian poetry, Andrew Taylor does not mention his own very substantial contribution to poetry in this state during the last couple of decades, and the other extremely deserving novelists, poets, short fiction writers, not to mention playwrights, whom it has been impossible to include are legion.

Nevertheless I hope that *Southwords* helps fill a gap in Australian literary criticism by giving credit to those authors whose work may not have received the attention it deserved because of the region in which or about which they happened to be writing. I also hope that the collection acknowledges the diversity of past and present South Australian writing, and helps to have that diversity valued as part of Australian literature as a whole. I hope that it allows South Australian readers to learn more about their fellows and themselves. And I hope that it allows all readers to learn more of the too-little explored cultural history of South Australia.

WORKS CITED

Anderson, Benedict. *Imagined Communities: Reflections on the Origin and Spread of Nationalism*. London: Verso, 1983.

Bennett, Bruce. *An Australian Compass: Essays on Place and Direction in Australian Literature*. South Fremantle: Fremantle Arts, 1991.

Jacka, Elizabeth. 'Australian Cinema: An Anachronism in the 1980s?' in Graeme Turner, ed., *Nation, Culture, Text*. London: Routledge, 1993.

Kinross-Smith, Graeme. *Australia's Writers*. West Melbourne, Vic.: Nelson, 1980.

Neale, Agnes [Caroline Agnes Leane]. *Sunbeams and Shadows*. Adelaide: Burden & Bonython, 1890.

Rushdie, Salman. 'At the Adelaide Festival', in his *Imaginary Homelands: Essays and Criticism 1981–1991*. London: Granta, 1991.

Taylor, Andrew, ed. *Unsettled Areas: Recent Short Fiction*. Netley, SA: Wakefield, 1986.

CHAPTER

1

A LANDSCAPE OF WRITING FOR CHILDREN

Barbara Wall

Who Killed Cockatoo?
I, said the Mawpawk,
With my tomahawk:
I killed Cockatoo.

With these words W.A. Cawthorne, schoolteacher, artist and businessman, began *Who Killed Cockatoo?*, which was probably the first Australian picture book for children – although not the first illustrated Australian children's book – and certainly the first landmark in what has proved to be the considerable contribution made by South Australian writers to the world of children's literature. The old 'Cock Robin' nursery rhyme translated well into the new landscape, with Cawthorne taking the opportunity to celebrate native birds and animals. These are shown witnessing the murder of Cockatoo, assembling for his funeral and plotting revenge on the mawpawk. Cawthorne was illustrator as well, and his little book – nineteen pages – has sixteen delicate and lovely engravings of the birds and animals of the story as well as enclosed decorative borders around each page. *Cockatoo* is remarkable not only for its attractive appearance but also for having – unlike most children's books of the time – no moral intentions whatsoever. It is in fact much more savage than the rhyme on which it is based.

O wicked Mawpawk!
We'll have you caught,
For the deed you have done;
We'll slyly creep
When you're fast asleep,
And break your bones ev'ry one.

'Yes Yes', said the Hawk
And the bird that can talk
'We'll strike off his head'.
'Ah, Ah', said the Owl,
'By fish, flesh and fowl,
'We'll bang! shoot him dead'.

Who Killed Cockatoo? was first published in Adelaide about 1865.[1] It was reproduced in facsimile, not very satisfactorily, by Casuarina Press in 1978. A new edition in 1988 with brilliant, if rather inappropriate, illustrations by Rodney McRae shows that the text still has life.

Cockatoo was not the first South Australian book written for children. In 1852 James Bonwick's *Bible Stories for Young Australians*, probably the first book of bible stories for children, was brought out in Adelaide. A second edition appeared in Melbourne in 1857. Bonwick's intention was to introduce his 'Dear Young Friends' to the Bible. He selected some of the 'pretty stories' from the Old Testament and concluded each episode with instructions to his readers to adore God and to do their duty in the world. In spite of its educational significance – Bonwick later published many educational textbooks in other states and over-seas – this little book, with its short dull prosy tales, has not withstood the test of time.

More interesting is J.R. Lockeyear's *Old Bunyip, the Australian River Monster*, which was published in Melbourne in 1871. This is in many ways a typical nineteenth-century moral tale for children. Good little

Mary Somerville meets a strange creature who talks of punishing the wicked and of the evils of drink. The creature, however, is a bunyip – a huge monster like an elephant, with fins like a whale. This is probably the first bunyip to appear in a printed story for children, and so deserves special mention. There is a distinctly Australian touch in the tale Mr Bunyip tells about the barrel of brandy which fell off a paddle-steamer and led to his becoming drunk and beating his wife, to say nothing of its effect on the fish: 'I have not tasted a drop of anything stronger than water from that day to this.' Mr Bunyip speaks in a cheerful, colloquial tone and never condescends to the girl who listens to his history. Though the story itself is slight, the tone is ahead of its time. Lockeyear is probably responsible for the fact that in Australian stories for white children, bunyips tend to be friendly creatures with a tendency to make jokes. Charles Barrett's study, *The Bunyip* (1946), makes it clear that for Aboriginal people the bunyip was always an object of fear. Lockeyear's book was successful enough to be reprinted in its first year under the title '*Mr Bunyip*' or *Mary Somerville's Ramble*, and again in 1891 and 1894.

Another step forward in Australian writing for children came with John Howard Clark's *Bertie and the Bullfrogs, An Australian Story for Big and Little Children*, which formed part of the Adelaide *Observer*'s Christmas supplement in 1873 and was privately printed in 1874. Though few children would have had access to the book, *Bertie* must have reached a wide audience in its newspaper form. It is modelled on *Alice's Adventures in Wonderland* (1865) and was dedicated to Lewis Carroll, Esq. Bertie's Alice-like adventures take place in an Australian landscape, and the tale is full of puns and other wordplay. Clark, unlike many English imitators of *Alice*, appreciated that Carroll was interested in fun and nonsense that appealed to all ages, and not at all in moral instruction. It is this aspect which gives Clark's work its significance in the history of Australian children's literature.

The 1890s saw the publication of a number of important South Australian books. Unlike the thin books published locally that have already been mentioned, these managed to find English publishers, perhaps because they were full-length stories and more nearly fitted established expectations. Elphinstone Davenport Cleland's *The White*

Kangaroo, a Tale of Colonial Life Founded on Fact (1890) is a holiday adventure story which, with its outback setting (a station in the north of South Australia), its encounters with Aborigines and its 'lost in the bush' episode, had something to offer British as well as Australian readers. In spite of these clichés the story is an entertaining one, and the two lads, Ralph and Ernest, are ordinary fun-loving boys who become lost partly through their own understandable mistakes. Cleland gives a detailed and believable picture of station life – he had lived in the area, and a muff made from the skin of the white kangaroo is still in existence – and this helps *The White Kangaroo* to stand out from the general run of adventure stories.

The second half of the nineteenth century was the period of what is often known as 'family reading'. Books with children as characters published originally for adults were frequently seen as suitable for parents to give to their children to read. When there were very few stories with local settings, a book like Maud Jeanne Franc's *Marian, or The Light of Some-One's Home* (1859), which is set in Mount Barker, Adelaide, and 'the bay', Glenelg, and deals with the introduction of a young immigrant governess to farm life, was seen as suitable for children, especially as it had a strong evangelical Christian theme. All fourteen of Franc's novels – the last, *The Master of Ralston*, being published in 1886 – were much read by young people.[2]

Other examples of 'family reading' can be found in the work of M. Ella Chaffey and Evelyn Goode. In publishing Chaffey's *The Youngsters of Murray Home* in 1896, Ward, Lock, a London firm with an office in Melbourne, no doubt hoped to repeat the success it had had with its first Australian children's book, Ethel Turner's *Seven Little Australians*. Unfortunately, *The Youngsters of Murray Home* lacks the sparkle of *Seven Little Australians*, and the narrator has some difficulty in finding the right tone. Sometimes the story is addressed specifically to children – 'Shall I tell you about some of these pretty things?' – but more often it is, as stated in the dedication, a 'story of child-life' rather than a story for children. Nevertheless it is an attractive account of a bunch of children living ordinary lives with supportive parents. The setting, a property near Renmark, is realistic and convincing, and the picture of family activities there is clearly written from experience. Evelyn Goode's two novels, *Days that Speak: A Story of Australian Childlife* (1908) and *The Childhood of Helen* (1913) are, like the work of Franc and Chaffey, often listed as stories for children, but they too are more accounts of the interaction between adults and children than they are genuine children's books. However, the setting on a farm some distance from Adelaide and the details of the daily lives of three engaging children made them not unsuitable reading for children. The number of copies that can still be found in secondhand shops suggests that they were much read and much loved.

Fairy stories and folk tales in Victorian times were popularly supposed to provide suitable reading for children. But to some writers the stories traditionally told to British children seemed uncomfortably alien in our very different landscape. Charles Marson and F. Atha Westbury,[3] while resident in Adelaide, made valiant though hardly successful efforts to put fairies into Australian life. Marson's *Faery: Stories* (1891) transports trolls, dwarfs and brownies into a weird land and sea world of magpies, 'sheaoaks' and 'leathern jackets'. Westbury's *Australian Fairy Tales* (1897), several of which were first published in Adelaide's *Pictorial Australian* in 1885, is much more substantial, but his fairy worlds are equally unconvincing; his attempt to introduce an Australian flavour into trite routine stories of magic did not produce memorable work or solve the problem of peopling the Australian landscape with non-human characters which suited it.

This was done by a writer who understood that genuine folk tales are the product of hundreds of years of story-telling and who did not invent stories but endeavoured to record those of Australia's indigenous people. K. Langloh Parker's *Australian Legendary Tales* (1896) has proved to be South Australia's outstanding nineteenth-century landmark in writing for children. Catherine Field, known as Katie, was born near Victor Harbor in 1856. She spent much of her childhood on her father's property on the Darling but returned to Adelaide when she was sixteen. In 1879 she married Langloh Parker and went to live with him at Bangate, a station in a remote area of northern New South Wales. Here she lived for twenty years, getting to know, respect and love the Aboriginal people of the area, the Noongahburrah branch of the Euahlayi people. She realised that the tales the parents told to their children were well worth preserving and, believing that Aboriginal culture was doomed to disappear, set herself to record them. She did her best to make her retellings of these stories accurate, and it was this scrupulous attitude which gave her work its distinction then and makes it still important today:

> I can safely say that every idea in the legends in my books is the idea of a real black – I am very careful to get them as truly as I can. First I get an old, old Black to tell it in his own language (he probably has little English). I get a younger one to tell it back to him in his language; he corrects what is wrong, then I get the younger one to tell it to me in English. I write it down, read it, and tell it back again to the old fellow with the help of the medium, for though I have a fair grasp of their language, I would not, in a thing like this, trust to my knowledge entirely. (173, see also 150)

Australian Legendary Tales was published in England with an introduction by Andrew Lang, who was famous as a collector of folk and fairy tales for children. Lang's brother, a doctor in the Corowa area of New South Wales, was lucky enough to come upon a sketchbook of some remarkable drawings done with a pointed stick dipped in ink by a local Aborigine known as Tommy Macrae. Lang sent the sketchbook to his brother, who suggested using the drawings as illustrations to Katie's book. The fact that Macrae was the first Aboriginal illustrator of a children's book has added further distinction to *Australian Legendary Tales*. The brusque, bare, sinewy style in which these stories are told has meant that they have not dated. They are as important and as relevant today, both to children's literature and to anthropology, as they were when they first appeared.

A second volume, *More Australian Legendary Tales*, appeared in 1898. After Parker's death, Katie married Percy Randolph Stow, returned to Adelaide and settled at Glenelg. In 1930, under the name Catherine Stow, she published a third volume of legends, *Woggheeguy*. She died in 1940. I should point out that Katie Parker's work was not the first retelling of Aboriginal stories for white children. Western Australian Mary Fitzgerald's *King Bungaree's Pyalla* (1891) preceded it, but these are stories filtered through a European culture and embroidered with inappropriate literary language. They do not stand comparison with the authenticity of Parker's work. A selection of Parker's stories edited by Henrietta Drake-Brockman received the Children's Book of the Year Award in 1954.

The first half of the twentieth century proved to be a lean time for children's literature throughout the English-speaking world. Among works by South Australians, perhaps only C.J. Dennis's *A Book for Kids* (1921), a provocative mixture of prose, verse, fantasy and nonsense, with zany illustrations by the author, deserves special mention, although many other writers wrote and published. Dennis's book, as attractive to parents as to children, remained a favourite for years. It was reissued in 1935 as *Roundabout*. Worth noting, though scarcely of literary value, were Kathleen Mellor's illustrated stories for pre-school children, probably the first stories published in Australia specifically for this age group. Mellor was the first director of the Lady Gowrie Child Centre and the first pre-school adviser to the Kindergarten Union of South Australia. The series of a dozen or so stories began with *Gee Up Bonny* in 1945.

Although original works were undistinguished at this time, South Australians continued to contribute to children's literature and children's reading in other ways. Indeed South Australia had always been a leader in the field, and the contributions of institutions, bibliographers, reviewers and publishers have continued to be outstanding right up to the present day. In 1889, at a time when there were few books for children, and almost none by local writers, the South Australian Education Department started a monthly paper for school children called *The Children's Hour*, with the intention of 'encourag[ing] a taste for reading'. This paper, sold very cheaply, had far-reaching effects, and not only in South Australia, for the idea was copied in other states until 'ultimately children across the continent received a school paper' (Bonnin 9). In 1915 one of the first children's libraries in Australia was established in the Public Library of South Australia with the Unitarian Miss A.B. Whitham, BA, as Librarian. The magnificent Children's Literature Research Collection housed in the State Library of South Australia was begun in 1959 and, with its 53,000 volumes, is now the major such collection in Australia. It specialises in Australian children's books from before early settlement times to the present day, but contains much material from overseas, especially nineteenth-century British children's books. It also includes books in languages other than English. It is a priceless resource for researchers.

In the 1960s there was a world-wide increase in interest in children's literature. Rosemary Wighton was at the forefront of this movement in Australia. 1963 was an important year: it saw the publication of Wighton's *Early Australian Children's Literature*, the first serious study of nineteenth-century Australian books for children. It was part of Oxford University Press's *Australian Writers and Their Work* series, edited by another South Australian, Geoffrey Dutton. Though slight, it was pathbreaking in its understanding of the subject and its matter-of-fact acceptance that books for children are part of literature. In the same year the new periodical *Australian Book Review*, edited by Max Harris, Dutton and Wighton, began to publish challenging reviews of children's books and to issue annual children's book supplements that gave children's books a much higher profile than they had enjoyed before. Indeed, Rosemary Wighton and Dennis Hall initiated a new era in the reviewing of children's books. Hall took reviewing very seriously; he spelled out his criteria for criticising children's books, and his fiercely provocative reviews stimulated debate about standards in writing for children, and made many parents and teachers realise that children's literature needed careful consideration. Wighton's collection of Australian stories for children, *Kangaroo Tales*, was also published in 1963. It was the first such collection, containing extracts from a number of early Australian stories for children, and was the first Australian Puffin.

The 1970s saw the publication of Marcie Muir's monumental *Bibliography of Australian Children's Books*, the first volume in 1970 and the second in 1976. These two indispensable volumes laid the foundation for the serious study of children's literature in Australia. Muir's efforts did not cease with the *Bibliography*, although she had surely already accomplished enough for one lifetime. Two other pathbreaking books by Muir were *Australian Children's Book Illustrators* in 1977 and *A History of Australian Children's Book Illustration* in 1982. She also published in 1980 a small study, *Charlotte Barton*, which identified the author of *A Mother's Offering*, the first Australian children's book.

Who Killed Cockatoo? may have been Australia's first picture book, but it was certainly not the last. Two South Australian publishing teams have made important contributions to the explosion in picture books that began in the 1970s and has continued until the present day. Together with outstanding local artists and writers, they have produced some brilliant and extraordinarily successful picture books.

In 1980 Rodney and Sandra Martin of Era Publications issued their first picture book, Rodney Martin's *There's a Dinosaur in the Park*, illustrated by John Siow. It is still in print, and has sold some 100,000 copies. In 1984 they published *Arthur*, written by Amanda Graham and illustrated by Donna Gynell. This engaging tale of a pet shop dog who wanted so much to be sold, to have his own family and some slippers to chew, appeals to the need in all of us, adults and children, to be wanted and loved. It has had enormous success, here and internationally, having sold nearly 250,000 copies. Era, which specialises in educational books, has continued to publish fine picture books, including the two sequels to *Arthur*, *Educating Arthur* (1987) and *Always Arthur* (1989).

In 1981 Jane Covernton and Sue Williams, former employees of Rigby, joined forces to publish children's books under the imprint of Omnibus Books and had their first prize-winning success with *One Woolly Wombat* (1982), a quirky counting book featuring Australian animals and birds, written by Kerry Argent and Rod Trinca and illustrated by Argent. In 1983 Mem Fox's *Possum Magic*, illustrated by Julie Vivas (a Victorian, although born in Adelaide), began its record-breaking career, winning international acclaim, and achieving cult status. This entertaining story of a female child possum who has enjoyed the invisibility brought about by her grandma's magic, but now must travel Australia to find what will make her visible again (vegemite and lamingtons among other things!) has been Australia's most successful picture book, selling nearly 800,000 copies. Fox's understanding of the reading process and her desire to make her picture books stepping stones for beginning readers has given her stories extra depth. She has consciously tried to contribute to the emotional understanding and growth of children by linking the very old with the very young, as in *Wilfred Gordon McDonald Partridge* (1984), and by introducing ideas of death and loss. She has helped to give books for the very young a high profile in Australia. Omnibus has published many fine picture books and has had considerable success with books for older children, including Helen Frances's *The Devil's Stone* (1983) and Gillian Rubinstein's prize-winning *Space Demons* (1986). Omnibus is now part of the Scholastic Australia Group.

The story of Omnibus and Era highlights the present day interest in picture books, a phenomenon of the 1980s, but the fifty years since the second world war saw a world-wide flourishing of all kinds of children's books. In Australia many notable writers emerged, a number of them in South Australia. The best-known names are those of Colin Thiele, Max Fatchen, Christobel Mattingley, Gillian Rubinstein and Eleanor Nilsson, but there are many others who have written worthwhile books, and new names – notably Josephine Croser, Caroline Macdonald, Peter MacFarlane and Daryll McCann – continue to appear.

While it is interesting and important to record what early writers in South Australia contributed to the development of writing for children, present day writers, living in our global village, should not be seen parochially as South Australian writers, but as Australian writers and in some cases as writers who take their place internationally. What South Australian writers can do, which nobody else can, and for which they must be valued as South Australian writers, is to bring alive the world in which South Australian child readers live, by showing them the past which underlies their present lives, by teaching them to use their eyes in their own time, by helping them to grasp and value imaginatively the history and the urban, rural and outback landscapes that are theirs and no one else's. Today's children need not be impoverished as, to some extent, were earlier generations, who grew up finding only foreign times and foreign landscapes in their fiction.

Of all South Australian writers Colin Thiele has not only been the best known, most respected and most loved over a period of forty years, but has also been the writer who has done most to bring alive the South Australian landscape. Although he has never been an innovative novelist, and many of his characters now seem to belong to a calmer, more stable world than the world we know today, he has a remarkable ability to create, in language accessible to children, a place or an environment, solid, three-dimensional, yet presented with imagination and sensitivity. A single quotation can do little to give an idea of his quality but the opening paragraphs of *Storm Boy* do give an indication of his brilliant, detailed, economical, evocative style.

> Storm Boy lived between the South Australian Coorong and the sea. His home was the long, long snout of sandhill and scrub that curves away south-eastwards from the Murray Mouth. A wild strip it is, windswept and tussocky, with the flat shallow water of the Coorong on one side and the endless slam of the Southern Ocean on the other. They call it the Ninety Mile Beach. From thousands of miles around the cold, wet underbelly of the world the waves come sweeping in towards the shore and pitch down in a terrible ruin of white water and spray. All day and all night they tumble and thunder. And when the wind rises it whips the sand up the beach and the white spray darts and writhes in the air like snakes of salt.
>
> Storm Boy lived with Hideaway Tom, his father. Their home was a rough little humpy made of wood and brush and flattened sheets of iron from old tins. It had a dirt floor, two blurry bits of glass for windows, and a little crooked chimney made of stove pipes and wire. It was hot in summer and cold in winter, and it shivered when the great storms bent the sedges, and shrieked through the bushes outside. But Storm Boy was happy there.

Thiele is often thought of as a regional novelist, and indeed he has made the area in the north Barossa Valley where he grew up – Eudunda, which he called in his stories Gonunda – a real and lively place for more than one generation of readers. In half-a-dozen novels, from *The Sun on the Stubble* (1961) to *Emma Keppler* (1991), he has celebrated the world of his childhood, a world of hard-working German-speaking farmers struggling through the depression years. *The Valley Between* (1981), which won a Children's Book of the Year Award in 1982, is characteristic, with its lad protagonist poised between school and manhood, learning to assume responsibility on the farm amidst feuding neighbours. Comic episodes dramatise the disasters which loom so large in adolescence. The 1930s live on in these tales; the carefree lives of the children, although frequently disrupted by hilarious misadventures or inevitable sadnesses, contrast strongly with the pressures which are part of the lives of present day children. It is an irony of Thiele's work that, without disguising the hardships, he has made the depression years seem a golden time.

Yet this is only one of the areas which he has brought to life. The Coorong of *Storm Boy* (1963) and the Port Lincoln with its wild seas of *Blue Fin* (1969) are the best known, but in more than thirty novels, some written for beginning readers, some for young independent readers, some for adolescents, he has brought our world alive. Sometimes it is the world of the past as well as a special place, as in *The Undercover Secret* (1982), where the 1930s live again in the Hackney area on the banks of the Torrens behind the zoo. Travelling by tram is an event and the first traffic lights in the state appear in King William Street. More frequently it is a world in which the characters are forced to face natural dangers and disasters. *Flash Flood* (1970) deals with the sudden rising of creek waters in the Flinders Ranges; *River Murray Mary* (1979) with the lives of blockers on the river, the sudden hail storms that ruin the grape harvest, and the disastrous 1931 floods; *Yellow-Jacket Jock* (1969) with the dangers that water skiers may bring to quiet river waters. In *The Fire in the Stone* (1973) he brings alive not only the bleak pitted landscape of Coober Pedy but also the reality of opal mining, in both past and present times, with its manifold dangers.

Thiele cares about children as much as he cares about writing, and he is always deliberately, if unobtrusively, an educator. He uses landscape and seascape not as scenery but as factors which shape human lives and develop human capabilities. His books are meticulously researched and full of simple geographical and geological lessons; he shows why the landscape is as it is, why disasters happen and what precautions human beings need to take to avoid causing or suffering such disasters. No child reading in *Chadwick's Chimney* (1979) of the sinkholes and caverns of the south-east would underestimate the dangers involved in caving, or the need for the most scrupulous attention to the details of equipment. No child reading in 'The Water Trolley' of Peter's ghastly journey through the arid and beautiful northern outback, with its difficulties and dangers, could fail to grasp the preciousness of water.[4] His novels plead for his readers to care for our environment and our wildlife. *The Sknuks* (1977) which, translated, won the Austrian Book Award in 1979, is a scathing indictment of human treatment of the planet.

Christobel Mattingley is another writer who has made an outstanding contribution to writing for children. She was one of the pioneers of books for what are now called 'junior' readers, books for newly independent readers. *The Picnic Dog* (1970) was one of the first Australian stories for this age group. In 1981 she won the first Junior Book of the Year Award for *Rummage*, which, with its copiously illustrated longer text, led the 1980s movement to bridge the gap from picture books to novels. Mattingley's *The Angel with a Mouth-Organ* (1984), a deeply moving story which recounts refugee experiences similar to those of many immigrants, was the first Australian picture book about the second world war. Although Mattingley usually works on a much smaller scale than Thiele, her stories are set firmly in local landscapes with local flora and fauna, like the parks in *The Battle of the Galah Trees* (1973) and *Emu Kite* (1972), the farm of *Windmill at Magpie Creek* (1971), and the back yard of *Worm Weather* (1971). Other stories are set in identifiable places, such as *The Jetty* (1978) at Tumby Bay, *The Long Walk* (1976) at Erindale, and *Queen of the Wheat Castles* (1973) over the border in the Wimmera, in a landscape of silos and railway sidings which has its counterpart in many areas of South Australia. What Mattingley has achieved in writing for the younger reader should not be underestimated. Her stories, though not without suspense, are gentle and reassuring and remarkable for making drama from uneventful everyday lives.

In spite of the fact that we are a nation of city dwellers, children's writers have tended to set their stories outside cities, often in the rural areas they themselves knew as children. A good example is Josephine Croser's *The Talking Stone* (1989), set north of Port Augusta in the days of the one teacher school. Gillian Rubinstein, however, who did not grow up in Australia, has brilliantly accepted the frenetic urban world in her computer-based fantasies, *Space Demons* (1986) and *Skymaze* (1989), and has suggested the savage brutality which underlies much city life in *Answers to Brut* (1988). She seems thoroughly at home in the city landscapes of schools, fun-fairs and multi-storey car parks. But in all her work, even in her Yorke Peninsula stories, *Beyond the Labyrinth* (1988) and *At Ardilla* (1991), both winners of Children's Book of the Year Awards, her chief concern is not with the setting, but with her characters and their relationships, with fractured families and social misfits. A more recent winner of a Children's Book of the Year Award, Eleanor Nilsson, in *The House Guest* (1992), has given life to the Blackwood area and to the Brighton beach in a way which brings satisfying feelings of recognition to those familiar with these places.

Many writers have recreated South Australian landscapes in their novels. Fewer have tried to recreate the past. Max Fatchen notably has done both, bringing back the old paddle-steamer days on the Murray, the riverboat men and their rivalries, and the old river towns in *The River Kings* (1966) and *Conquest of the River* (1970). *The Spirit Wind* (1973), a turn of the century tale, tells of the escape of a boy sailor from the bullying mate of a squarerigger coming to Port Victoria for a cargo of wheat, and of his encounters with an Aborigine, a man of great dignity and spirituality. This novel is remarkable for its portrayal of an early violent era and for its strong girl characters.

There have been some noteworthy stories of the very early days of South Australia. Phyllis Piddington's *Southern Rainbow* (1982) is set in the late 1830s when the journey between the beach where the Pobble family have landed and the scarcely established town of Adelaide is a major undertaking. Much authentic detail enables this book to give a rare glimpse of the hardships experienced in the ordinary run of early colonial life. Elizabeth Wilton's *A Ridiculous Idea* (1967) shows how young Quaker children, stranded without adults, learn to cope as farmers on a small farm not far from Adelaide. The strong realisation of the family's Quaker background gives distinction to this historical tale. Past and present are juxtaposed in Helen Frances's *The Devil's Stone* (1983), which traces a family through generations from 1851 when the first members arrive to clear land on Fifth Creek, near what is now Cherryville in the Adelaide Hills, until some strange happenings in 1982.

These stories and others begin to give some idea of what the times which underlie the present day were like. The writings of authors like Thiele and Fatchen draw attention to what is peculiarly ours in the landscape. But the history of South Australia is a rich field for imaginative investigation and our landscape, in its historical as well as its present aspect, still has much to offer young readers. South Australia will continue to produce writers who, because of the quality and the universality of their work, will be seen as leaders in the field of writing for children. It is to be hoped that some will also set out to realise the world of South Australia.

WORKS CITED

Bonnin, Heather. *Hours to Remember: Reflections on Life in South Australia 1889–1929*. Adelaide: South Australian Government Printer, 1987.

W.A.C. [W.A. Cawthorne]. *Who Killed Cockatoo?* Adelaide: J.H. Lewis, printer, [1865].

Franc, Maud Jean. *Marian, or the Light of Some-One's Home*. Mount Barker: Alfred Waddy, 1859.

Muir, Marcie. *Bibliography of Australian Children's Books*. London: Deutsch, vol. 1 (1970), vol. 2 (1976).

_____. *Australian Children's Book Illustrators*. South Melbourne, Vic. : Sun, 1977.

_____. *Charlotte Barton*. Sydney: Wentworth, 1980.

_____. *A History of Australian Children's Book Illustration*. Melbourne: Oxford, 1982.

_____. *My Bush Book*. Adelaide: Rigby, 1982.

Thiele, Colin. *The Rim of the Morning*. Adelaide: Rigby, 1966.

Wighton, Rosemary. *Early Australian Children's Literature*. Melbourne: Lansdowne, 1963.

NOTES

1. This is usually dated 1870, but recent evidence makes the earlier date likely.
2. This was published originally in four shilling parts. Maud Jean or Jeanne Franc was the pseudonym of Matilda Jane Evans, neé Congreve.
3. Westbury, who used the pseudonym 'Atha', has often been assumed to have been a woman. He was almost certainly the F.A. Westbury who was a land agent in Adelaide from 1881 to 1887. He was a friend of G.E. Loyau and contributed the biographical note on Loyau to the latter's *Notable South Australians* (1885).
4. Published in *The Rim of the Morning*.

CHAPTER

FIDELIA HILL

FINDING A PUBLIC VOICE

Philip Butterss

To say that Fidelia Hill, the first woman and the first 'South Australian' to publish a book of poems in Australia, is not a household name would be an understatement. Even in Adelaide, a city as interested in its own origins as any other Australian capital, she is almost entirely unknown.[1] The only memorial to Fidelia Hill can be found in The *Buffalo Seafood Restaurant and Museum* at Glenelg, located aboard a replica of the *Buffalo*, the ship on which she came to the colony. The restaurant serves a desert known as a 'Fidelia Hill': a baked walnut and banana pudding served with a warm caramel sauce and macadamia nut icecream. Here she is memorialised not because of her position in Australian literary history, of which the proprietor was unaware, but because when he was choosing names for dishes from the passenger list he thought hers sounded appropriate for a dessert.[2]

It is now a commonplace that women who published in the nineteenth century were contravening, if in a licensed way, an ideology that operated to constrain them to domestic activities and the private sphere. Robert Dixon's examination of women's private writings demonstrates that 'respectable' women such as Elizabeth Macarthur went to considerable lengths to locate their speaking position as within the family and the home (130–31). Publishing one's writing – moving into the public sphere – required some negotiation of the prevailing ideological boundaries. As Mary Poovey, discussing nineteenth-century novelists, has noted:

> Writing for publication . . . jeopardises modesty, that critical keystone of feminine propriety; for it not only 'hazard[s] . . . disgrace' but cultivates and calls attention to the woman as subject, as initiator of direct action, as a person deserving of notice for her own sake. (36)

In her preface to *Poems and Recollections of the Past*, the single volume she published in 1840, Fidelia Hill uses several of the common strategies employed by women to make the transition from the privacy of their writing desks to the public reading world, strategies playing down her role as a speaking subject in the wider culture. Certainly these were formulaic, but many women evidently felt that such gestures were necessary. The preface is written in the third person (a grammatical self-effacement); it makes reference to 'defects' in the poetry; and it states, perhaps paradoxically, that it is the author's *private* situation which has led to her venturing into the public domain:

> [T]he writer of these pages . . . pleads the pressure of circumstances as her only apology for intruding on the notice of the public. – She trusts that a charitable allowance will be made for defects of which she is conscious, the poems having been written during seasons unfavorable to composition, of severe domestic calamity, and bodily suffering. Several of them were suggested by the singular reverses of fortune, which it has of late, been the writer's portion to experience.

An examination of the surviving biographical information gives an idea of the extent of those calamities, sufferings, and 'singular reverses of fortune'. Fidelia Hill was born in Yorkshire, probably in 1790. The first of her setbacks appears to have occurred in Kingston, Jamaica, where she and her husband, Robert Keate Hill, an ambitious captain in the East

India Company's service, had moved, perhaps in 1831.[3] The Hills appear to have lived a comfortable life in this tropical colony: Robert was employed in what he was later to describe as a 'lucrative situation', and they evidently owned 'valuable property' (State Records Office, GRG 24/1 1838/235). It was in Jamaica, however, that Fidelia's brother, Richard Munkhouse, the oldest boy in the family, died of an unspecified tropical disease, and this was an event which affected her very deeply. The brother, known to the family as 'Thornton', had evidently been a childhood friend of Robert Hill, and had followed his sister and her husband to Jamaica. Some sense of guilt may be part of the reason that she was to publish as many as five poems on this subject.[4]

In spite of the 'peril, pain, and hardship' they had experienced in Jamaica, the Hills left with what Fidelia described as 'brightest hopes', because Robert had been promised the position of Harbour Master in the new colony of South Australia, a post bringing the very attractive salary of £200 per annum to its incumbent. When they reached England, some time after the middle of 1835, however, they found that Thomas Lipson had already been appointed Harbour Master. Robert Hill claims to have then been assured that, if he proceeded to South Australia in the brig *Rapid* with Colonel William Light, he would have 'an appointment at salary equal to that of Harbour Master'. In November 1838, more than two years after his arrival in the colony, he would write, with more than a trace of bitterness: 'Depending on this promise I quitted England but the appointment has not yet been made' (State Records Office, GRG 24/1 1838/235).

Robert Hill left England in May 1836 as third officer on the *Rapid*. One of his fellow officers, William Pullen, later described him, giving prominence to what he considered the primary cause of the 'reverses of fortune' referred to by Fidelia. In Pullen's words, Robert Hill was a:

> rough good humoured old fellow, very much given to drinking deep. Grog I really believe had walked away with one half of his liver, poor fellow. He used to be very bad at times. He done little good for himself. All his misfortunes may be attributed to his fondness for drinks of the most potent kind.[5] (4)

Knowledge of his alcoholism among the colonial administration is likely to have been the reason that Robert Hill did not achieve high office while in the colony, and it may well have been relevant to the fact that he was not appointed Harbour Master in the first place.

Fidelia Hill followed her husband to South Australia, leaving England in July 1836 on the *Buffalo*, and arriving in Holdfast Bay on 28 December. A few days later she was taken to a tent set up on the river Torrens by her husband, and from there the couple soon moved to what must have been one of the first houses in Adelaide – a dwelling in Hindley Street – although whether the change in accomodation alleviated or contributed to Fidelia Hill's 'bodily suffering' is by no means certain. In May 1837 the house was sold to the Colonial Goverment as an Infirmary and Dispensary, and comments made by Thomas Young Cotter, the Colonial Surgeon, about its state give an idea of the conditions Fidelia Hill experienced. He noted that the roof was incomplete when the building was bought, and later stated publicly that it was 'ill constructed and badly ventilated, and in every respect unfit for the reception of sick persons' (*Southern Australian*, 1 September 1838, 4). One of the house's problems was the sanitary arrangements, a description of which Cotter included in a letter dated 27 July:

> In consequence of there being no chamber utensils or watercloset in the building the patients are compelled to go into the bush when their bowels require evacuating, and Geo Trollop who has not either the strength or at all times the sense, to do so, is frequently in such a state as to be quite a nuisance to the other patients . . . The want of these things not only interferes physically with the well doings [sic] of the patients but likewise acts upon their minds and is calculated to render them unhappy and discontented. (State Records Office, GRG 24/1 257)

For much of 1837 Robert Hill was working as Deputy Storekeeper, a post earning him a salary of £15 per quarter – hardly the well-remunerated and influential position they had desired (State Records Office, GRG 48/8). To augment his income he became a constable, but this, too, was the cause of some degree of 'domestic calamity', as John Woodford, the surgeon from the *Rapid*, indicates in his journal entry for Thursday 25 March:

after [dinner] I was taking a stroll when I saw a number of men hurrying along led by Mr Mann, the Attorney-General, and Hill, my old messmate, who has been sworn in Constable. Upon my going up to the latter and enquiring the cause of the row, he very civilly pressed me in the King's Name, to assist in taking into custody some seamen of the 'Buffalo' who had been guilty of some disturbance (these men are on shore building a house for the Governor). I accordingly joined them 'nolens volens', and in a few moments had a job cut out for me, for these men being intoxicated had no idea of Civil Law, and treated poor Hill very uncivilly by knocking him down with a bludgeon and laying open his temporal artery. I have just helped carry him home, dressed his wound and left him pretty comfortable, but not over well pleased with his warlike expedition.

The couple's decline continued with the termination of Robert Hill's employment as Deputy Storekeeper in October 1837 (State Records Office, GRG 48/8). By the end of 1838 he realised that there was to be no bright future for him in South Australia and probably sailed from the colony as Chief Officer on the *Pestonjee Bomanjee* (Mayo Papers, Series 1, 89). When Fidelia Hill left Adelaide is not certain, although she may have remained until the latter part of 1839.[6] She was certainly in Sydney in May 1840 when she wrote the preface to *Poems and Recollections of the Past*, describing herself as 'Late of Adelaide, South Australia'.

There is no doubt that the apologia quoted above from Fidelia Hill's preface was conventional for its period, and there is an evident tension between the self-effacement and a strong desire to be a speaking subject within public culture. This desire emerges distinctly at a number of points in the preface. She begins by stating that 'the writer of these pages previously to quitting her native land, received the most flattering encouragement from one of the first booksellers in London, to publish a Volume of Poems'. Fidelia Hill was not reticent about her place in the history of Australian literature, describing herself as 'the *first* who has ventured to lay claim to the title of Authoress' – the italics to make sure no one missed the point. That laying claim to authorship was no trifle is indicated by the number of women who chose anonymity or pseudonymity as their strategy for entering the public sphere, including Anna Maria Bunn, whose *The Guardian: A Tale* was published two years earlier. Evidently intending this to be the beginning of something of a career in the public world of letters, Hill concludes the preface hoping for 'a continuation of patronage and support' from 'the highly respectable and numerous' subscribers to her volume. Nor are even her references to personal misfortunes entirely distinct from the world of public poetry, for, as Angela Leighton, writing about Victorian women's poetry, has pointed out:

> Renunciation, rejection and despair are . . . gestures loaded with inherited, mythic meaning for the woman poet who, in the wake of high Romanticism, was still very conscious that being a poet was not simply a professional occupation, but an idea to be invented and lived out. (5)

Hill's references to her personal experiences, and to the fact that several of the poems had been suggested by her recent 'reverses of fortune', are likely to have been read as an indication that the volume would address private and domestic themes, another common means of negotiating the move into the public sphere. In fact this is so, for much of the volume. The twenty-two poems which are not identifiably Australian, and which were probably at least the bulk of what she was urged to publish before she left England, fall largely into two categories – private/domestic pieces such as 'Lines to my Sister, with a Chysanthemum', or fragments of metrical romance.

One of the four poems which can be identified as having been composed in Australia falls into the former category: it is a musing on the coincidence that the *Sir Charles McCarthy*, the ship which had taken the Hills to the West Indies in more hopeful times, arrived at Port Adelaide in mid-1838, for use as a storeship (Sexton 42). The poem contains the kind of personal reflection which the preface heralds, finding it sadly ironic that the 'proud and gallant bark' should have had a fall in status which mirrored her own. Hill wrote, remembering the earlier voyage to the far Atlantic:

> I thought not, as I walked thy deck
> That I such varied ills should see,
> That thou so soon, shouldst prove a wreck
> And linked with thine, my destiny. (36)

However, because she was in South Australia at a self-evidently 'historical' moment Fidelia Hill felt authorised to write much more public poems than she had previously produced. Probably the first of her South Australian pieces was 'Adelaide', a dream vision of what the city might eventually become:

> . . . all that soul could wish, or eye could see
> For comfort, ease, convenience, or for cheer –
> Treasures for time, and for eternity,
> Seemed as by magic art concentred here. (43)

In 'Lines to the Memory of Col. Light' Hill shifts from writing the future to writing self-conscious public history, arguing that the multi-talented city planner should be memorialised, and concluding with the performative lines:

> With that of South Australia, proudly write
> On history's page – the honor'd name of LIGHT! (62)

Although her personal knowledge of Light allows her to enter this public discourse, in the body of the poem she feels compelled to reduce her own presence: she writes that the Colonel is 'long remembered by a faithful band, / Who prized their gallant leader as they ought'. The 'faithful band' is glossed as 'His Officers, Surveyors, &c., chiefly those who sailed with him, in the Surveying Brig "Rapid"'. The closest Hill comes to self reference is in the space not encompassed by the term 'chiefly', or perhaps in what is included in the '&c.' But there are other oblique references, including the poem's epigraph, which points to its author's personal connection with the object of her public history: 'Who living honor'd thee, and being dead / We yet may meet again!' It is clear, too, that Hill sees strong parallels between the public career of Light, and her and her husband's personal experiences in the colony. Lines such as the following have strong personal resonances for her:

> While base ingratitude disgrac'd the way:–
> As thou wast singled out to be the prey
> Of malice, envy, unrequited love:–
> Of disappointed hope to own the sway,
> And of fell treachery the victim prove. (61)

In 'Recollections', the last poem in the collection, Hill is audacious enough to write herself overtly into the public sphere, but the poem also seems to reveal a deep ambivalence about holding such a position. It opens with a passage alluding to Wordsworth's 'Lines Composed Above Tintern Abbey':

> Yes, South Australia! three years have elapsed
> Of dreary banishment, since I became
> In thee a sojourner; nor can I choose
> But sometimes think on thee; and tho' thou art
> A fertile source of unavailing woe,
> Thou dost awaken deepest interest still. (64)

Morris Miller has taken these lines to mean that Hill spent three years of 'dreary banishment' in Sydney while she pined for Adelaide (195), but, as the biographical details outlined above indicate, this was not so. For Hill, South Australia is 'a fertile source of unavailing woe' on a personal level, but she retains a 'deepest interest' at a more public level. Having introduced the poem with the lines just quoted, she describes the first moments of colonisation, obliquely connecting herself with this historical event: one footnote establishes that 'Holdfast Bay', where the ship anchored, was named by 'the husband of the Writer'; another makes clear that the 'we' in the body of the poem refers to those on board the 'H.M.S. *Buffalo* – commanded by Captain Hindmarsh, R.N. and Governor of South Australia'. Alongside the public descriptions of the 'novel scene' where

> . . . toil was cheer'd, and labour render'd light,
> Privations welcom'd, every hardship brav'd,
> In the blest anticipation of reward: –

is an excursion into private disgruntlement: 'reward / (Which some indeed deserv'd, but ne'er obtain'd)' (65). After half a dozen more lines on injustices to some of those who worked 'unceasingly . . . to promote / The interests of the rising Colony', Hill shifts back from the personal to the public, placing herself centre stage:

> They bore me to the future Capitol,
> Ere yet 'twas more than desart [sic] – a few tents,
> Scatter'd at intervals, 'mid forest trees,
> Marked the abode of men . . .
> 'Twas then they hail'd me as the *first* white lady
> That ever yet had enter'd Adelaide. –
> Can time e'er teach me to forget the sound,
> Or gratulations that assail'd me then,
> And cheer'd me at the moment, or efface
> The welcome bland of the distinguish'd one –
> Who fix'd the site, and form'd the extensive plan
> Of that young City? (65–66)

Setting herself firmly at the centre of attention in such a public moment seems not to be an entirely comfortable action. The lack of agency which Hill allows herself in the passage is striking: 'They bore' her; they 'hail'd' her, they congratulated her, they 'cheer'd' her, they welcomed her. The poem shifts quickly away from herself and her role in South Australian history, and then returns in its final section to the more comfortable terrain of the personal and the domestic, remembering the tent that her husband had pitched for her on the Torrens:

> This, this methought shall be my happy home!
> Here may I dwell, and by experience prove,
> That tents with love, yield more substantial bliss
> Than Palaces without it, can bestow. (66)

There are probably a number of reasons why Hill failed in her efforts to write herself into literary or South Australian history in any long-lasting way. In an interesting essay on the autobiographies of five publicly successful women at the turn of the century, Jane Marcus has argued that these women enacted 'a deliberate resignation from the public world and patriarchal history, which had already erased or was expected to erase their names and their works, [by re/signing] their private lives into domestic discourse', aiming to reach a community of women readers. The women Marcus discusses recognised the inability of 'male public discourse . . . to include their voices in its history' (114). Hill's move into the public sphere, therefore, was a foray into an area where erasure was always likely. There is no doubt that the fact that Fidelia Hill's Australian poems were more specifically South Australian poems has been relevant. The early volumes of verse written by men in New South Wales have been republished, and their authors, Barron Field, W.C. Wentworth and Charles Tompson, have been the subject of considerable research. It is also true that the absence of biographical material relating to Hill in the Mitchell Library has hindered a number of researchers. And it is probably fair to say that the 'defects' which she herself mentioned may have been relevant to her lack of recognition.

But these factors do not adequately explain her absence from South Australian histories. It may well be that it was the presence of the private or, more accurately, the *nature* of Hill's private experiences, which prevented her from being allowed a place in those histories. The early public accounts of South Australia and its origins were, not surprisingly, tales of success, of mastery of the landscape, of financial reward. It is the personal which allows Fidelia Hill to lay claim to authorship and to a public speaking position, and yet her personal narrative is one of misfortune, not of fortune; and it is too explicitly critical of the colonial public sphere to allow her a place in the early public histories.

WORKS CITED

Bunn, Anna Maria. *The Guardian: A Tale.* 1838; Canberra: Mulini, 1994.

Dixon, Robert. 'Public and Private Voices: Non-Fictional Prose', in Laurie Hergenhan *et al.* ed., *The Penguin New Literary History of Australia.* Ringwood: Penguin, 1988.

Hill, Fidelia. *Poems and Recollections of the Past.* Sydney, 1840.

Leighton, Angela. *Victorian Women Poets: Writing Against the Heart.* New York: Harvester Wheatsheaf, 1992.

Marcus, Jane. 'Invincible Mediocrity: The Private Selves of Public Women', in Shari Benstock, ed., *The Private Self: Theory and Practice of Women's Autobiographical Writings.* London: Routledge, 1988.

Mayo Papers, Mortlock Library, PRG 1, Series 1.

Miller, Morris. *Australian Literature 1795–1938*. Melbourne: MUP, 1940.

Poovey, Mary. *The Proper Lady and the Woman Writer*. Chicago: University of Chicago Press, 1984.

Pullen, William. Memoir. Mortlock Library, South Australian Archives 4.

Sexton, Robert. *Shipping Arrivals and Departures: South Australia 1627–1850*. Gould Books/Roebuck Society, 1990.

Woodforde, John. 'Abstract of a voyage to South Australia in the surveying Brig "Rapid"'. Mortlock Library, PRG 502.

NOTES

1. I would like gratefully to acknowledge the helpful suggestions of David Elder and Robert Sexton.

2. Fidelia Hill's work is becoming better known: two of her poems were published by Richard Jordan and Peter Pierce in *The Poets' Discovery*, Melbourne: MUP, 1990; four of her poems were published in Fidelia Hill, *'Adelaide' and Other Poems of South Australia*, Cook, A.C.T.: Mulini, 1992; and it is hoped that Wakefield Press will be able to republish the entire volume of *Poems and Recollections of the Past*.

3. *Lloyd's Register*, London, 1833 records a journey by the *Sir Charles McCarthy* to Jamaica in 1831.

4. 'Thornton', 'My Brother', two of the poems titled 'Recollections', and 'To a Departed Relative' are probably all concerned with Richard Munkhouse's death.

5. I am indebted to Robert Sexton for his transcription of this quotation. Pullen wrote the passage on 7 January 1842.

6. The line 'Destined on these far shores a fate to find' in 'Lines to the Memory of Col. Light' conceivably indicates she was writing in the same place as Light died.

CHAPTER

3

CATHERINE HELEN SPENCE

NOVELIST

Susan Magarey

Introduction: Catherine Spence 1825–1910

'Do you remember Miss Spence's novel *Clara Morison*,' Miles Franklin asked her good friend Alice Henry in September 1930. 'I had no idea the dear old valiant was of such stature in that direction. For a literary artist to be drawn away by causes is a form of infidelity and has its punishment.'[1]

The subject of Miles Franklin's query was Catherine Helen Spence, for whom Alice Henry had written an obituary in 1910 entitled 'The Grand Old Woman of Australia'. A Scot who had emigrated to South Australia with her family in 1839, when she was thirteen years old and the newest invasion of Aboriginal territory by British settlers not quite three, Catherine Spence had, over the ensuing seventy-one years, developed a five-fold career as a novelist, a highly accomplished journalist, a preacher in the Unitarian church, a voluntary welfare worker and, during the last two decades of her eighty-five years, a renowned and widely admired public speaker for electoral reform. At a public gathering to celebrate her eightieth birthday in Adelaide, in October 1905, South

Australia's chief justice declared that she was 'the most distinguished woman they had had in Australia . . . There was no one in the whole Commonwealth', he went on, 'whose career covered so wide a ground'.[2]

Miles Franklin had learned about Catherine Spence from two friends Spence had made in the last, and most public, decades of her life. Journalist and welfare worker Alice Henry first sought a meeting with her in 1893 when Catherine Spence, aged sixty-seven, was passing through Melbourne on her way to the United States of America where, having been appointed Government Commissioner and delegate to the Great World's Fair Congresses in Chicago, she spent almost a year giving public lectures and sermons and attending meetings (*Autobiography* 69; Kirkby 47–50, 55–60). Rose Scott, leader of the campaign for women's suffrage in New South Wales, invited her to stay and held a reception for her in 1900 when Catherine Spence first visited Sydney to address public meetings and join Scott on platforms calling for votes for women (*Autobiography* 20, 53, 87, 91–93). Miles Franklin found, she noted years later, that Miss Scott would turn aside hero worship offered to her by insisting that 'Miss Spence . . . was unquestionably the leading woman of Australia' (Untitled Talk 253f). Knowing of her only through Henry and Scott, it is hardly surprising that Franklin knew of Spence as a 'dear old valiant' rather than, like Franklin herself, a novelist, for Catherine Spence had stopped writing fiction in the 1880s, before she met them. The work that Franklin had chanced upon was Spence's first published novel, written in 1854, a quarter of a century before Miles Franklin was born.

I   Clara Morison

This was *Clara Morison: A Tale of South Australia during the Gold Fever*,[3] a narrative with, as its title suggests, two subjects. One is the heroine, Clara Morison. Her story combines two elements. It is an instance of the feminine form of romance: a tale of courtship and marriage. It also contains elements of the *bildungsroman* or 'novel of education': the hapless orphaned young Scotswoman, despatched to South Australia by a stingy uncle, preserves her respectability and fine moral and social sensitivity through a succession of testing vicissitudes to emerge triumphant, though less from greater knowledge of herself (as in traditional examples of this genre) than from the seasoning of experience.

The second subject is the colony of South Australia. Its story also combines two elements: a realist depiction of life in the colony during the period when most of its men left it for the gold-diggings in Victoria, and a social purpose argument advanced through the characters and their interactions with each other about the best kind of society to be established in this outpost of the British empire. The realism was important to Spence's social purpose: she wanted to combat the impression created by Thackeray who had, she recalled, 'written about an emigrant vessel taking a lot of women to Australia, as if these were all to be gentlemen's wives – as if there was such a scarcity of educated women there, that anything wearing petticoats had the prospect of a great rise in position' (*Autobiography* 22). In the letter that accompanied the novel to England in search of a publisher, Catherine Spence asserted its truth to life:

> the domestic life represented in my tale is the sort of life I have led – the people are such as I have come in contact with – the politics are what I hear talked of – the letters from the diggings are like those I have seen – the opinions I give are what may be considered a faithful transcript of life in the Colony. (Letter to Smith, Elder & Co.)

She may have emphasised the novel's documentary value to make it more attractive to publishers. She was trying to earn a livelihood with her pen: 'I had an idea', she noted, 'that, as there was so much interest in Australia and its gold, I might get £100 for the novel' (*Autobiography* 22). But she was not making an exaggerated claim. Events in the novel follow events in the colony so closely as to suggest that she wrote with copies of the *Government Gazette* and the daily newspapers beside her.

The central characters, too, were drawn from life. 'Of course, Mr Reginald was Mr John Taylor, the only squatter I knew', she acknowledged; he was the friend who took the manuscript of the novel to England for her (*Autobiography* 22, 26). She herself was Margaret Elliot, the sister who 'was full of what she herself called *elbows*, – salient points which people who did not know her very well were apt to find inconvenient', considered a bluestocking for her wide-ranging and industrious intelligence, her fondness for 'singing something wise and stirring to the tunes of love-songs', and her preference for the company of gentlemen rather than ladies, a preference, notes the author, that was not reciprocated: 'for gentlemen did not like a girl who thought for herself, and spoke out as boldly as she thought, without desiring to be led by their superior judgement' (I:205). Spence denied that she was identified with her heroine, though readers have found elements of her in Clara Morison's refuge from the loneliness and drudgery of her life as a domestic servant – writing imaginary conversations, and even sermons, in her journal (*Autobiography* 26; Green I:222). Spence said, too, that she shrank from the notion that she might be capable of 'taking off' her acquaintances in her fiction. But such shrinking may well have been prompted by consideration for the originals of such targets of her social satire as Mr and Mrs Bantam, Miss Withering, Mr Humberstone and Mrs Tubbins, all of whom are most appropriately named; she also reflected, with some satisfaction I would surmise, that: 'There must have been some lifelike presentation of my characters, or they could not have been recognised' (*Autobiography* 26).

Catherine Spence achieved this remarkable fusion of 'transcript' and romance, *bildungsroman* and social purpose fiction, focused on a principal protagonist who was a woman, by writing what is primarily a domestic novel. Clara Morison spends most of the novel in kitchens, parlours and bedrooms, with very occasional ventures through the streets of Adelaide on errands to Macnab's drapery store, and a long journey to the Beauforts' station in the north. This allows Spence to demonstrate her conviction of the central importance of the household and the relationships between the members of a household, and their visitors, to the values and behaviours to be found in the colony's society as a whole. But if the main action of the novel occurs almost exclusively on the colony's hearthstones, it is nevertheless set in a much wider context.

Clara Morison does not encounter the diggers who marry in dozens at the Port, nor the tradesmen's daughters who dance at the public house with Harris, nor the pastoralists who attend 'at homes' at the viceregal Government House with Chaloner. The characters with whom she becomes close friends do not make fortunes from grazing sheep and mining copper, and then return to England to live among the landed gentry, like Dent. Nor do they die of desertion and disease like Miss Kerr. But she and her friends – and the novel's readers – learn of all of these people and activities through the stories told by their visitors, through their own visits to other colonists, and through letters, some sent from pastoral properties in the South Australian countryside, others from Melbourne, yet others from the Victorian gold-fields. The totality of the society in which Clara makes her place is richly varied, as Catherine Spence noted when she compared the society that she depicted with that in Jane Austen's novels. Austen's 'circle', she observed, 'was as narrow as mine, indeed narrower . . . She represented well-to-do grown-up people, and them alone . . . The life I led had more breadth and wider interests. The life of Miss Austen's heroines, though delightful to read about, would have been deadly dull to endure' (*Autobiography* 26). Miles Franklin agreed with her, commenting that Spence's circle was not only wider than Austen's but also more socially fluid, and that conversation in her novel could range over:

> the differential calculus, all of politics including the Mexican constitution, the current sermons, housing, the price of commodities, the scarcity of domestic helpers and the changes of vocations for young men and women. Nothing was taboo apparently except bad language. (*Laughter* 61–63)

But this social range is almost always perceived as though framed by the doorways or windows of a household. And this framing serves to mark a boundary not only between the domestic world, which is the novel's focus, and the wider public world of elections, wheat sales and stock exchanges, but also between the kind of colonist who will contribute most to the fruitful development of the colony, and the rest. It is a boundary made also of values.

Catherine Spence had been brought up on Maria Edgeworth's moral tales, and she knew Bunyan's *Pilgrim's Progress* so well that later in her life she would write her own version of it. She believed that fiction should be improving as well as entertaining.[4] In *Clara Morison*, the values of the central characters are continually contrasted with those of other colonists, always to the advantage of the former.

The central characters have much in common with the literate provincial middle classes of early nineteenth-century Britain, not unlike some of the characters in the novels of Elizabeth Gaskell. They win their bread by hard work, they are only moderately successful at the gold-diggings, they cook, wash, scrub their own floors, chop their own wood and mend their own fences. They subscribe to the library, read the newly-published works of Dickens and Thackeray as they arrive in instalments from England, entertain their guests by playing the piano and singing, go to concerts at the exchange, and attend informative quarterly conversaziones at the Mechanics' Institute. They read the *Government Gazette*, discuss colonial politics, annotate their newspapers and devise letters to the editor. They prize solid worth and despise shallowness and show. They believe, with Minnie Hodges and against Miss Withering, that marriage should be founded in love and mutual esteem, rather than in financially advantageous connections: Miss Withering is resolved, she says: 'to remain single unless I could marry a gentleman worth at least eighteen hundred a year' (I:121, 170). The central characters have a strong sense of vocation and, unlike many of the lesser characters, follow it. Margaret tells Clara: 'Your vocation is marriage . . . All your little talents are pleasure-giving; you have feeling, and taste, and tact, and I can fancy your husband finding new charms in you every day' (II:17). Margaret's vocation is not marriage; at the end of the novel she is planning to set up in a small cottage and study law with her brother Gilbert (II:260). (Miss Withering's vocation, Clara decides, is to set people tasks [II:83].) Above all, the characters are committed to the growth and well-being of the colony. Margaret is critical of the Tubbinses' use of their new-found wealth, commenting severely, 'South Australia is none the better for that family' (II:105). Her own family, by contrast, contributes to the colony, as she tells Gilbert:

> we came here not to make our fortunes and leave the colony forthwith, but to grow up and settle in it; we have all rather more than average abilities; we have had good principles instilled in us from our early youth; we have all a deep feeling of our accountability to God for both our private and public conduct; we have all, I think, a love for the country of our adoption, and a wish to serve it . . . (II:255)

This aspect of *Clara Morison* could have been forbiddingly earnest. It is certainly serious. But it is also, often, extremely funny. The self-portrait rendered in the figure of Margaret Elliot is splendidly ironic. Minnie Hodges's engagement with Miss Withering in what one discerning critic likened to 'a verbal War of Independence' (I:ch. 11; Daniels 39); Mr Humberstone's proposal to first Grace and then Margaret Elliot, after his night on the booze (II:68–70); and Mrs Tubbins's pleasure in her new grand piano, on which she puts the children to bed at night (II:100–105) – all are verbal exchanges in which Spence's prose has 'a Jane Austen sparkle and economy' (Daniels 22). It is little wonder that Miles Franklin seized upon this work as 'the greatest Australian novel of the time – a novel which has since been surpassed by few if any others'.[5]

Catherine Spence was to write a further five novels, a short story, a novella and a religious allegory over the following quarter century. All are engaging reading, and the last full-length novel and the novella are pioneering adventures into a genre of utopian future-vision fiction. But her career as a novelist was hardly a raging success. Only one novel, *Tender and True* (1856), achieved a second printing during her lifetime; one *Gathered In* (1881–1882), was serialised in the Adelaide *Observer*, but not published as a book until almost a century later, in 1977; and the last full-length novel that she wrote, *Handfasted* (1880), did not achieve print until 1984. When she began writing fiction, she had hoped that she might make her living with her novels, but altogether over twenty-five years they earned her no more than £105. 'Novel writing,' she remarked, 'had not been for me a lucrative occupation' (*Autobiography* 23). It was less the 'causes' that led her away from her literary talent, as Miles Franklin had imagined, than this discouraging lack of reward and her need to earn her own bread. By the time she gave up writing fiction in the 1880s, she was gaining great satisfaction in making a living as a journalist and social commentator (*Autobiography* 55–56). By the 1880s she was, she recalled, 'earning by my pen a very decent income' (*Autobiography* 61).

II Re-Discovering Catherine Spence the Novelist

So small a financial return, and her difficulty in finding publishers for her later novels, could be seen as reflecting on the literary merit of Spence's fiction.

Of course Spence herself suffered doubts about the quality of her novels. I have recounted these in *Unbridling the Tongues of Women: A Biography of Catherine Spence* (ch 2, esp. 56–57), so I will not rehearse them again here. But it should be noted that Spence, like literary historian H.M. Green, considered that there were particular difficulties in being a colonial writer. Reflecting on her literary reputation at the end of her life, she felt, she recalled, 'that though Australia was to be a great country, there was no market for literary work, and the handicap of distance from the [British] reading world was great' (*Autobiography* 23; Green I:220). Such difficulties could be overcome, but only, in Spence's view, by 'great genius'. The only Australian novelist of genius that she knew of, she said, was 'my friend Miss Mackay' – Catherine Martin (*Autobiography* 64; Allen 264). Martin's novels were not to gain any greater favour with the radical nationalists of the 1890s, and those literary critics of the twentieth century who created a legend of the radical nationalists' writing, than did those of Spence. When Spence once again sought a publisher for *Gathered In* in Sydney in 1900, she was assured that 'the only novels worth publishing in Australia were sporting or political novels' (*Autobiography* 93). In 1902 she was moved to protest: 'In modern novels provincialism seems to have run a little mad' ('Dialect'). She was not about to try to emulate them. On the contrary, she considered the dominance in Australian writing of 'the "dead-beat" – the remittance man, the gaunt shepherd with his starving flocks and herds, the free selector on an arid patch, the drink shanty where the rouseabouts and shearers knock down their cheques, the race meeting where high and low, rich and poor, are filled with the gambler's ill luck' – as 'false in the impression they make on the outside world and on ourselves'. Better, she believed, 'to see Australia steadily and see it whole'.[6]

That view serves to mark a clear distinction between Catherine Spence's novels and those canonised as specifically 'Australian' works for much of the twentieth century – masculine romances of the bush and roving, droving bushmen, writing to their mates with their thumbnails dipped in tar. Writing in 1990, literary historian Joy Hooton described a narrowing of the concept of what represented 'Australian' literature, and of what properly constituted the 'literary', lasting for at least seventy years in this century. (The chief exception in her analysis was the literary historian, Henry Green, whose compendious *History of Australian Literature*, published in 1961, included high praise for the portrayal of the Lindsays in *The Author's Daughter*, and for the secondary narrative in *Handfasted*, the entrancing story of Marguerite de Launay, compelling reading even in the late twentieth century [Hooton 312–13; Green I:225].) In the mid-nineteenth century, definitions of both 'the literary' and 'the Australian' were more capacious. And in that period, Spence's fiction could gain serious attention and warm approval.

As early as 1856, Frederick Sinnett, a journalist working on the Melbourne *Argus*, surveyed 'The Fiction Fields of Australia', judging 'most Australian stories' to be '*too* Australian' – 'instead of human life, we have only "manners and customs" portrayed in them' – but then declared *Clara Morison*: 'Decidedly the best Australian novel that we have met with . . . deserving careful criticism and much praise.' He approved the characterisation: 'The personages are not mere wooden figures pulled about by perceptible wires, but, with few exceptions are full of life and truth.' While disliking 'the abruptness of Mr Reginald's literary love making' he admired the women that Spence had created. 'Female writers, like the author of *Clara Morison*,' he observed, 'have an advantage in not being afflicted by the necessity, under which most male writers seem to labor, of making all their agreeable feminine characters fit to be fallen in love with by anybody at a moment's notice.' He approved of the novel's realism, considering that the circumstances shaping the characters' lives 'seem to follow one another like the events of real life in a natural sequence'. But his highest praise was for the fact that, while 'being Australian', the novel was 'quite alone among all Australian stories yet published, in that it is free from the defect of being a book of travels in disguise'. While 'being Australian', he considered, it was also 'a work of art'.[7]

In the late twentieth century, developments in both cultural studies and feminist literary criticism, engendering critiques of the seventy-year obsession with the bush and what Anne Summers characterised as the 'epochal dimensions' of our history – convict colony, exploration, gold rushes, land selection, Anzac, and so on, what Hooton called 'a familiar national monomyth' – have created once again more capacious definitions of both 'Australian' and 'literature'.[8] These provide a context in which the artistry of Catherine Spence's novels can once again be considered seriously.

The 1970s and 1980s have seen all but two of Spence's novels, and the religious allegory, either published or reprinted (see Works Cited). And in the 1980s, new critical assessments have located Spence's work in a newly-defined Australian context: Drusilla Modjeska identifies Spence as the founder of a genre of realist fiction in Australia; Susan Sheridan places her at the beginning of 'a feminine (though not feminist) tradition' in Australian literature; Patrick Morgan describes *Clara Morison* as inaugurating 'the line of middle-class novels of society developed later by Rosa Praed, "Tasma", Henry Handel Richardson and Norman Lindsay'.[9] Fiona Giles expands that Australian context to include the development of realist fiction in Europe, and Elizabeth Perkins considers *Clara Morison* to be 'the first colonial work that may fairly be compared with that of George Eliot or Elizabeth Gaskell' (Giles, 'Romance' 225; Perkins 145–46). Yet others have claimed for Spence a place in a tradition of feminist writing, noting her depiction of a gender segmented labour market unjustly refusing the means of earning a livelihood to middle-class women, in *Clara Morison* and *Mr Hogarth's Will*, and her critique of marriage in *Tender and True*, *Gathered In* and most particularly *Handfasted*. The judges of the competition to which Spence submitted *Handfasted* rejected it on the grounds that 'it was calculated to loosen the marriage tie – it was too socialistic, and consequently dangerous'.[10] Indeed *Handfasted* can be located at the beginning of an international tradition of feminist future-vision fiction which has usually traced its origin to north American feminist writer, Charlotte Perkins Gilman, and her novel *Herland*, published thirty years later than Spence's work was written (*Unbridling* 69–71; 'Feminist Visions').

In such a context, it is no longer necessary to make a case for Spence's novels even to be read, or simply to read them as extrusions from her biography. It is now possible to explore, as Lesley Ljungdahl does in her illuminating introduction to the 1987 reprint of *A Week in the Future*, the sources of Spence's social theories; or as Fiona Giles does, ways of reading Spence's novels that can learn from late twentieth-century theories of postcolonialism (Ljungdahl; Giles, 'Finding a Shiftingness').

III Reading Spence's Novels in the Twenty-first Century

There are, I hazard to guess, three elements that will gain fresh attention in readings of Catherine Spence's novels in the near future. One relates to the politico-social purposes of her novels. Another is the intertextuality of her fiction. The third is her feminism. All are interconnected. There is not space, here, to do more than glance at each in relation to *Clara Morison*.

The colonists among whom Clara Morison finds herself when she arrives in Adelaide serve as a reminder of the ethnic variety of settler Australians. Clara herself is Scots, and on one occasion is rejected as a governess on the grounds that her Latin is marred by her accent. The company that she encounters in Mrs Handy's boarding-house includes, as Charles Reginald points out to her, 'English, Scotch, and Irish, and the German gentleman at your other hand' (I:34). Moreover, while the fine moral distinctions drawn in the process of establishing the qualities of the ideal colonist certainly favour the Scots – the Elliots are Scottish too – these distinctions do not operate prejudicially against ethnic or national stereotypes: the characters who drink too much, or throw their money about, are not stereotyped Irish; the depiction of German Mr Haussen as feckless is balanced by the brief appearance in the novel of his superseded German fiancée, the noble Sophie Werner; even the Scottish Elliots find a counterweight in the figure of keeper of the drapery store, Mr Macnab, whose conversational anality exceeds his financial meanness (the author takes revenge on Macnab by marrying him to Miss Withering). And while the horrifically English Miss Withering could suggest a more than probable Scottish antipathy, even her nationality is off-set by that of Charles Reginald, the romantic hero.

But if the ethnic politics of this text can be described, in the language of some social policies in the late twentieth century, as 'inclusive', the racial politics are not. Aboriginal Australians appear in this novel on two occasions. On the first, Miss Withering has, 'with great condescension', bestowed upon Clara, in her capacity of domestic servant in the Bantams' household, an old gown. Clara, being really 'a lady', burns with resentment, longing to refuse the gift. But this would blow her cover and lose her her job, so she 'swallow[s] down her proud heart', 'heroically' thanks Miss Withering, and vengefully resolves 'to give it to the first woman who might come to chop wood'. The gown:

> was old and oddly made, but her acquaintance, Black Mary, would make no objection, and would be very much the better for a gown, for she had nothing at present but an opossum skin rug, and an old drawn silk bonnet, which had once been white. The dress was a morning wrapper, and drew in with strings, so it would be sure to fit; and it also had a capacious pocket, which would charm Mary's heart. (I:167)

On the second, two sheep farmers discuss the possibilities of employing Aboriginal Australians as shepherds, and conclude against their reliability (I:237). These are accounts included to show, as James Baldwin said once of depictions of poor whites in the United States, where the bottom is; there is no consciousness at all in the careful social discriminations in this text that these proud colonials might all be invaders of land with which Black Mary in her opossum skin cloak, and the recalcitrant shepherds, already had a relationship closer and more complex than 'settler' concepts of ownership.

In relation to class, though, this text is more complicated. There are countless examples of Spence's crashing snobbery. But it is not a snobbery that prizes aristocratic birth, 'blue blood', and access to the vice-regal circles emanating from Government House. The Society of Rosa Praed's Queensland finds no place in Catherine Spence's South Australia. Nor is it, simply, a snobbery that identifies all virtue in the respectability of the middle class. Rather, it is a snobbery which delights in drawing fine moral distinctions *within* the respectable middle classes. And it is with these distinctions that Spence conveys the social purpose of this novel.

Her social purpose is, also, imbricated in the novel's intertextuality. *Clara Morison* is self-conscious about its own textual status, and this forms one of the principal means by which its social purpose argument, and its plot, are advanced. Charles Reginald establishes himself as a 'gentleman' within a page of his appearance by, in Sinnett's amused representation, 'talking modern literature, and displaying a highly cultivated mind with a promptitude and pertinacity frightful to contemplate' (I:33; Sinnett 23). Clara and Reginald forge their initial alliance with each other, and against the other boarders in Mrs Handy's establishment, first by discussing possible endings to Thackeray's Pendennis, still arriving in South Australia in the monthly instalments in which it first appeared, later by engaging in a discussion incorporating Shakespeare, Byron and Walter Scott (I:33–35).[11] Clara's status as a 'lady', despite her employment as Mrs Bantam's maid, is established for the pastoralist's daughter Minnie Hodges when Clara recites Tennyson to her – and this also forms a bond between them (I:147, 158, 162, 183). Clara, Margaret Elliot and Charles Reginald discuss the recently published poetry of Elizabeth Barrett Browning and admire Bulwer Lytton's fiction, whereas Humberstone rejects The Caxtons as 'hundreds of pages of rigmarole', Mrs Haussen reads only yellow books and Julia Marston a French novel (I:187, 238–39, II:8–9, 58). Reginald cements his status as the rightful claimant to Clara's heart when he sends her Elizabeth Barrett Browning's sonnets, and this gesture shows him to be not merely a gentleman of fine taste, but an exceptional masculine sensibility: 'In these matter-of-fact days, how rare it is to see a vein of poetical feeling running through a man's nature,' reflects Clara (I:238–39, II:9). And he demonstrates himself to be a desirable husband – for a woman who has already shown herself capable of finding a living independently – in a discussion comparing Milton's Eve with the Eve of Elizabeth Barrett Browning, dismissing Milton's Eve's 'entire dependence' on her husband (II:58). Such richness of intertextual references serves as well not only to locate Spence's novel firmly in its context of Anglophone literature of its period – a context in which comparisons with the works of Austen, Brontë, Gaskell, Eliot and Dickens are far from inappropriate – but also to present the feminist considerations about work and marriage which, while far more pronounced in her later fiction, are nevertheless present in Clara Morison.

Definitions of feminism have always been controversial; they are particularly so in the late twentieth century. Moreover, some scholars have pointed out that the term 'feminist' did not enter popular discourse until the late nineteenth century. It is not difficult, though, to see that there is a far longer history for analyses of power differences between women and men, the feminine and the masculine – however each might be defined culturally and historically – and commitment to eliminating those differences in power.[12] Catherine Spence herself looked to Mary Astell's *Essay in Defence of the Female Sex*, written in 1696, and Mary Wollstonecraft's *Vindication of the Rights of Woman*, published in 1792, as early clarion calls in the struggle for women's rights (Spence, 'Woman's Suffrage'). Late twentieth-century readers might well find in Margaret Elliot's resolve to study law with her brother, in order to further his career, but not to seek a career in the law herself, an instance of the limitations of Spence's capacity to imagine a society in which differences in opportunity for income-earning work between women and men had disappeared. But a reading of *Mr Hogarth's Will*, if nothing else, makes it clear that Margaret's solution did not proceed from any deficiencies in Spence's imagination, but rather from her realism. And her depiction of the characters in *Clara Morison* suggests strongly a commitment to changing the conventional relationships between women and men.

The principal male characters learn, mainly through the need to provide for themselves at the gold-diggings, what a labour washing and cooking can be, and thereby turn themselves into desirable husbands (II:41–42, 88–89). Reginald does not go through this particular test, but he passes all the tests of literariness and then sensibility, fidelity, and an untrammelled chivalry, to become a worthy suitor to Clara. The principal female characters, who occupy the centre-stage of this novel (as they do in all of Spence's novels), establish themselves as desirable wives by proving their capacity to earn a living in extremely difficult circumstances (Clara), and to manage their household independently while the men are away at the gold-diggings (the Elliot sisters). Moreover, Clara (like all of Spence's heroines) is a rebel. Miles Franklin thought she would still be considered a rebel a century later, for she 'hated crochet and despised worsted work' (*Laughter* 53). Cast as a conventional romantic heroine, encountering situations which, in different hands, would reduce such a figure to illness, destitution or moral ruin on the Beaufort property, Clara, instead, finds work, makes friends and defends herself competently against sexual harassment.

In the South Australia in which young Catherine Spence had to defend her younger sister from the opprobrium that might be associated with the notion that she wrote for the daily press, even anonymously (as Spence did) (*Autobiography* 22), Clara Morison was a figure to challenge many proprieties. But in the literary world she was an instance of a new wave. Clara asks Reginald, during one of their literary discussions, 'Is not Jane Eyre, who is neither handsome nor what is called good, a more interesting and natural character than you will find in men's books?' (II:59). Over a century later, north American literary critic Elaine Showalter observed:

> The influence of *Jane Eyre* on Victorian heroines was felt to have been revolutionary. The post-Jane heroine, according to the periodicals, was plain, rebellious, and passionate; she was likely to be a governess, and she was usually the narrator of her own story. (Showalter 122)

None of Spence's heroines narrate their own stories. Neither Clara, nor the wonderful Jessie Lindsay in *The Author's Daughter*, who proposes to George Copeland on her way to do the milking, nor Jane Melville in *Mr Hogarth's Will*, the novel in which, Spence said, she 'took up the woman question of the time – the difficulty of a woman earning a livelihood, even when she had as much ability, industry, and perseverance as a man' (*Autobiography* 25), nor even brilliant, independent Liliard Abercrombie, speak for themselves through Spence's narratives. But they are often plain, often governesses (or housekeepers, who had similar status difficulties), sometimes passionate about public affairs, and always – however mildly – rebellious. All of these characters are unconventional, when compared with Thackeray's schemers or Dickens' insipid and virtuous beauties. They are as unconventional as was Sybylla Melvyn, heroine of Miles Franklin's first novel, *My Brilliant Career*, published in 1901, almost half a century after *Clara Morison*.

It is little wonder, then, that Miles Franklin should have fallen upon *Clara Morison* with such glee. For this novel connected her, and her fiction, with what she could see as a literary origin in Australian feminism. As Marjorie Barnard was to observe:

> Now in Alice Henry [Franklin] met another . . . woman, who, in her turn had lit her torch at the flame of yet another Australian, Catherine Helen Spence, writer, pamphleteer, social reformer . . . Catherine Spence was born in Scotland in 1825: Rose Scott was born in the Hunter Valley, Australia, in 1847: Alice Henry in 1847. Miles Franklin in 1857. There was, you see, quite a dynasty of women, all unmarried, all practical philanthropists and reformers, all deeply interested in the cause of women, each in turn linked to another. Catherine Spence became one of Miles's heroines both as reformer and writer. (Barnard 43)

WORKS CITED

Allen, Margaret. 'Three South Australian Women Writers, 1854–1923: Matilda Evans, Catherine Spence and Catherine Martin'. PhD thesis, Flinders University, 1991.

Anonymous. 'Catherine Helen Spence 1825–1905'. Pamphlet reprinted from the *Register*, Adelaide, 1905.

Barnard, Marjorie. *Miles Franklin*. Melbourne: Hill of Content, 1967.

Daniels, V.K. 'History and Literature: A Study of the Novels of C.H. Spence'. BA Hons. thesis, University of Adelaide, 1962.

Delmar, Rosaline. 'What is Feminism?'. *What is Feminism?* Ed. Juliet Mitchell and Ann Oakley. Oxford: Basil Blackwell, 1986.

Docker, John. *In a Critical Condition: Reading Australian Literature*. Ringwood: Penguin, 1984.

Eade [Magarey], Susan. 'A Study of Catherine Helen Spence 1825–1919'. MA thesis, Australian National University, 1971.

Franklin, Miles. Untitled undated talk. MS. Miles Franklin Papers. ML MSS 364/63.
_____. Letter to Alice Henry, 22 September 1930. Miles Franklin Papers, General Correspondence 1908–1949. Mitchell Library [ML] MSS 364/11.
_____. *Laughter, Not for a Cage*. Sydney: Angus & Robertson, 1956.

Giles, Fiona. 'Finding a Shiftingness: Situating the Nineteenth-Century Anglo-Australian Female Subject'. *New Literatures Review* 18 (1989).

_____. 'Romance: An Embarrassing Subject'. *Penguin New Literary History*. Ed. Hergenhan et al.

Green, H.M. *A History of Australian Literature Pure and Applied*. 2 vols. 1st pub. 1961, revised by Dorothy Green. Sydney: Angus & Robertson, 1984.

Henry, Alice. 'Catherine Helen Spence: The Grand Old Woman of Australia'. *Survey* (New York), 16 April 1910.

Hergenhan, Laurie, Bruce Bennett, Martin Duwell, Brian Matthews, Peter Pierce and Elizabeth Webby Eds. *The Penguin New Literary History of Australia*. Ringwood: Penguin, 1988.

Hooton, Joy. 'Australian Literary History and Some Colonial Women Novelists'. *Southerly* 50.3 (1990).

Kirkby, Diane. *Alice Henry: The Power of Pen and Voice: The Life of an Australian-American Labor Reformer*. Cambridge: Cambridge University Press, 1991.

Ljungdahl, Lesley Durrell . 'Prologue'. Spence. *A Week in the Future*.

Magarey, Susan. 'Radical Woman Catherine Spence'. *Rebels and Radicals*. Ed. Eric Fry. Sydney: Allen & Unwin, 1983.

_____. *Unbridling the Tongues of Women: A Biography of Catherine Helen Spence*. Sydney: Hale & Iremonger, 1985.

_____. 'Feminist Visions across the Pacific: Catherine Helen Spence's *Handfasted*'. *Antipodes: A North American Journal of Australian Literature* 3.1 (1989).

Modjeska, Drusilla. *Exiles at Home: Australian Women Writers 1925–1945*. North Ryde: Angus & Robertson, 1981. Repr. 1991.

Morgan, Patrick. 'Realism and Documentary: Lowering One's Sights'. *The Penguin New Literary History of Australia*. Ed. Hergenhan et al.

Perkins, Elizabeth. 'Colonial Transformations: Writing and the Dilemma of Colonisation'. *Penguin New Literary History*. Ed. Hergenhan et al.

Roe, Jill, ed. *My Congenials: Miles Franklin & Friends in Letters*. 2 vols. Sydney: Angus & Robertson, 1993.

Sheridan, Susan. 'Ada Cambridge and the Female Literary Tradition'. *Nellie Melba, Ginger Meggs and Friends: Essays in Australian Cultural History*. Eds Susan Dermody, John Docker and Drusilla Modjeska. Malmsbury: Kibble Books, 1982.

Showalter, Elaine. *A Literature of Their Own*. Princeton: Princeton UP, 1977.

Sinnett, Frederick. 'Fiction Fields of Australia'. *The Writer in Australia: A Collection of Literary Documents 1856 to 1964*. Ed. John Barnes. Melbourne: Oxford UP, 1969.

Spence, Catherine Helen. Anonymous letter in Catherine Spence's handwriting. To Smith, Elder and Company. 1 August 1853. ML, MS (A111).

————. *Clara Morison: A Tale of South Australia during the Gold Fever*. 1854. Facsimile edition Adelaide: Wakefield Press, 1986.

————. *Tender and True: A Colonial Tale*. London: Smith, Elder, 1856.

————. *The Author's Daughter*. London: R. Bently, 1868.

————. *An Agnostic's Progress from the Known to the Unknown*. London: Williams and Norgate, 1884.

————. 'Woman's Suffrage and Effective Voting, A Paper read at a Drawing-Room Meeting at Glenelg'. *Voice*, 9 December 1892.

————. Writing as A Colonist of 1839. 'Dialect – A Protest'. Galley Proofs, ML.

————. 'The Australian in Literature'. *Register*, 22 November 1902. The article is anonymous, but it is among Spence's papers in its printed form, marked 'C.H.S.' in her handwriting, ML.

————. *An Autobiography*. Reprinted from the *Register*, Adelaide, 1910. Reproduced by the Libraries Board of South Australia, Australiana Facsimile Editions, no. 199, Adelaide, 1975.

————. *Gathered In: A Novel*. Intro. B.L. Waters and G.A. Wilkes. Sydney: Sydney UP, 1977.

————. *Handfasted*. Ed., Preface and Afterword Helen Thomson. Ringwood: Penguin, 1984.

————. *A Week in the Future*. Intro. and Notes Lesley Durrell Ljungdahl. Sydney: Hale & Iremonger, 1987.

————. *Mr. Hogarth's Will*. Intro. Helen Thomson. Ringwood: Penguin, 1988.

Spender, Dale. *Writing A New World: Two Centuries of Australian Women Writers*. London: Pandora, 1988.

Summers, Anne. *Damned Whores and God's Police*. Ringwood: Penguin, 1975. New revised edition 1994.

Thomson, Helen. 'Love and Labour: Marriage and Work in the Novels of Catherine Helen Spence'. *A Bright and Fiery Troop: Australian Women Writers of the Nineteenth Century*. Ed. Debra Adelaide. Ringwood: Penguin, 1988.

NOTES

1. Stella Franklin to Alice Henry, 22 September 1930, Miles Franklin Papers, General Correspondence 1908–49, Mitchell Library [ML] MSS 364/11.

2. 'Catherine Helen Spence 1825–1905', pamphlet reprinted from the *Register*, Adelaide, 1905; C.H. Spence, *An Autobiography*, reprinted from the *Register*, Adelaide, 1910, reproduced by the Libraries Board of South Australia, Australiana Facsimile Editions, no. 199, Adelaide, 1975; the last eight chapters of Spence's *Autobiography* were, in fact, written by her friend and colleague Jeanne F. Young; see also Susan Magarey, *Unbridling the Tongues of Women*.

3. This novel has appeared in a number of different editions. It was first published in 1854 by Rigby Limited, Adelaide, who also published a second edition in 1971, with an introduction and notes on the text by Susan Eade (Magarey); facsimile edition by Wakefield Press, Adelaide, 1986 with revised introduction and notes on the text by Susan Magarey; also as a volume of the Portable Australian Authors series *Catherine Helen Spence*, ed. with intro. by Helen Thomson, St Lucia: University of Queensland Press, 1987.

4. *An Agnostic's Progress; Autobiography* 11; *Unbridling* ch. 3; Allen ch. 9.

5. Miles Franklin to Lucy Spence Morice, 10 August 1936 in Roe I:338.

6. 'The Australian in Literature', *Register*, 22 November 1902; the article is anonymous, but it is among Spence's papers in its printed form, marked 'C.H.S.' in her handwriting, ML; *Autobiography*, 97.

7. Frederick Sinnett, 'Fiction Fields of Australia', first printed in two parts in the *Journal of Australasia*, September and November 1856, reprinted in *The Writer in Australia: A Collection of Literary Documents 1856 to 1964*, edited by John Barnes.

8. Summers ch. 1; Hooton 310; see also, for example, Drusilla Modjeska, *Exiles At Home: Australian Women Writers 1925–1945*, esp. 8–9; Susan Sheridan, 'Ada Cambridge and the Female Literary Tradition', esp. pp. 162– 66; John Docker, *In a Critical Condition*.

9. Modjeska 121; Sheridan 166; Morgan 241.

10. Susan Eade [Magarey], 'A Study of Catherine Helen Spence 1825–1919'; Susan Magarey, 'Radical Woman Catherine Spence'; Magarey, *Unbridling*, ch. 2; Helen Thomson, 'Love and Labour'; Dale Spender, *Writing A New World*:176–181; Perkins, 'Colonial Transformations', 146.

11. See also notes on the text in the Rigby and Wakefield Press editions.

12 See, for example, Rosalind Delmar, 'What is Feminism?'.

CHAPTER

4

READING CATHERINE MARTIN'S
AN AUSTRALIAN GIRL

Margaret Allen

'A true child of the age we live in,' wrote Catherine Spence of her friend and fellow South Australian writer, Catherine Martin (1848–1937) (Spence 2). Martin was in many ways in tune with the intellectual climate of the last decades of the nineteenth century, during which period two of her major works, *An Australian Girl* (1890) and *The Silent Sea* (1892), and a number of her serial stories and short stories appeared.[1] This was the era of 'the revolt against positivism' and 'the turn towards the subjective' (Hughes 34). Much of Martin's work is characterised by a critique of positivistic and mechanistic philosophies and takes a sceptical view of many of the religious and social reform positions espoused so unilaterally by South Australian writers from an earlier generation – namely Matilda Jane Evans and Catherine Helen Spence (see Allen).

While Martin's works can be seen as congruent with some of the intellectual movements of the last decade of the nineteenth century, the rejection of positivism in her works draws strongly upon the ideas of German romanticism and idealism which permeated her own education and reading. It is intriguing that Martin, born Catherine Mackay in Skye in 1848, the daughter of a poor crofter family which emigrated to South Australia in 1855, should, with the assistance of a philanthropic organisation, have gained such an intellectual education. Her education has been described as 'private, in an up-country district in South Australia, but she was a diligent student of literature, and made herself familiar not only with the great German poets, but with the works of Kant, Fichte, and Hegel' (Plarr 726).[2] The romanticism and idealism which Martin imbibed from her studies were sharply divergent from the rationalist and positivist notions that dominated much Western European thought in the century after the Enlightenment. Much nineteenth-century German thought was critical of ideas important to the Western European Enlightenment, in particular the utilitarian attitude towards knowledge, the idea that one gained knowledge in order to manipulate and change the world. Just as the world defied total scientific categorisation and scientific manipulation, the individual was also seen as richly complex and ultimately infinite and unknowable.

Martin's work bears the marks of a close study of the novels of George Eliot. Just as George Eliot's *Middlemarch* has been seen as history, sketching out the complexities of social change in nineteenth-century England, Martin, in *An Australian Girl* and *The Silent Sea*, portrays a large panoramic vista of contemporary Australian society, as well as, in part, that of Europe. Many stories are told, allowing the reader to see various aspects of the social order. In *An Australian Girl* we meet wealthy pastoralists, Anglican clergy, some *nouveau riche*, philanthrophic women, missionaries, German scholars, and rural workers. We visit the Mallee, Melbourne and the homes of rich and poor in Adelaide. The many elements of these novels come together in symphonic form. The authorial voice is not fixed and didactic; rather it is ironic and detached, only rarely advocating a particular view.

Martin's works demonstrate the complexity of the world and of people, and there is little movement towards closure in texts such as *An Australian Girl*. Some of the complexity of Martin's development of character can be seen in the character of Stella Courtland, heroine of *An Australian Girl*, a 'character that is still growing when the book ends' (Byrnes 23). The reader is aware that Stella is influenced by forces beyond her conscious knowledge and control. She is a paradoxical figure – wary of marriage, but then marries precipitately. She is critical of those who engage in social reform, but feels intensely the sorrow and misery of the poor. She has had a wide education and has read deeply in religion and philosophy, but is ignorant of the baseness of the character of others and is thus ill-equipped to survive material and practical pressures. This helps to bring her to grief and to personal and psychological crisis. The nature of her character is unfolded within the larger structure of the novel, which is based upon elements of the quest and also the two suitor novel, in which contrasting suitors offer contrasting possible lives for the heroine.

Martin engages with the conventional generic structures of nineteenth-century literature, which she moulds and shapes to her own ends. She rearranges, reverses and at times denies these devices. In the classic style of the quest novel, *An Australian Girl* focuses upon Stella Courtland during the period from when she is in the bosom of the family, through a time of indecision about whether and whom she will marry, to marriage and apparent installation in society as the wife of a wealthy landed proprietor in South Australia. Stella changes from being a cynic about important social issues and institutions such as marriage and social reform, to someone committed to the wider society, including activity in social reform. She also submits to social conventions about marriage. The two suitor convention and the development of the heroine's character chart the oppositions and possible synthesis of the material world on one hand, and the life of the mind and the spirit on the other. Martin also uses the two suitor convention to explore ideas about another dualism, Australian identity *vis-a-vis* that of Europe.

As the novel opens, Stella Courtland is twenty-three, the daughter of a comfortably placed Adelaide family. Her mother is the widow of an Anglican clergyman, who has invested an inheritance in a station in Victoria, Lullaboolagana, which is run by her older sons. Stella's brother Cuthbert is also an Anglican clergyman, and one sister is the wife of yet another Anglican clergyman. An older sister, Esther, is the widow of a pastoralist and lives on her station in the south-east of the colony. Alice, only eighteen months older than Stella, is engaged to be married but, in middle-class style, is waiting for her fiancé, a rising young professional man, an architect, to be able to afford marriage. Tom, the youngest son, is a lawyer. Stella's siblings have made their decisions about the direction of their lives, and have gained adult status. Stella, the youngest, is beautiful and by some accounts 'spoiled'.

Stella is introduced to the reader with a description which shows the combination of beauty and high intelligence, the material and the spiritual, with which she is endowed:

> The eyes were extremely beautiful – starry, large, deep and liquid. When we try to describe eyes or flowers, we find that language is extremely destitute in precise colour terms. They were dark gray-blue – sea-blue is, perhaps, the term that most nearly approximates to the hue of this girl's eyes . . . They were as sensitive to her moods as the surface of the water is to the sky's influence. Thus it will be seen that their range of expression was infinite. The same might be said of the whole countenance. When moved or animated, it glowed and sparkled as if a light shone through it. The brow was singularly noble, and gave promise of unusual mental power. The complexion was very fair and clear, and when she talked it was often tinged with swift delicate rose-pink, that died away very slowly, leaving a soft warm glow in the cheeks like that often seen in a moist sea-shell. It was a face whose every line and feature indicated that Stella was endowed with rare qualities of intellect and imagination, quick to feel, to see, to think. And yet a very woman, far from indifferent to admiration and the sense of power that the homage of men gives a girl. Yet, withal, liable to that quick disdain of the more frivolous aspects of life, which to those who understood but one side of her complex nature appeared in the light of wilful caprice. (I:14–15)

Stella is more complex than any quick summation might indicate, her range of expression is 'infinite'. An important key to understanding her position is the fact that she has 'rare qualities of intellect and imagination' but is 'yet a very woman', subject to the dangers and weaknesses that society puts in woman's way, including the danger of enjoying the rather doubtful power that men's admiration gives her. Her seriousness, her 'disdain of the more frivolous aspects of life', is misunderstood and seen as 'wilful caprice'.

Stella's mind has a 'brooding introspective undercurrent', derived from both her relationship with the Australian landscape and from her speculative investigations of the meaning of existence (I:88). Stella is well-read, particularly in German literature and philosophy.[3] Her studies of Kant and Goethe are not conducive to her submitting to the social rounds assigned a well-bred young lady in colonial society. We understand that her social situation is not large enough for her nature. The similarity between Stella and some of George Eliot's heroines, notably Maggie Tulliver and Dorothea Brooke, is striking.[4] In the Prelude to *Middlemarch*, Eliot writes of Saint Theresa, whose story evidently influenced her in the creation of Dorothea Brooke, the heroine of *Middlemarch*:

> Theresa's passionate, ideal nature demanded an epic life: what were many volumed romances of chivalry and the social conquests of a brilliant girl to her? Her flame quickly burned up that light fuel; and fed from within, soared after some illimitable satisfaction, some object which would never justify weariness, which would reconcile self-despair with the rapturous consciousness of life beyond self . . . Many Theresas have been born who found for themselves no epic life wherein there was a constant unfolding of far-resonant action; perhaps only a life of mistakes, the offspring of a certain spiritual grandeur ill-matched with the meanness of opportunity. (3)

Stella, who refers to Saint Teresa (as Martin spells it) a number of times, similarly yearns for something greater than what surrounds her. Throughout the novel there are various reminders of the contrast between the breadth of Stella's nature and education and the 'meanness of opportunity', the narrow social role open to her, between her spiritual nature and yearnings and the material reality. Thus she thinks of Kant's 'The Kritik of Pure Reason' (sic) when the hairdresser comes to do her hair before a ball. She listens to the scholarly talk of her friends, Dr Stein and Professor Kellwitz, as they discuss 'the early twilight of man's history on earth' and a new work on the narrowness of man's freedom. Later Stella recalls her thoughts:

> I was sewing in a desultory dejected way – and gradually a sense of being very ignorant stole over me – of wasting my time on a foolish

shirt for a preposterous baby who should never have been born! But then I reflected that my metier is to please – not to be learned – and that the more foolish I am the more charming I may be. This reflection comforted me marvellously. I feel it in me to be perennially foolish. I went on sewing with redoubled speed. (I:181)

In this novel Stella does not stand astride the action. Martin creates characters somewhat in the style of George Eliot, characters who are buffeted by mighty elements. Throughout the novel there are a number of suggestions that events are not wholly within her power. She has a number of premonitions of misery or of some catastrophe in the future (see for example I:33, II:260–63).

Stella has a deep nature and struggles to find something more than the prosaic surface of life. She had some years previously undergone dramatic changes in her religious beliefs. Raised in the Anglican Church, Stella, in preparing for confirmation at the age of seventeen, became dissatisfied with that creed and with the smug assurances of her teacher, her clergyman godfather. Previously indifferent, if not 'slightly antagonistic' to religion, she now throws herself into the study and observances of Catholicism, an anathema to those around her. She reads works such as Cousin's *Jacqueline Pascal*, Newman's *Apologia*, St Teresa's letters and 'a book about the Spanish Saints, which I loved very much'. She becomes very pious, separating herself from the material world:

I began the practice of rising at certain hours in the night to pray and meditate. It was like an ecstasy, that strange new power of rising in transports of prayer above all the things of earth. When my heart glowed, and my whole mind was borne as if beyond the barriers of sense, I felt ready for any sacrifice. (I:96)

She attends the Catholic church, but her mother forbids her to become a Catholic before she is twenty. Stella's enthusiasm can be read as evidence of her spiritual yearnings: 'How entirely, how sincerely, I offered up my whole life as I lay prostrate in spirit, adoring God for the heavenly mysteries at which I was permitted to assist' (I:99). However, she shortly becomes disillusioned with Catholicism and moves from this strong faith to disenchantment as she begins to question the absolute claims of religion: 'How many besides Christ have been reputed to be of mystical birth?' (I:105)

Stella's critical faculties are re-awakened when, worshipping before the Virgin and Child, she now notices that 'her crown was fly-marked, and her pink sarcenet robe tawdry and duststained' (I:110). Being introduced to Kant by her German teacher and friend, Pastor Fiedler, Stella begins a process of disengagement from her blind faith. Kant argued that it is impossible to know through reason whether there is or is not a supreme being. Stella points out Kant's conclusion, 'we may hope, but we may not know'.

It is not only in regard to religion that Stella confounds the expectations of her family. She is very critical of the institution of marriage, saying that since childhood she has been 'convinced that marriage is the most foolish, faulty old institution going' (I:63). She has, however, been courted almost since childhood by Ted Ritchie, a friend of the family. The son of Sir Edward Ritchie, a man of lowly birth who has prospered in Australia, Ted has come into a great deal of money and owns a vast property, Strathaye in the south-east of South Australia. He very much represents the material side of life. He is an attractive young man:

> The young man was good-looking in a not uncommon and distinctly unintellectual way. He was close on six feet in height, with a well-knit athletic figure, a sun-bronzed face, inclining to be florid. The forehead was low and square . . . it was the face of a man who could be firm and determined in action, yet morally lacking in force of will. (I:15–16)

Ted is easy-going and does not share any of Stella's intellectual and spiritual concerns: 'Nothing in books, or the destiny of the race, or the life of the soul, had ever moved him. But, then, he was not without a horse or two that had achieved something wonderful, or was just going to do so, or might do it if they chose' (I:67). With 'a limited outlook on life', he seems an unlikely suitor. He sees the 'chief end of man' to 'sell on the rise and have a good time' (I:23). Stella finds Ted's prosaic nature amusing and, given her lack of any real kindred soul, it is not surprising that at times she falls back on the relationship with this childhood friend. He adores her and she laughingly heads off his marriage proposals. They share a love of horses and the outdoors, and go on long morning rides together. Stella has:

> a passionate love of being in the open air, of riding, of getting away from people who were, more or less, tiresome – she herself, at times, most of all. On horseback, more completely than anywhere else, she threw every haunting shade of troubled thought to the winds. Life then became a glorious ecstasy – a glad, bounding motion in which simply to be was enough, without any foolish looking before and after. (II:10)

She has become aware that her brother Cuthbert, previously a close confidante, disapproves of her critical and questioning nature. She teases him about her inability to become a 'bread-and-butter miss': 'I should dearly like to be a facsimile of the good little pig that stayed at home; but nature is too strong' (I:239, 241). However, when he becomes engaged to Dora, a sweet and very proper daughter of an English clergyman, Stella feels very jealous and isolated from her brother. Dora has the 'sweet untroubled faith of childhood' and: 'Dora was very pretty; fair and *mignonne*, with pale gold hair in crisp wavelets, a pure English complexion, and large blue eyes that had something of the expression of a child's who has suddenly been told a pleasant piece of news' (II:1). Stella is aware that her friendship with her brother, 'the chief attachment of my life', is crumbling away. When she visits Dora's family, Cuthbert notes critically that Stella is 'bored in this exquisitely refined Christian home and yet tolerant of Ritchie as a lover!' He upbraids her for her association with Ted and Stella retorts, 'You see, we Australians understand one another! We have a wicked love of enjoyment, of horses, and sunshine, and the seashore' (II:9).

Just below the surface at times is a clearer articulation of Stella's sexual attraction to Ted than these discussions of their mutual love of horses. She thinks of what reason she should give in refusing his proposals:

> And then a little panic seized her, that no reason she could offer would stand the tide of Ted's remonstrances. She did not

acknowledge it to herself, and yet a vague consciousness underlay her musings, that the masterful way he had held her hands, and looked at her with ardent eyes, made some hitherto unknown chord of her nature vibrate in unison with his will. Perhaps it was a faint reminiscence in her blood of the remote ancestresses of pre-civilisation, who were knocked on the head if they did not fall in with the marriage arrangements made for them. (II:27)

Stella has a sparring, mocking relationship with Ted as she refuses his numerous offers of marriage. At times she is overcome with remorse at the realisation that she has failed to help Ted, that she has: 'relin-quished those ardent dreams of being a power for good in the lives of those to whom she was dear . . . Her face grew hot as she recalled the frivolous way in which she had met his half-expressed resolution of giving up horse-racing . . . she had almost mocked his recoil from his past devotion to the racecourse' (I:143). She becomes accustomed to Ted with all his faults, and sees the consolations that his wealth will bring, 'I begin to see that Ted is my fate. I shall have to succumb. On the whole, it will be less tiresome. And then I want to go to Rome and places' (I:62–63). There are a number of hints throughout the book that Ted is even more earthy than Stella suspects, for he is addicted to alcohol (e.g. I:30, 133–38). Stella does not pick up these clues. When her friend makes a disastrous marriage to an alcoholic who beats her, Stella helps her, but does not transfer this knowledge to her own situation. With her spiritual and intellectual leanings, she is not experienced in coping with the material world. Stella is critical of marriage, but does not make it clear to Ted that she does not plan to marry him. She plays with his feelings. While she is opposed to marriage, she does not take any steps to plan her life without it.

The other suitor, Anselm, responds to the more spiritual and intel-lectual side of Stella's character. He shares her interests in books and ideas and is very different from the men she has previously met. He 'had the look of one so much – how shall I say it? – devoted to ideas, and not jostled up with the meanness of ordinary life. And then his mind had an alert literary kind of side to it . . . you know, one gets so wonderfully weary of the commercial stamp of mind and face, one quickly recognises the difference' (I:279). An English doctor, visiting Australia for a year and well-read in English and German literature and philosophy, Anselm represents European culture, while Ted represents a materialistic Australia. He is also involved in reform, has ministered to the poor in London and is dedicated to the notion of service to the needs of the less fortunate in society. With him, Stella enjoys for the first time what is for her the ideal relationship between a man and a woman, that is, a relationship of friendship. Later they fall in love and discuss marriage. But first Anselm must visit Europe to set his affairs in order. Unbeknown to Stella, this involves ascertaining that his long-estranged wife is dead.

Stella falls prey to Ted's sister, the scheming and social-climbing Laurette Tareling, who wants Stella to marry Ted for her – Laurette's – own financial gain. Laurette has a keen understanding of the weaknesses in Stella's character. Aware that Stella is in love with Anselm, she alters one of his letters to make it appear that he has a loving wife waiting for him in Europe, anxious for reconciliation. The altered letter also suggests that it was Stella who had made the first move towards declaration of their love. Stella is devastated by these revelations and in particular her pride is hurt:

> It was the bitter humiliation of this that stung her beyond endurance. Sorrow in any other form she might have borne – but this scorched her, degraded her, bit into her like some virulent immaterial poison which nourishes the blood in order that it may consume the soul. Jealous of a man's wife! These were the words that came to her perpetually more venomous than the hiss of a serpent. (III:6–7)

Abandoning all her higher aspirations, Stella decides precipitately to marry Ted: 'A marriage in which some kind of friendship was possible – in which travel, movement, variety, were open to her – this was the least objectionable scheme that remained to her. Ted's allegiance was so unshaken – he exacted so little' (III:7). Marriage to Ted will make Stella wealthy. She is impatient to enter adult status and cannot stand the thought of having to return to her childhood home to live with her mother and widowed sister – to take up 'a faded, insipid existence'. Naive about the real world and little able to plumb the deviousness of a person such as Laurette, Stella acts impulsively. She accepts the strange letter unsuspectingly and remains curiously unsuspecting even though, soon after, she sees a play in which letters are similarly stolen (III:33).

Shortly after her marriage she discovers that Ted is a heavy drinker, a 'dipsomaniac'. Laurette had kept this information from Stella, although Ted believed that she knew about it. Stella turns against Ted, telling him that they cannot live as man and wife. Although he vows to rehabilitate himself, she sees him as totally unable to reform. Ted and Stella travel to Europe on their honeymoon trip and in Berlin she meets Anselm by chance and discovers that she has been tricked, that Anselm still loves her and that his wife is dead, just as he suspected. She suffers a nervous collapse.

Both Ted and Anselm try to aid her recovery. Ted is solicitous and gentle. Anselm does not push his suit, but seeks to involve Stella in visiting poor children in a hostel and editing his treatise on factory working conditions.[5] Here the authorial voice pronounces:

> To think exclusively of our selves or our own concerns, even under our best aspects, is, as a rule, to become sad, weary, and discouraged. But to be immured in such thoughts, when the thrill and joy of life are gone, when its best promises are mildewed with disillusionment, is to poison the very source of sane existence and healthy endeavour. It had been so with Stella, and in the lowest depths of her unhappiness there yet opened the lower deep, that the misery which had overtaken her like a flood was so largely her own doing. (III:243)

Even as Stella recovers and immerses herself in charitable work, she begins to understand the forces in her personality which had led her to the hasty decision to marry the 'wrong' man.

With such a plot, there are a number of possible outcomes (Kennard). In a similar situation, having married the wrong man, many heroines of conventional two suitor novels simply expire. Stella, however, recovers. Another possibility, involving decisions rarely made in nineteenth-century novels, is that she leave Ted and attach herself to Anselm. Anselm suggests to her that her marriage to Ted is but a sham and that, as she was tricked into it, she need feel no obligation. However, he advises her to restore her health before making any decisions about the future. Recovered, Stella decides to travel with Anselm, and to stay with him. Initially happy with her decision to end her marriage, to go against 'authority and tradition', later she finds difficulty in justifying the decision. She thinks of how she will explain it to her mother. She has a great personal crisis when she sees Cardinal Newman officiating at Mass: 'She heard nothing – saw nothing but that pale, spiritual presence; the high, noble brow – the austere, ascetic countenance, furrowed with years and sorrows – a face keenly symbolical of a life consecrated to the service of God and man' (III:303). Stella weeps, deeply aware of her spiritual yearnings. Her experience in the church is mysterious and evades rational comprehension: 'There are experiences of the soul that cannot be fathomed. They are beyond the reach of any plummet that is within our grasp – being part of the inscrutable union of matter and spirit' (III:304). She is pierced by the knowledge that:

> her own pride and vanity and impatience of suffering had been at the root of the evil that had overtaken her. A scorching sense of shame at her infidelity to the higher loyalties of justice, and self-sacrifice, and generosity overcame her. Waves of cutting remorse swept over her as she reviewed her conduct in her relationship with her husband. (III:305)

She thinks of her indifference and hardness towards Ted and realises how she had justified leaving Ted by a conviction that he was inherently unable to change himself and that he was irrevocably determined by the material side of his nature: 'She recalled how, in speaking of him she had even inferred that he could not help himself – assuming that the spirit of man, no more than his body, can have any source of impulse or action apart from the inexorable links of material causes' (III:306). She had been viewing Ted as a type or a category, not as a unique individual with vast possibilities. As she realises that she has been happy to assume that Ted is really worthless and of no concern to her, she thinks of something she had once read that summarised the moral influence that one ought to have on others: 'He had so keen an appreciation of what was good in people – quick to perceive how men's failings and vices are often a forced rather than a wilful product. Always he expected them to live

down the evil – to hold to and cultivate the better side of their nature'
(III:306). Resolving to help Ted reform, she rejects any finite nature of
human character, as well as the contemporary notion that alcoholics are
incapable of reform.

In deciding to rise above her personal sorrow, Stella is aided by her
realisation of the great social problems abounding in European cities,
and decides to devote herself to serving others. Her experiences of
socialist circles in Berlin have shocked her. The hatred and bitterness of
the poor women there have disturbed her. She is mistrustful of the
socialism that these women adopt, of 'universal schemes of social bet-
terment', and wary of the belief that there is 'any one system of social
change that could minister so widely, so universally to the evils from
which men suffer' (III:155). She believes that she can help work for better
solutions. Thus the heroine decides to endure. She sees her personal,
emotional crisis in a larger social perspective and decides that her
problems are trifling in comparison. As she tells the distressed Anselm
of her decision, she alludes to the vastness of the universe and the
importance of bringing a good influence to bear in one's own vicinity:

> Yet the day can never come in which we shall be indifferent to each
> other. And in the same way we may know, with a conviction beyond
> dispute, that behind all the confusion and mystery of life there runs
> a great sane purpose with which we may join our wills and lives. In
> the end the most we can hope to do must be limited to a small
> patch of the world, and as far as our personal influence can reach. To
> spoil that for the sake of any happiness. (III:319–20)

Stella and Ted set sail for home, where Stella will set up a scheme to
settle some poor but worthy European families on some of the couple's
Australian property.[6] This unusual ending is consistent with the philosophies and discourses that inform the novel. Stella, it appears, has
achieved a way of relating her spiritual yearnings to the real world.
She has in fact become a Catholic: 'I knew that though I may never be
an orthodox Catholic, yet the old faith had so far revived as to be an
inspiring rule of life, to give a vivifying motive to every exertion' (III:319).
As well as this new religious awareness, Stella also dedicates herself to
serve others. The example of Anselm's commitment to others and her

own experiences with the poor both in London and Berlin help to rekindle her interest in such endeavours. She is now able to work in the world in a practical way to help others. She sees herself now as being able to live with Ted and to help him bring out his better qualities. Stella has also transcended her own situation and sees herself within a larger order. Her happiness is to be neither bounded nor limited by the man to whom she is married. There is a sense in which Stella now does not need a man to define her. She is now larger and too autonomous for that.

Here the two suitors convention, then, has been given an interesting turn. Stella attains a greater understanding of herself and the motivation of some of her behaviour. This makes her resolve to turn her back upon the man she loves, and with whom she has had great intellectual companionship, to take on a larger social role, as well as to commit herself to Ted, the 'wrong man'. Now Stella, indeed, looks forward to the day when she will be able to tell Ted about herself and Anselm – that is, she anticipates that she and Ted will be able to have a real understanding of each other. Ted is viewed as being redeemable, as having boundless potential.

Stella's decision to stay with Ted, and in particular her resolve to remedy his poor education, can be compared to similar situations in other South Australian novels. It is like Marian Herbert's civilising of Allen Burton in Matilda Evans's *Marian* and Amy Staunton's tutoring of Alan Lindsay in Catherine Helen Spence's *The Author's Daughter*. A woman is seen as being able to redeem Australian manhood – able to foster the appropriate mix of culture and practicality. Significantly, of these three characters, Stella is the only Australian girl.

Catherine Martin was as, Catherine Spence noted, 'a true child of her age', conversant with contemporary ideas, and touched by a rising Australian nationalism. But her work also drew upon other, older sources, including a close reading of the works of George Eliot and her youthful immersion in the literature of German romanticism.

WORKS CITED

Allen, Margaret. 'Three South Australian Women Writers, 1854–1923: Matilda Evans, Catherine Spence and Catherine Martin'. PhD thesis, Flinders University, 1991.

Byrnes, John V. 'Catherine Martin and the Critics'. *Australian Letters* 3.4 (1961).

Eliot, G. *Middlemarch*. Ed. D. Carroll. Oxford & New York: Oxford University Press, 1988.

Hughes, H. Stuart. *Consciousness and Society: The Re-orientation of European Social Thought 1880–1930*. New York: Vintage, 1958.

Kennard, Jean. *Victims of Convention*. Archon Books: Hamden, Conn., 1978.

Martin, Catherine. *An Australian Girl*. 1890. 3 vols. London: Bentley, 1890.

———. *Border Watch*. 2 February 1920.

Martin, E.C. 'George Eliot's Life'. *The Victorian Review*. 12 (June 1885). 162–89.

Plarr, Victor G. *Men and Women of Our Time: A Dictionary of Contemporaries*. 15th ed. Revised and brought down to the present time. London: George Routledge and Sons, 1899.

Robertson, J.G. *A History of German Literature*. 5th Edition. Edinburgh & London: Wm Blackwood & Sons, 1966.

Spence, Catherine Helen. Review of *The Silent Sea*. *The Voice*, 9 December 1892. 2.

NOTES

1   Her other publications include *The Explorers and Other Poems* (1874), *The Old Roof Tree* (1906) and *The Incredible Journey* (1923) as well as numerous other pieces, short stories, travel writing, serial stories and verse in newspapers.

2.   It appears that C.H. Spence encouraged Martin to submit an entry to Plarr's publication (Spence, Diary, August 1894). Martin referred to the works of Goethe, Schiller, Lessing, Herder, Novalis, Teick, Jean Paul Richter as 'some of the noblest productions of human genius' (*Border Watch*, 2 February 1920).

3.   In 1889 Catherine Martin submitted a manuscript entitled 'Letters of Stella von Arnim' to Macmillan (Macmillan records Reel 64 part 2). This indicates a possible source of the name Stella. Bettina von Arnim (née Brentano) 1785–1859 was a friend of Goethe's and corresponded with him over five years. Like her brother and husband she was a writer involved in the romantic

movement in Germany in the early nineteenth century. She was 'one of the prominent women writers of her time' (Robertson 374, 391, 433). Goethe wrote a work entitled 'Stella'. It appears that that the manuscript submitted to Macmillan was a forerunner of *An Australian Girl*.

4. In a biographical entry, presumably contributed by Martin, there is acknowledgment of the influence of George Eliot in *An Australian Girl* and *The Silent Sea* (Plarr 726). See also E.C. Martin, 'George Eliot's Life', *The Victorian Review*, 12 (June 1885): 162–89 (in table of contents listed as by Mrs Frederic Martin).

5. Here it is interesting to note another connection with *Middlemarch*. In Eliot's novel, Causubon is opposed to Dorothea assisting him in his work, while Anselm encourages Stella.

6. This appears to be a revisiting of *Middlemarch*, where Dorothea builds cottages for the poor.

CHAPTER

ELLEN LISTON'S 'DOCTOR' AND THE ELLISTON INCIDENT

Rick Hosking

A useful insight into the typical valorisation of some of the experiences of the settler-colonist through a conscious process of selective reporting can be found in the short story 'Doctor', which was written by the South Australian writer Ellen Liston, and first published in the Adelaide *Observer* on 17 June 1882.[1]

Liston[2] was born in London on 25 March 1838, and came to South Australia in 1850. In 1869 she travelled to one of the remotest edges of Britain's empire, the west coast of South Australia, to work as a governess on John Chipp Hamp's Nilkerloo (now called Chickerloo) Station, where she not only fulfilled her duties as the teacher of Hamp's children, but also helped with the station work, experience which she later used in a number of short stories and serial novels which were published through the 1870s and 1880s. It appears that Liston began writing in earnest on Nilkerloo, and contributed short stories and verse to the Adelaide *Observer* and to other periodicals. She left the West Coast in 1872, returned to Adelaide, trained as a teacher, taught at East Wellington on the Murray River and then applied for work with the

Posts and Telegraphs Department. After working for some time in the GPO in Adelaide as, it is asserted, the first woman telegraphist in South Australia, Liston was appointed Post and Telegraph Mistress at Watervale. In 1878 she was transferred to the Post Office at Marrabel. She died at Harkness on 19 August 1885, and is buried in the Kapunda Church of Christ cemetery.

In the early 1880s, while living at Marrabel (and possibly inspired by a piece of fanciful 'ficto-history' published in the Adelaide *Observer*), Liston attempted a sequence of stories about the fluctuating fortunes of a married 'pioneer' couple nearly twenty years before Henry Lawson was to attempt the same in his 'Joe Wilson' sequence. 'Doctor', the first in the sequence, was written at Marrabel in 1882. The second Kit and Jack story, 'Our Baggage-Mule', was also written at Marrabel in 1882, and later published in the Adelaide *Observer* on 30 June 1883, while the third, 'Our Domestic Helps', was written in Marrabel in July 1882 but not published until 1936. Given that all three published stories were written so close together, it is perhaps reasonable to assume that Liston was attempting a novel which plotted the progress of a young couple from a hut on the frontiers of the colony to a middle age of affluence in Adelaide's suburbs – exploring the now-contentious paradigm of the settler-colonists' rise to riches.

'Doctor' is Ellen Liston's most powerful short fiction. At first glance, it seems to challenge some of the orthodoxies of masculine writing about the 'outback' in late nineteenth-century 'Australian Literature'. In a short preface to the story 'Doctor', Fiona Giles justly draws the comparison with some of Barbara Baynton's stories, and notes that both writers represent the Bush as a powerfully Gothic site where mysterious and violent events occur:

> Kit is the first white woman in the district. She has nerve and compassion, generously adopting a phantom dog when there is little enough food to spare for her husband and child. This environment is similar to the one depicted by Barbara Baynton in her stories, peopled with isolated wanderers and settlers; some good, some threatening. Here the overtones are also mysterious, but it is the good which is often more unaccountable than the bad.

Although this story was written in 1882, it is set earlier in the century (Giles 132).

Both Liston and Baynton write about the woman alone in a Bush setting which is variously represented as threatening, dangerous, and mysterious. Both represent the Bush as a site for sensational happenings. Both Liston and Baynton describe the sexual threat to the woman posed by the isolation from 'civilisation' and by predatory males in particular, a threat seen as an essential aspect of women's experience on the empire's periphery.

It is possible to detect the influence of popular British sensational and thriller fiction on both writers. Liston wrote a handful of 'crime stories' in which events or characters are presented in ways that at first appear to be mysterious and even supernatural, but are later revealed to be mundane and everyday. It can be argued that Liston's late nineteenth-century fictions show some allegiance to the 'School of Terror' initiated by Ann Radcliffe in the late eighteenth century, where the reader is at first encouraged to suspect supernatural agencies at work, but then reassured by rational explanations for them. Certainly this narrative strategy re-emerged in the later nineteenth century with the boom in the popular publishing of short fictions all around the world – Conan Doyle's first Sherlock Holmes story appeared in 1887, suggesting that Liston (in just a handful of stories) was well placed to use her experience at Nilkerloo as a basis for the kinds of thriller or crime fiction which, as Stephen Knight has shown, dominated Australian popular writing in the last four decades of the century.[3] It can be asserted that Liston might have assumed she was writing popular (even ephemeral) pieces for publishing in local Adelaide newspapers, occasional writings which, read against her own steady output of fanciful and now mostly unreadable romances through the 1860s and 1870s, signal something of a change in direction late in her writing career to attempt her own versions of these newly-popular crime fictions.

'Doctor' opens with the arrival of the half-mastiff, half-Newfoundland[4] dog at the family's remote hut on a station named Three Peaks. The time is twenty-seven years before the narrator's present. Kit reveals that she is a soft touch where dogs are concerned, for which Jack 'was always twitting [her] . . . in the early years of . . . married life' (133).[5] She feeds the dog and it disappears for a day or two. She is delighted to see it return, for Jack is often away with their other dogs with the stock, and Kit feels that this mysterious dog would be good company for herself and her son. It is clear that Kit is pleased to welcome her canine friend and companion, for reasons that (although unstated) can be deduced from a long expository reflection, where it is made clear that Three Peaks is 'no place for a nervous lady':

> You colonists[6] of today have very little idea, if any, of what our life as pioneers in the far bush was in those days. We were one and forty miles from the most embryo township, and that was in the very wilds itself; from it we had to get all the necessaries of life; the luxuries that fell to our lot were very small, excepting our meat that, of course, we grew. The drays went down from the Three Peaks twice a year for the shearing stores and then with the wool; and ours went with them, as the more company the better when the blacks were numerous and ofttimes troublesome. Our sheep used to be shorn at the Three Peaks, as we were only small beginners, and had no shed.
>
> Mine was an exceptional case, too. I was the first white woman in that district, and the only one for some time; but when I married Jack I had no mind to be parted from him almost directly and be left in the comparative comfort and safety of the township, while he went to the wilds alone to establish our future home. I was young, with plenty of strength and nerve, and as I was to share the ease and independence we meant to gain, I elected also to take a little of the preliminary hardships and discomforts. Our hut was on the border of a pretty she-oak flat; but all round for many miles was almost limitless light scrub. It was broken in many places by patches of she-oak country, and far away towards the distant ranges it grew more wooded. Sometimes, on still, quiet days, the solitude would seem almost oppressive; a vast and terrible stillness seemed to lie over everything; frequently it would press so heavily upon me that I was tempted to flee away shrieking as from some unholy presence. (134–5)

This is a typical description of what many Australians still like to think they remember as the grim and difficult actualities of the colonist's life. Conventional 'literary-historical' readings of such a passage might well note that Liston's ideas about the Bush anticipate some of Henry Lawson's influential remarks in 'The Drover's Wife' or Barbara Baynton's stories like 'Squeaker's Mate' or 'The Chosen Vessel'. What emerges is the idea that to celebrate the achievements of the settler-colonist, one must accept a linear view of history, where the effort, application and bravery of (usually) male but here (perhaps uncharacteristically) female pioneers have shaped the safe and secure domestic worlds of those who follow them. There may have been (usually unacknowledged) casualties along the way – for example, the dispossessed Aborigines – but in the long run Aboriginal suffering and dispossession does not matter in the face of the greater good which has flowed to those who come later and who have directly benefited from the colonial enterprise. To read the later two 'Kit and Jack' stories is to realise this point. The fact that the third story, 'Our Domestic Helps', represents Kit and Jack as having travelled a long way from the wilds and melancholies of the West Coast to a comfortable middle-class existence in Adelaide's northern suburbs suggests a linear, evolutionary progress from barbarism to civilisation which Liston and her contemporaries obviously considered as justifying the entire colonising enterprise. As the opening paragraph to 'Doctor' makes clear, Kit and Jack now live in the city, but they owe their financial security and their standing to the fact of their having braved the wilds – and in the story 'Our Domestic Helps', it is clear that the family still owns a run on the Murray.

Of greater interest are the highly charged descriptions of the nature of the landscape and the way in which Liston insists Kit responds to the pressures it induces: 'a vast and terrible stillness' that pressed so heavily upon her that she was 'tempted to flee away shrieking as from some unholy presence'.[7] It seems to me that this representation of Kit's feeling can be read as something more significant than merely asserting yet again the *difference*, the incomprehensible alterity of this particular sub-species of the 'Australian landscape'. What is there to fear in this amiable limestone country, which today is marked by property after property of grazing land, by wheat and barley paddocks, by Fred Williams hilltops carrying dead she-oaks, by patches of mallee scrub, by old freestone walls and the ruins of shepherd's huts, all mapped, surveyed and sign-posted, with Telecom repeater towers on the higher hills, pipelines, small towns, silos? Kit seems to feel some kind of 'nervous expectation . . . a psychological, oppressive unease' (Healy 21).

What precisely might be read into this awareness of 'unholy presence' may be revealed in the central episode of 'Doctor', 'the one horror' of Kit's life. Jack is away with sheep, and due back in the evening. Kit is left to shepherd the home flock. By the time the sheep are yarded it is dark, the child Johnnie is ill, and the sheep dog Lassie uneasy. Coomultie[8] appears in the doorway:

My back was towards the door, which suddenly went shut, and an uncomfortable presence seemed to fill the hut. I turned hastily round, to meet the grinning gaze of a powerful blackfellow. He was stark naked, and carried a waddie; the whites of his eyes and his teeth looked horrible in the light of my tallow candles and the fire. I knew him – Coomultie by name, and by report one of the worst and most brutal of his tribe. If hearts ever do stop beating in the midst of life, mine did for a second, but I retained my outward self-possession; if he was one by himself he might not mean any harm, though from his character I mistrusted him.

'My lubra sit down directly,' I said, wanting to make him under-stand Jack would soon be there, but he shook his head with a hateful grin. 'Loose him pony, lubra comalong.' And he stood a pace or two forward, putting out a hand to grasp me. I shrank back, and poor little Johnnie set up a terrified cry. Coomultie snatched him up with one hand, and swung his waddie round with the other.

You have read of the tiger that leaped into the camp and rescued her chained-up cub. I think I must have felt like she did, as with a rush forward I tore the boy away, and put the table between us and our assailant. It was only a temporary respite; I knew it by his ugly look and angry mutter.

What could I do? Useless to make a dash for the door, for it was behind Coomultie, as also was the entrance into the bedroom, where our firearms were. Then I remembered Jack had taken the gun to try and get a wild turkey, and the pistol was useless, for we were out of caps to fit it. Not even a knife on my side of the room; and what would it have availed against a stalwart black with a waddie?

Where was Lassie? Where was Jack? Ah! he was going to finish us.

He stepped back, and poised his weapon. Whether he meant to throw it, or spring on us and beat us down, I don't know. Involuntarily I bent forward over my closely-clutched boy, and raised my arm to parry the blow. From under my arm I saw him advance one step – two. There was a sudden rush of something through the window behind me, and over the table a hoarse growl from a dog, and a yell from Coomultie. The waddie went shivering amongst some bottles on a shelf above my head, as the black went down borne forcibly to the ground by the swift assault of the 'mangy cur', who was seeking to fix his teeth in the fellow's throat.

'Hold him, Hector. Hold him, good dog,' I said. But he needed no encouragement. His eyes were red with rage, and the bristles on his back erect.

It was an awful struggle, and I shudder now to think of it, but I did not then, although my heart sickened. Still, it was dear life for Johnnie and myself if the dog did not gain the mastery. How long the conflict lasted I could never tell. It appeared hours, but could not have been anything like one. But it was terrible to witness, yet I could not turn my eyes away. Once having got a hold, all Coomultie's desperate efforts to free himself were in vain. I believe you might have torn the dog limb from limb before he would have let go.

Gradually the struggles grew fainter and fainter till they finally ceased, and Hector, cautiously releasing his fangs, stood on guard. I could not stop in the hut. Holding my boy tight (I had kept his face covered during the dreadful scene), I hurried past the dead black and outside, calling Hector to follow, which he did. The first thing I stumbled over midway between the hut and the yards was poor Lassie's stiffening corpse with a spear sticking through her; then I recognised why her bark had ceased so suddenly, and why she had apparently deserted me.

The moon was just rising, and I made away down the track by which I knew Jack would come. I had gone about a mile when I heard his horse cantering sharply along, and I stood still to await his coming, and Hector lay at my feet. Poor fellow, he was weary. Jack pulled up sharply, with surprise.

'Why, Kit; is that you? Did you think I was late? What; the phantom dog back again? What's the matter, wife?'

I, feeling perfectly safe now he had come, burst into tears. I hate to think it is what a woman generally does, but I could not help it. It was a little time before I could tell what had happened, and I hardly knew my husband's face when I had ended. 'Good old dog; brave old dog,' he said over and over again, caressing my gaunt saviour.

He lifted Johnnie and me on to the horse, and putting both barrels of his gun on half-cock, we went back.

'I wonder how the black devil knew my horse was lost; I was two hours looking for him this evening. That made me late. He must have crossed his tracks – perhaps drove him away; but I think he would have speared him had he seen him. I can't think what Coomultie was doing by himself, either; there must be others in the neighbourhood. Not close about though, or the dog would scent them; good old fellow, dear old fellow, don't leave us again. Whilst we have a sheep you shall have half, and all our gratitude through life.'

As he spoke to Hector the dog looked up at me with his whine of pleasure.

I could not go near the hut; it was too full of horrors, so Jack fetched out the rugs and things, and made a camp by the sheep-yard; got me some hot tea and baked some bread.

'I must take you into the Three Peaks tomorrow, Kit, this has quite unnerved you,' he said with much concern, and I unwillingly admitted that it had.

Neither of us slept that night; later on, when I was more calm, he left me with Hector on guard, and went down to the hut. We had a big pile of wood, drawn together at leisure times; this Jack set fire to and dragging out the dead body of Coomultie, threw it on, and gave him the rites of cremation, but he buried Lassie down in our garden. When he came back all his comment on the proceedings was to fervently kiss Johnnie and myself, and caress anew good Hector; that there were tears in his eyes I was sure, and I felt he could not trust himself to speak.

It was just dawn when we started for the Three Peaks. We had but the one horse then, so Jack walked. We left the sheep in the yard, knowing we could get a man on horseback to return and take them over to our other place. Hector went with us, and in about four hours we reached the station. The first words that greeted us were that the blacks had robbed the hut about six miles from our home the previous day and murdered the hutkeeper. The shepherd on arriving home had found him dead, and immediately started off to the head station with the intelligence. He had seen the blacks whilst out on the run. Coomultie was amongst them. 'Coomultie will not rob nor murder any more,' said Jack grimly, as he patted Hector's head, and lifted me from the horse. All was bustle and excitement at the Three Peaks, but in a few hours after our arrival I knew nothing for a long time.

When I again came to my proper senses I found my baby had been born and buried, and I owed my recovery to the unremitting devotion of my Jack and a good woman who had only arrived at the station with her husband the week before we came. I learned there had been a muster of hands from several stations, and they had gone in for a crusade against the natives. They cannot be blamed, for we were too far from civilisation to depend on lawful redress, though without doubt many of the unoffending suffered with the guilty, but that is not a result confined to dealings of whites with blacks – it tells both ways. (137–39)

It is clear that Kit knows Coomultie, in that she can name him, and the fact that he speaks some English suggests that he has been living on the edges of this settlement for some time, albeit 'by report one of the worst and most brutal of his tribe'. The words exchanged between the two are beguiling. Why does Kit refer to her husband Jack as 'My lubra' (137)? On one level the degenerate and mangled English used in the exchange may be intended to suggest Kit's innocence, where she subconsciously reverses the traditional gender roles, in ways which are echoed in the dog Doctor/Hector[9] revealing himself to be a woman's best friend. On another level the exchange suggests the extent to which the Aborigines are denied speaking rights in Liston's representation of the contact zone, and the only communication possible is that conducted in what Kit understands as the English one speaks to Aborigines.

It is also revealing that Coomultie is not the only Aborigine living in reasonably close proximity to the young family. When Kit does her best to persuade the mysterious dog to remain close by, she does so in the awareness that 'Jack and the boy [my emphasis] we had were away all day with the sheep, and of course [the sheepdogs] Lassie and Bob went with them' (134). It can be assumed that 'the boy' is Aboriginal: in a letter home from Nilkerloo, Liston mentions that in 'Mr Hamp's absence I was promoted to Overseer and had to superintend the watering of the flocks and counting of them, the boys and lubras shepherding' (quoted in O'Dea 7).

There are thus two models of Aboriginal male behaviour available for Kit's discerning gaze. The fact that Coomultie refuses to act as the loyal and submissive servant, as we assume 'the boy' does, justifies the former's representation as implacable and Manichean savage. It is clear that initially Kit reads Coomultie's threat as sexual – he is described as 'stark naked', and he reaches out a hand to grasp her. However, it is the direct threat to her son Johnnie – the representative of the rising Australian generation, the 'coming man' – that provokes Kit's tigerish defence, in that her natural wish to defend her innocent child inspires her to grab him back from Coomultie and then raise her arm against him. Coomultie is elsewhere in the story described as 'the black devil', and his inscrutable actions, which threaten the very basis of Kit's growing family unit, can only be opposed by the equally inscrutable actions of the mysterious dog, the 'Doctor'. It is worth noting that on several occasions Jack (even if jokingly) describes the mysterious dog as 'phantom', 'not a canny dog', 'spirit dog', 'as hungry as Beelzebub', a dog who 'vanished into the limbo of uncertainties', 'Diabolus', 'a mystery'. But it is Coomultie who, in the context of this narrative, is discovered to be evil, the creature of darkness, the unholy presence, not the Doctor.

We quite understand that Kit might have found it impossible to return to the 'hut . . . full of horrors', but there are one or two details about how the pair 'clean up' after the event that are intriguing. Jack wonders why Coomultie acted alone.[10] Surely the event on which the story turns – the fortuitous appearance of Doctor/Hector – would not have worked in plot terms had Coomultie been accompanied, as the dog would not have been able to deal with more than one attacker. Then Jack drags Coomultie's body from the hut, puts it on a big pile of wood and gives him 'the rites of cremation', but Lassie the sheepdog is buried in the garden. The detail suggests that the cremation proceeded with at least some ceremony, the only moment in the story when Coomultie's humanity is recognised. But perhaps Kit and Jack want to get rid of the evidence.

Significantly, Kit and Jack are *not* shown as wondering why Coomultie acted as he did. Contemporary readers might be tempted to think that Coomultie might have reached the point where he was driven to violence out of a recognition of the threat posed by the settlers to his own culture.[11] His intentions or motivations are not discussed, and any extenuating circumstances are simply not considered. In the absence of any such discussion, the reader is left with the impression that Aborigines are by nature randomly violent, impetuous, treacherous. These stereotypical and Manichean categories stress the dangerous 'otherness' of the black and thus justify not only the violence done in return but, of course, also the dispossession of the lands of the Aborigines.

In this regard Coomultie's attack on Kit can be seen as a much more complex action than merely random violence. He personifies the 'unholy presence' that Kit feels in this frontier landscape – it is tempting to read Kit's response to landscape as a subconscious awareness of the reality of Aboriginal dispossession. Narratives interrogating colonisation and empire are fundamentally political in the sense that they deal with power relationships between people which (if not left unresolved) are often contested through violence, guerilla skirmishing and even organised and deliberate warfare. An empire built on hierarchies which reflect Manichean allegories about race obviously will (sooner or later) be contested by those (like Coomultie) demonised by such hierarchies. Conflict provoked by a perceived sense of racial difference and by unquestioned assumptions about racial hierarchies may well be the typical experience of the most obvious consequences of the early stages of colonisation and empire-building. As Abdul JanMohamed has observed, the political context of culture and history will be revealed in 'an analysis of the domination, manipulation, exploitation, and disenfranchisement that are inevitably involved in the construction of any cultural artefact or relationship' (59).

Whatever Coomultie's motives, he can be understood as reacting violently to the prevailing and enduring European construction of possible and permitted relationships between settlers and Aborigines. Liston at least is more revealing than most of her contemporaries in representing the violence that so often lay behind the establishing of the settler-colonist's enterprise in the 'contact zone'. She hints at a further violent colonial moment – a 'crusade' against the natives with unstated numbers of casualties:

> When I again came to my proper senses I found my baby had been born and buried, and I owed my recovery to the unremitting devotion of my Jack and a good woman who had only arrived at the station with her husband the week before we came. *I learned there had been a muster of hands from several stations, and they had gone in for a crusade against the natives. They cannot be blamed, for we were too far from civilisation to depend on lawful redress, though without doubt many of the unoffending suffered with the guilty, but that is not a result confined to dealings of whites with blacks – it tells both ways.*[12] [my emphasis] (139)

This detail should be one of haunting and resonating meaning and importance for all (South) Australians. Any attempt to celebrate and valorise 'the woman's experience' in 'Doctor' (and no one could deny Kit acts bravely and resourcefully, and naturally we feel sympathy for the loss of her child) must also confront the fact that her strength of character is revealed as a direct consequence of the Aboriginal Coomultie's death. The attempted attack on Kit precipitates what she describes as a 'crusade' against mostly innocent Aboriginal people of the Three Peaks district – an interesting choice of words for a massacre.

Why should the simple word 'crusade' haunt (South) Australians? As a child on the West Coast I grew up with stories about the so-called 'Elliston (or Waterloo Bay) Massacre'. Liston must have known many of the typically brutal stories about the settlement of Eyre Peninsula by Europeans in the two or three decades before she arrived at Nilkerloo in early 1869, and especially those 'affrays' occurring in 1848 and 1849, culminating in what one version of the 'legend' asserts was the massacre of as many as 260 Aboriginal people near Elliston in a 'drive' or 'muster' conducted by the settlers who drove them over the cliffs into what is now known as Waterloo Bay.

The debates about whether the Elliston massacre actually happened have been proceeding since the 1880s, the most recent public manifestation occurring in 1970, when, in an attempt to bring mainstream Australian attention to the significance of celebrating 200 years of history since Captain Cook landed on Australia's east coast, the Federal Council for the Advancement of Aborigines and Torres Strait Islanders approached the Elliston District Council for permission to erect a cairn to 'commemorate the massacre of about 250 Aborigines in 1846 [sic] at Waterloo Bay near Elliston'.[13] J.B. Cameron, the Chairman of the Elliston District Council, responded by saying that the council would agree to the cairn being erected if it could be proven by 'history' that the massacre actually took place. John Moriarty, the president of the Aborigines Progress Association, in answer to Cameron, asserted that the Aboriginal view was that the massacre did happen, and for a number of weeks controversy raged in Adelaide's two newspapers. It is my contention that Ellen Liston's story 'Doctor' offers previously unnoticed evidence in support of the contemporary Aboriginal view that a massacre did take place.

It may well be that the incident at the centre of Liston's 'Doctor' is loosely based on the murder of the shepherd's wife, Anne [or Annie] Easton, at Lake Hamilton, south of Elliston. It is inconceivable that Liston would not have known of the circumstances of her death. The Adelaide *Observer* published 'A Reminiscence of Port Lincoln' by 'H.J.C.' (Henry John Congreve)[14] on 14 August 1880 (281) – two years before Liston's 'Doctor' was published. 'A Reminiscence of Port Lincoln' – which, incidentally, was published in 'The Miscellany' section of the Adelaide *Observer* – is a fanciful and sometimes wildly inaccurate account of the events of 1848 and 1849. In lurid and sensational fashion, and often in fictional form, the piece describes three murders by an Aborigine called Multulti: of 'Captain B – ', the 'young and pretty wife' of a shepherd[15] and a hutkeeper who was surprised while cutting wood and subsequently decapitated with his crosscut saw.

I think we can assume that Liston saw the piece, because in the same issue of the Adelaide *Observer* (283) she published a poem 'The Fire King: A Reminiscence of 1851'.[16] Furthermore, she probably heard the story of Annie Easton's death from her Nilkerloo employer, John Chipp Hamp, who is often quoted as re-telling the story of his father's death.[17] Whether Liston's story 'Doctor' was written in response to Congreve's 'A Reminiscence of Port Lincoln' or whether she attempted to fictionalise the stories she must have heard at Nilkerloo is impossible to determine. Save for the obvious fact that the historical Annie Easton died (and is buried at Lake Hamilton), Liston's version is closer to the historical truth, suggesting that she based 'Doctor' on anecdotes she heard at Nilkerloo between 1869 and 1872, and that she may have written 'Doctor' partly in response to Congreve's more fanciful version. Congreve, for example, does not stress the fact that it was the 'hands' who were responsible for the 'crusade', the telling detail in Liston's version.

In trying to deal with violence in the contact zone between European settlers and Aborigines, Liston's story 'Doctor' reveals what J.J. Healy hints at, 'the great rich fictional unease of nineteenth-century Australian fiction' (Healy xv), which elsewhere Hodge and Mishra have described as suggesting the dark side of the Australian Dream. In this regard Kit's refusal (or inability) to describe exactly what happened is significant. It does not occur to her to ask Jack or any of the 'hands' what happened: perhaps such matters are not women's business. The 1880 *Register* piece is full of admittedly sensational details which Liston might have used if she had forgotten any of the stories she must have heard from her employer John Hamp. The fact that she chooses not to dwell on what the 'hands' did may be read as clearly suggesting the role Liston was determined to play in maintaining the silence and, by so doing, in demonstrating her complicity in the creation of a discursive regime, a discourse which privileges the colonist's position. When Liston participates in the process of deliberate and systematic forgetfulness, we remember that Kit tells us that she and Jack 'are rich today' (135), twenty-seven years after Coomultie's death.

Kit's assertion that many innocents died in the 'crusade' is justified on the grounds that 'it tells both ways'. On the one hand this suggests a morally bankrupt view, but a typical one in any debate about the excesses on the edge of empire provoked by the scramble for land and the wealth the land produced; Liston's character Kit's refusal to resurrect the details of what happened can be seen against the historical background of unreported (or evasively reported) violence on the frontier. We might read her refusal as implying that the Aborigines got what they deserved as a punishment for not just Jack's and her ordeal but also for the miscarriage of her child.

However, a defensive note must also be heard in the phrase 'it tells both ways'. There is here an ambivalence about frontier violence, an awareness of Aboriginal presence which the 1936 editors of *A Book of South Australia: Women in the First Hundred Years* must have sensed when preparing 'Doctor' for republication and wished to edit out. J.J. Healy records that he:

> began to see an Aboriginal subject that cut right into the centre of their doubts, fears, hopes, traumas; a penetration so massively reflected upon that their [i.e. *some* nineteenth-century Australian writers'] fictions became narrative battlegrounds in which conscience fought itself into a kind of consciousness. I was struck by how often a consciousness of who they themselves were became tied into the quality of their contact with Aborigines. It occurred to me that the novel itself was a field of consciousness, one which had been alerted into existence by a disturbing experience; the working through of the experience became possible only through the form of the novel. (xv)

The valorisation of Kit – the celebration of her story – can only be accepted by sidestepping the consequences of the episode described in 'Doctor'. At issue is, of course, the nature of the colonial enterprise in Australia. As Henry Reynolds's researches have shown, coercive and repressive measures were used as a matter of course against the Aborigines. In spite of the legal fiction of *terra nullius*, which asserted that 'Australia was a colony of settlement not of conquest', there was in fact a frontier conflict which even at the time was understood as a 'kind of war', a 'sort of warfare', a guerilla war against the invaders (Reynolds 4, 5–6). We will never know how many Aboriginal people died defending their lands[18] or as a direct consequence of contact with European civilisation, because such knowledge has been either actively suppressed or eroded from the public memory by a combination of amnesia and guilt.

Liston's lack of specificity is revealing, and we should be immediately reminded of the preface to the 1893 South Australian novel *Paving the Way: A Romance of the Australian Bush*, in which Simpson Newland enters the debate about 'history' and the writer's role in preserving representations of the contested sites on the edges of empire:

> As, in a work on Australian pioneer life such as . . . *Paving the Way* purports to be, it might be difficult to present bare facts in an acceptable form to the general public, my object has been to blend truth and fiction in a connected narrative. That it partakes largely of a romance is certain, but the incidents, though so romantic, are mainly authentic; for these lives have been lived and these deaths have been died. It is not alone on the familiar ground of the Old World that heroic deeds have been performed or suffering nobly endured.
>
> To particularise too closely would not add interest to the story for the public, though it might in the opinion of those acquainted with many of the occurrences alluded to or more or less related. I have endeavoured to wound as few susceptibilities and tread on as few toes as possible; the time has not yet arrived in the life of Australia when the historian or novelist can write with an untrammelled pen.

The nineteenth-century writer consciously seeks to play a part in representing history, and although she is prepared to admit that such 'crusades' occurred, Liston's character decides to remain silent about the details. She suggests that what gives her the right to make such judgements is her colonial status as an individual who had endured not only solitude but also the 'awfulness' of wild blacks.[19] Such courage and endurance endows the right to call the bush 'ours'. Coomultie no longer lives to offer a rival claim – he has been literally written out of sight, and his story (incomplete as it is) is understood by Liston as nowhere near as significant as Kit's 'her-story'. Coomultie's Manichean behaviour is seen by Liston as justifying the crusade against innocent Aboriginal people, and their deaths would no doubt have been understood by late nine-teenth-century readers as inevitable. If the guns of the hands had not killed them, they would have died out anyway in competition with the relentless advance of the European settlers and their diseases and alcohol, flocks and firearms. The writer is thus an active participant in not only suppressing certain aspects of 'her story', but in sanctioning others' silences and evasions.

WORKS CITED

Across the Bar to Waterloo Bay: Elliston 1878–1978. Elliston Centenary Committee, 1978.

Bennett, David. 'PC Panic, the Press and the Academy', in *Cultural Studies: Pluralism and Theory*. David Bennett, ed. Melbourne University Literary and Cultural Studies. Vol. 2. Melbourne: Department of English, University of Melbourne, 1993.

Brown, Louise, Beatrix Ch. de Crespigny, Mary P. Harris, Kathleen Kyffin Thomas and Phebe N. Watson, eds. *A Book of South Australia: Women in the First Hundred Years*. Adelaide: Rigby, 1936.

Charter, Greg. *Frontier Violence, Vengeance and Myths: A Study of Aboriginal Resistance to European Occupation of the Eyre Peninsula 1839–1885, and an Assessment of the Later Writings Pertaining to the Conflict*. Unpublished Honours Thesis, School of Social Sciences, Flinders University of South Australia, 1989.

Cockburn, Rodney. *What's in a Name? Nomenclature of South Australia: Authoritative Derivations of Some 4000 Historically Significant Place Names*. 1908. Rev. Stewart Cockburn. Adelaide: Ferguson Publications, 1984.

_____. *Pastoral Pioneers of South Australia* [Facsimile ed.] indexed by A. Dorothy Aldersey. Adelaide: Publishers Limited, 1925–27.

Depasquale, Paul. *A Critical History of South Australian Literature 1836–1930. With Subjectively Annotated Bibliographies*. Warradale, SA: Pioneer Books, 1978.

Giles, Fiona. ed. *From the Verandah: Stories of Love and Landscape by Nineteenth Century Australian Women*. Fitzroy: McPhee Gribble, 1987.

Harwood, Ellen A. ed. *Pioneers: Stories by Ellen Liston*. Adelaide: Hassel Press, 1936.

Healy, J.J. *Literature and the Aborigine in Australia*. [1978] St Lucia: University of Queensland Press, 1989.

Hodge, Bob and Vijay Mishra. *Dark Side of the Dream: Australian Literature and the Post Colonial Mind*. Sydney: Allen & Unwin, 1991.

JanMohamed, Abdul. 'The Economy of Manichean Allegory: The Function of Racial Difference in Colonialist Literature'. *Critical Inquiry* 12.1 (1985): 59–87.

Knight, Stephen. 'The Case of the Missing Genre: In Search of Australian Crime Fiction'. *Southerly* 48.3 (1988): 235–49.

_____. 'Introduction' *Dead Witness*. Ringwood, Vic.: Penguin Books, 1989.

_____. 'Sterling Settlement and Colonial Currency: Post Colonial Patterns in Australian Crime Fiction'. Working Papers in Australian Studies No. 82, Sir Robert Menzies Centre for Australian Studies, Institute of Commonwealth Studies, University of London, 1992.

Liston, E.M.H. 'Preface', in *Pioneers: Stories by Ellen Liston*. Ed. Ellen A. Harwood. Adelaide: Hassell Press, 1936.

Muecke, Stephen. *Textual Spaces: Aboriginality & Cultural Studies*. Kensington, NSW: New South Wales UP, 1992.

Nosworthy, Maureen and Bill Nosworthy. *Tjeiringa: The Story of the Sheringa District*. Sheringa: Sheringa History Committee, 1988.

O'Dea, J.F. 'Elliston: A Brief Outline of the History of This Area of Eyre Peninsula'. pamphlet, Mortlock Library, nd.

Pope, Alan. *Resistance and Retaliation: Aboriginal-European Relations in Early Colonial South Australia*. Bridgewater, SA: Heritage Action, 1989.

Reynolds, Henry. *The Other Side of the Frontier: Aboriginal Resistance to the European Invasion of Australia*. Ringwood, Vic: Penguin, 1982.

Thompson, Neil. *The Elliston Incident*. London: Hale [1969].

Thompson, Neil and Val Thompson, eds. *The Streaky Bay: A History of the Streaky Bay District Council Area*. Streaky Bay, SA: The Streaky Bay District Council, 1988.

NOTES

1. A revised version of 'Doctor' was published (with significant editorial changes) in the anthology compiled by Louise Brown et al., *A Book of South Australia: Women in the First Hundred Years*. It was reprinted (in its original 1882 *Observer* version) in Ellen A. Harwood's *Pioneers: Stories by Ellen Liston*. It has been most recently published (in its original *Observer* version) in Fiona Giles's *From the Verandah: Stories of Love and Landscape by Nineteenth-Century Australian Women*.

2. Biographical information about Ellen Liston has been drawn from several sources: from the Liston family, and from Mr John Liston, to whom I owe particular thanks; from the Preface to *Pioneers* written by her niece E.M.H. Liston; and from notes by Constance C. Darling in the possession of the Liston family.

3. See Stephen Knight, 'Sterling Settlement and Colonial Currency: Post Colonial Patterns in Australian Crime Fiction'. Knight has published extensively on Australian crime fiction, including 'The Case of the Missing Genre: In Search of Australian Crime Fiction', and the 'Introduction' to *Dead Witness*.

4. This is not the first Newfoundland cross to appear in Liston's fiction (there are at least two others: Pluto in the serial novel *The Stauntons*, and Lartius in the short story of the same name). It is reasonable therefore to assume that the Hamps kept such a dog at Nilkerloo. As 'Doctor' implies, such large dogs were kept on stations for the express purpose of driving off any Aborigines who appeared, and were trained to attack such 'intruders' on sight. In her short story 'Our Baggage Mule', the second of the Kit and Jack sequence, Liston has Kit address the reader as follows: 'You might think it not very pleasant for a woman often alone with two children, but one gets used to most things, and after the dog Doctor, whose history I have told, installed himself with us, I should not have feared a dozen [evil-eyed men with a scowl or a leer], and Jack was never away of a night' (140).

   The barbarous method used to train such dogs for the task of driving off Aborigines I heard described on the West Coast as late as the 1970s, and was certainly still in use in the 1960s, and given the numbers of large dogs in front yards in towns like Ceduna and Port Lincoln, it may be that the training methods are still in use. To read widely in contemporary accounts of black-white contact in South Australia is to come across numbers of references to dogs attacking Aborigines. In 1845 there were at least two incidents in and around Streaky Bay that resulted in the deaths of Aborigines.

5. Page numbers refer to Giles's publication of the story.

6. We should note in passing that Liston uses the term 'colonist' rather than the much more problematic term 'settler'.

7. To read *stillness* as presence may remind us of the conventional nineteenth-century trope about the Australian landscape which Marcus Clarke famously described as 'weird melancholy'.

8. Given where the story is set, Coomultie must be either Wirangu or Kukatha. The balance of evidence suggests that if this story does allude to one of the events which provoked the Elliston 'affray', then it may have been that Coomultie was a Kukatha, whose lands covered most of central northern Eyre Peninsula. Although the Kukatha spent much of the year in and around what is now the Gawler Ranges, they would travel northwest as far as Ooldea, and as far south as Elliston, depending upon seasonal food and water supplies and ceremonial needs. Charles Mann was the acting judge of the South Australian Supreme Court who sat in judgement on Bakilta and Putarpintye, who were charged with Easton's murder, but acquitted. In a letter to the Colonial Secretary, Mann describes the accused as members of the Anargetti tribe (GRG 24/6/1849/1893, 3). The unnamed writer of 'The Elliston Massacre 1869 [sic]' notes that his father told him that 'the natives who on walkabout periodically arrived from the Gawler Ranges [and] . . . seemed quite familiar with the hunting areas, particularly around the lakes, and the fishing spots at the reefs below the cliffs (where they speared rock fish and crayfish, and collected shellfish' (*Across the Bar to Waterloo Bay* 10). However, in *The South Australian Register*, 3 October 1849 there is a letter to the Editor from James Easton about the acquittal of Pakilte [sic] in which Easton accuses Pastor Clamor Schürmann, the court-appointed interpreter, of both ignorance and prejudice for not being able to speak the 'particular dialect used by the natives of the western coast of Port Lincoln' (4) (therefore Wirangu?), that is, by those accused of his wife's murder:

In the cases against the natives for the murders of Mr Beevor and Mr Hamp, the native witnesses, having often been in Port Lincoln, were better able to understand Mr Schurmann, and the blacks were in conse-quence convicted, which would have been the case with Pakilte, had there been a competent person to interpret, and who could have been procured from Port Lincoln.

This remark seems to assert that the alleged perpetrators were Wirangu, whose lands stretched from the Head of the Bight along the coast to Cape Blanche, and inland as far as Ooldea. This is also evidence for the 'detribal-isation' of the Aboriginal communities which, manifestly, was well advanced by the late 1840s. It appears likely that the Aborigines involved in the various incidents between 1848–1851 were displaced from their country, or had (for whatever reason) chosen to leave it, in that those responsible for the deaths of Hamp, Beevor and Easton committed those murders in country to which they did not belong.

9. I am grateful to Phil Butterss for his suggestion that Liston drew on J.W. Bull's *Early Experiences of Colonial Life in South Australia*, where an 1837 episode is described in which a 'fine kangaroo dog [called] Hector' growls at Aborigines who threaten the party, and then captures a wounded swan before one of the black youths can reach it, threatening the Aborigine with his fangs. Bull's reminiscences were published in 1878, some four years before Liston's story appeared in the *Observer*. The connection with Bull's *Early Experiences* suggests an interesting reciprocity between prose fiction and the traveller's narrative.

10. The deaths of John Hamp, Captain Beevor and Anne (or Annie) Easton were all committed by numbers of Aborigines, as the court records make clear.

11. If this story does (even in passing) build on West Coast contact history, then it is worth noting that there was considerable speculation that the outburst of frontier violence in the late 1840s was caused by the fact that the Aborigines were starving and desperate. Colonial Secretary Charles Sturt wrote to the Commissioner of Police on 29 May 1851 'attributing these out-rages to their suffering for want of food' (GRG 24/4/1851/305). George Dashwood, the Commissioner of Police, wrote back on 10 June 1851 to agree. Dashwood argued that the most efficient method of stopping the frontier violence would be to issue rations and clothing to the Aborigines:

We see the Native driven from his hunting grounds and his food, by the lawful intrusion of the white man, starving, and in want of water: we see the white man in possession of food and water in abundance, that, indeed, which the Native requires to keep body and soul together; we see this ines-timable prize, this unendurable want, I regret to say, in many instances, but ill protected, and in some cases left quite exposed, and the results are murder and robbery.

Dashwood suggested that 1/2 lb. of flour and 1/2 lb. meat *per diem* should be issued from Police Stations on a certain day each week (GRG 24/6/1851/1733). One might reflect that the cycle of poverty and dependency begins in 1852 with such seemingly philanthropical gestures by government.

12. It is interesting to note that one of the two published versions of 'Doctor' to appear in 1936 does not contain the lines given in italics here. Given the story appeared in an anthology intended to celebrate a centenary of achievements, Louise Brown, Beatrix Ch. de Crespigny, Mary P. Harris, Kathleen Kyffin Thomas and Phebe N. Watson, eds., 1936. *A Book of South Australia: Women in the First Hundred Years*, it is hardly surprising that any references to the 'dark side of the dream' should have been excised.

13. Max Fatchen, *The Advertiser*, Wednesday 25 March 1970.

14. Henry John Congreve (1829–1918) was the brother of the writer 'Maud Jean Franc'. Congreve arrived in South Australia in 1849 on the 'Trafalgar', and worked variously as a doctor, bullock driver and newspaper editor. He lived in Port Lincoln, Burra and Gawler. I am grateful to Margaret Allen for this information.

15. The relevant section from 'A Reminiscence of Port Lincoln' is quoted in full:

From thence in a body, they proceeded to the next station, Lake Hamilton, eighteen miles distant, where a man, with his young and pretty wife, had charge of a flock of sheep. Multulti, the chief of the tribe whose misdeeds I am narrating, was a thorough villain, and his character was stamped upon his face. He was of the usual height, but from an accident in childhood had been crippled in one foot. He was strong, muscular, and energetic, and had been the instigator of many dark deeds. He had two lubras, old and ugly, and was on the look out for another, young and handsome, to add to his family. This shepherd's wife had attracted his eye and inflamed his passions, and I have been assured by a native of another tribe that the present outbreak was occasioned by his desire to expel the whites from the country and obtain the object of his fierce wishes. I believe this was his motive. To the shepherd's wife, Mary, he had shown repeated acts of kindness foreign to his nature; but she, getting suspicious, had told her husband, and he had driven him from the station, warning him that if he appeared there again he would be shot. Multulti nursed his revenge, and stirred up the blood of his tribe until it had now burst forth. Now – with revengeful feelings, he was on his way to the hut. The poor woman, unsuspicious of the fate that awaited her, was merrily singing while preparing some little bush dainty for her husband on his return. Suddenly the door of the hut was darkened, and looking up she beheld the naked form of Multulti and his followers. With a faint cry she seized a spear made of a shear blade, fastened to a short stick, and rushed to the door to bar the entrance. At the first movement of Multulti she made a thrust at him, which he parried with ease, and wrenching the weapon from her hand, plunged it into her body, and she fell fainting to the ground. Speedily she was aroused by the cries of her child, who had been snatched by her murderer from its slumbers, and he now stood by the stone-chimney poising the child by its heels, ere striking the blow which should rob it of its life. With a scream poor Mary tried to rise to the succour of her babe; but the effort was in vain, and she saw the scoundrel dash out its brains against the mantel. The next moment a heavy blow fell upon her own head, shutting out the light of life for ever. After robbing the hut, the savages proceeded to another a few miles distance on the other side of the lake.

16. I am grateful to Margaret Allen for the bibliographic evidence to make this point.

17. See *The Register*, 6 March 1926, for Archie Beviss's recollections, *The Register*, 24 October 1929, 6, *The Adelaide Chronicle*, July 18, 1935, 4.

18. Reynolds suggests a figure of 10,000 blacks killed in north Queensland between 1861 and the early 1930s (165). The figure for all of Australia from 1788 to 1939 must be in the many tens of thousands.

19. See Cockburn's *Pastoral Pioneers of South Australia* for the full pantheon of colonial heroes (no women included). The brief biographical sketches which constitute the collection hint at dozens of narratives that might be told about violent relations between blacks and whites on the South Australian frontier.

CHAPTER

DAVID UNAIPON

HIS STORY

Susan Hosking

It is difficult to tell David Unaipon's story. There are some dates, some documents, some newspaper reports telling who, when and what David Unaipon was. But different stories emerge depending on how this information is assembled and, of course, who assembles it. It has been argued that David Unaipon both was and was not a white man's puppet.[1] Certainly he was approved by white authorities for ways in which he did *not* represent his race; he was applauded as an example of what a black man could *become* if he embraced the white man's ways of living and thinking. But to see David Unaipon as a mere pawn in the colonial power games of white men is surely to insult the intelligence of a remarkably sensitive man who had a vision for a harmonious future for black and white Australians.

David Unaipon was not the first Aboriginal writer. The first writings by Aboriginal people (Walter George Arthur, Peter Bruny and David Bruny) appeared in 1837 in Tasmania in *The Flinders Island (Weekly) Chronicle* (Narogin 18–19). Like the first writers, Unaipon was the product of a Christian mission, and his writing was controlled by his white mentors and editors. But even the earliest Aboriginal writing served to some extent to convey Aboriginal protest and expression of Aboriginal experience. David Unaipon, writing in the twentieth century, and drawing upon the basis of the British, Christian, literary education he had acquired at the Point McLeay Mission School, was in a more advantageous position to explore the space between Aboriginal and British colonial cultures; he did this with remarkable creativity, producing 'fictions' of a kind that defy categorisation. David Unaipon wrote from within what might be called a 'contact zone'[2] between two races, where understandings and practices interlocked and customary perspectives were challenged. Indeed, he may be seen as the first Aboriginal writer whose work demonstrates the creative possibilities and difficulties of the 'contact zone' – possibilities and difficulties which Aboriginal writers today are still facing as they create literary hybrids which often fail to please either of the cultures which contribute to their making. There is no doubt that in David Unaipon's life and in his writing there are mysteries and contradictions that defy simple explanation. As Mudrooroo insists in *Writing from the Fringe* (1990), new kinds of literature require new approaches. The same could be said for the lives of those who occupy the 'contact zone', for David Unaipon's life is as much a text for interpretation as is his writing – more so, perhaps.

In 1951, David Unaipon's story ('My Life Story') was published in the *Aborigines' Friends Association Annual Report*. Unaipon initially related his story to the president, who read it to the annual meeting in March. Two years later, David Unaipon spoke directly to the annual meeting and his talk appeared once again in the *AFA Annual Report* under the title 'Leaves of Memory'. The life that emerges from these two narratives is fascinating and problematic.

David Unaipon was born in 1872 'in a native wurley', he says, along the banks of the River Murray at Tailem Bend. His parents were 'full-blood aborigines', which made him also a 'full-blood aborigine', as newspaper reports were to stress again and again, in professed amazement at his achievements.

At the age of seventy-nine, recalling his childhood, Unaipon speaks of the customs of the Lower Murray tribes as 'primitive'. Yet he pays his respects to 'old man Murray', whose waters had sustained his people since time unremembered. He vividly recalls tracking animals, especially possums in the moonlight, and he remembers swimming and boating for fun, and locating birds' eggs and finding honey.

Just as vivid, however, is Unaipon's recall of the great disturbance caused to home life by the 'advent of the white man into tribal lands'. He says that the movements of the white man were 'keenly watched' and knowledge of their whereabouts spread 'by means of smoke fires and other agencies'. Interviewed on a much earlier occasion (the *Observer*, 10 October 1925) about smoke signals, David Unaipon had asserted that Aboriginal people were capable of communicating with each other 'across a distance which no speech could bridge'. This, he said, was:

> a matter of telepathy. There is nothing in the smoke. It is simply like the ringing of the telephone bell, to call your attention. You sit down and concentrate until you receive the message. The message on a stick is much the same. There is little in the signs themselves, but when my brother takes a stick from a messenger and is told it comes from me, he looks at it and thinks a while, and then says, 'David, he wants some spears and a boomerang.'

David Unaipon insisted that telepathic powers were latent in all his people and developed through the processes of initiation. He claimed that these powers were lost whenever 'one of my people comes under the influence of civilisation'. He felt this power latent in himself, but undeveloped: 'To a very slight extent I can transmit my thoughts, but not as my people do in their natural state. If my brother or any one dear to me receives a sudden shock, or is in danger, and thinks of me, I know it.'

Unaipon's personal narratives and responses to interviews reveal shifts in cultural identification. In the 1925 interview in the *Observer*, Unaipon states that he 'undoubtedly preferred his present state ["civilisation"]' to 'the primitive life which would have been his lot but for the coming of the whites'. He is reported as saying: 'My pleasure in knowledge and in using my mental powers are things I prize exceedingly . . . The coming of the white man was in itself a blessing. We were isolated from the world's culture. It is true that my people could not adapt themselves to civilisation, but that is because it came too suddenly for us.'

The published life-story narratives, while sustaining a conciliatory tone (appropriate for their audience) and stressing 'the want of understanding' on the part of the white man and the blackfellow alike, nevertheless convey a strong sense of white intrusion and disruption. 'My Life Story' tells of the great resentment against the 'newcomer'. 'Leaves of Memory' speaks of bitterness, invasion, appropriation, tragedies, resentment and opposition. In both narratives, however, 'a better feeling' and a 'new state of affairs' are attributed to the coming of the missionaries, most particularly George Taplin who 'gradually persuaded the natives to adopt civilised ways, and leave their old-fashioned wurleys and live in houses like the white people' ('Leaves of Memory'). George Taplin was especially interested in 'the young natives' and opened a school for their education and a dormitory for them to live in 'where they were trained in civilised ways'. There, David Unaipon learned to eat with a knife and fork, 'say grace and adopt table manners'. According to Unaipon, Taplin secured the co-operation of the old men of the tribes, including James Unaipon (Ngaiponi), David's father. James became a resident at Point McLeay, 'one of the first deacons of the church built by native labour'. There he erected a stone cottage with the help of his younger brother. Taplin was so pleased with James that he chose him to be one of the evangelists to work among the tribes in the district.

David Unaipon was educated at the Point McLeay Mission. There the 'natives', including David himself, were trained 'for useful service'. In 'Leaves of Memory' are listed the names of 'men who made good' as shearers, carpenters, masons, blacksmiths, bootmakers, bakers, dairymen, boatmen, stockmen, fishermen, teachers, shorthand writers and craftsmen. David Unaipon was 'set to mend boots', but the work did not 'suit' him and he abandoned it after a short time.

The young David took music lessons, and proved to be so gifted that he was appointed the church organist at Point McLeay. Describing himself as 'ambitious', he was determined to play 'something more than the usual church tunes' and obtained copies of 'The Messiah' and other more advanced music. He read books and journals sent to the Station, 'especially the scientific works which showed the new inventions which were coming into the world' ('My Life Story'). He decided to become an inventor and, despite his lack of mathematical training, succeeded in patenting an improved handpiece for a sheep-shearing machine used by an Adelaide firm. However, Unaipon says with remarkable restraint, 'not being properly protected I lost financially any material gain arising from this discovery, as this was passed to others who made use of my invention without giving me any compensation'. The shearing handpiece was only one of several inventions he patented. Unaipon read the writings of Newton to increase his knowledge of mechanics. He was fascinated with the problem of perpetual motion and over the years made several models to illustrate it. At seventy-nine he was still pursuing the problem and trying to perfect a model.

Unaipon speaks also of his desire as a young man to mount the pulpit. Repositioning himself in 'Leaves of Memory' in the kind of cultural shift that is common in his personal narratives, Unaipon describes how 'the natives' ('they') were particularly fond of some of the Bible stories, such as the flight of the children of Israel from Egyptian bondage 'and their forty years walkabout in the wilderness'. 'They' also liked the story of Joshua 'requesting the sun to stand still until he had defeated his enemies' and the story of Ruth and Naomi. In the New Testament the stories of the Lord's supper and the resurrection, among others, were favourites because they 'bore some resemblance to items in *their* own tribal lore' (my emphasis). In 'My Life Story', however, Unaipon freely admits to being 'thrilled' himself by stories in the Bible which give 'the blackfellow' entry into 'the past history of the human race':

> In various places of the Bible I found the blackfellow playing a part in life's programme. I found it was a blackfellow that befriended the prophet Jeremiah when he was unjustly cast into prison. It was a blackfellow who was there at the right moment to relieve Jesus by bearing the cross when the Saviour fell beneath its weight. It was in this Book I learned that God made all nations of one blood and that in Christ Jesus colour and racial distinctions disappeared. This helped me many times when I was refused accommodation because of my colour and race.

Unaipon comments in 'Leaves of Memory' that the natives trained on the mission to be preachers showed 'great originality' in their interpretations of the scriptures. But in order to mount the pulpit himself,

Unaipon first learnt by heart some sermons of the nineteenth-century evangelist, Thomas De Witt Talmage. Later, he wrote his own sermons.

When the needs and achievements of the Point McLeay mission became widely known, David Unaipon began to feel that he would 'like to move about in the white man's world' ('Leaves of Memory'). Initially efforts were made, he says, to detain him at the mission, in the bootmaking shop and later in the store. However, his interest in science and in preaching and his sense of obligation to his race provided strong motivation for his 'walkabout among the white race' ('Leaves of Memory'), and for many years he travelled throughout Australia, speaking in the pulpits of various denominations, especially in South Australia and Victoria. He also visited Sydney, where he was permitted to speak in the cathedral and in some other churches in New South Wales. At the same time he sold booklets prepared by the Aborigines' Friends Association. He wrote some legends (*Native Legends*) for the purpose, he claimed, of 'awaken[ing] interest in the aboriginal problem'. On his tours he took with him an instrument designed to demonstrate per-petual motion, and in 'Leaves of Memory' he claims that this instrument enabled him to interest audiences in the welfare of his people.

Among the important influences that shaped his life, David Unaipon claims the Christian example of his father, who was the first convert to the Christian faith among the Narringeri (Ngarrindjeri) and who became a liaison officer between the white and black races. David's father took him into the solitude of the bush, read the Bible to him and prayed that David might grow up 'to be a good man and live at peace with all men'. David Unaipon also expressed his indebtedness to the Aborigines' Friends Association (as of course he would, when address-ing them). He insisted that he had received assistance 'in ways beyond counting' from the Association, which had been his 'refuge in every time of trouble'.

'My Life Story' concludes with David Unaipon's statement on how best to deal with 'the aboriginal problem'. He makes a plea for co-operation: 'Colour and race prejudice should be be laid aside and equal rights given to both black and white Australians. Sympathetic co-operation is the keystone to success in solving the native problem.' He insists that, since he is a product of missionary work, he has a duty to testify to its value: 'the only hope for the improvement of my race lies along the line of properly-conducted missionary enterprise, which goes down to the fundamental needs of the aborigines and gives them the inner power to reconstruct their lives which have become shattered by contact with white civilisation'.

There is no doubt that David Unaipon won the respect of white authorities in south-eastern Australia, and in the 1920s and 1930s he influenced government policy pertaining to Aboriginal peoples. That he was accepted as his people's spokesman was problematic, for white Australia seized upon him as an example of the 'improving' powers of church and government on 'primitive' peoples. David Unaipon was not approved because he was Aboriginal, but because he confounded the expectations of whites who thought they knew the limitations of 'natives'. Unaipon was not celebrated for his Aboriginality, but rather as 'an Aboriginal intellectual', a 'black genius' and an 'Australian Leonardo'. The reporter who interviewed Unaipon for the *Observer* in 1925 expressed the shock of confrontation with 'a man from the Stone Age' who addressed him in 'cultured tones and proceeded to discuss the harnessing of gravity and the poetry of Milton'. Anyone, he suggests, would have the same reaction:

> A full-blooded aboriginal, Mr. Unaipon presents in physical structure an unmistakeable resemblance to those reconstructions of the older human types which scientists have sometimes supplied with the help of a tooth and a mouldering jawbone. Only the eyes, flashing with quick thought, limpid, friendly, give the lie to your impression. In manner, he is courteous and dignified, and an almost English purity of accent characterises his cultured voice.

David Unaipon did not have 'the answer' to 'the aboriginal problem'. No one had 'the answer' to conflict in the 'contact zone' where two previously separated races found themselves interacting. Yet his writing, representing as it did a synthesis of different knowledges, might have been (but was not) celebrated as a metaphor for creative and potentially harmonious interaction.

David Unaipon expressed his appreciation 'of the kindness shown me during my long lifetime by members of the white race' ('Leaves of

Memory'). Yet his life was not without frustration, sadness and discrimination: his talents were not used as he wished them to be. He needed the haven afforded him by the Mission; on his travels he was sometimes refused accommodation because of his colour; his patented inventions were used unscrupulously by others; additional legends by Unaipon were commissioned and published by the anthropologist W. Ramsay Smith without acknowledgement of their authorship in *Myths and Legends of the Australian Aboriginals* (1930). The absence of published complaint on Unaipon's part – an absence that in later years earned him some criticism – testifies to his firm belief in co-operation. In 'My Life Story' he endorses the words of one Professor Aggery, whom he quotes:

> I am proud . . . of my colour. I stand for co-operation with the white man, not amalgamation, not conflict but co-operation. You can play a tune of sorts on the white keys of the piano, you can play a tune of sorts on the black keys, but for harmony you must use both the black and the white.

Nevertheless, in both his life-story narratives, Unaipon's last words underline his commitment to the rights of Aboriginal people, who, he believed, should occupy 'a more worthy place in the life of the nation' ('My Life Story').

My Story

> *Do you think that, in a sense, I can legitimately take an interest in things to do with Aboriginal culture if I tell my own story, don't pretend to tell theirs?*
>   Yes. I think that is an appropriate procedure, but bear in mind how easily that story can be told by you while the Other continues to be unable to speak. (Stephen Muecke, *Textual Spaces*)

Alice was short and grumpy. Her hair was luxuriantly curly. Noreen was tall and raw-boned. She was quiet. Her hair was dead straight – dry and split and bleached at the ends. Neither of them smiled much. I liked Noreen. Alice didn't like me. Alice and Noreen failed their mental arithmetic. Alice failed nearly everything. I don't remember what Noreen failed because I liked her. Noreen could run, like a dream, in bare feet. Alice had a sharp tongue.

Alice and Noreen lived in Colbrook Home on Shepherd's Hill Road. It was a huge house. There wasn't much of a garden. It seemed very clean but bare from the outside. I never went inside. I was never invited. Why would Alice invite me home? She didn't like me. And Noreen did what Alice said. That house isn't there any more – not a sign of it. You can drive past where it used to be on the way to a dump near the railway line at Eden Hills. I wondered why there were so many of these children all living together in a huge house with verandahs, but I didn't wonder very hard. That was in 1954.

Sometimes Alice would sulk. And once Noreen was crying. I was sorry because I liked her. She said she wanted to go home. I thought she meant to Colbrook Home, but she meant another place. I thought she was an orphan. I thought all the children at Colbrook Home were orphans.

They didn't stay at school very long. Was it more than a year? They disappeared. And so did the boy in another class. I think he was Noreen's brother. I missed Noreen, for a while, and then I forgot her. I didn't think about Noreen and Alice for many, many years.

Once, in a pub toilet in Port Adelaide, an Aboriginal woman asked me for a pill because she didn't want to have a baby. I said I didn't have a pill – that you had to take lots of pills not to have a baby. She didn't believe me. I wondered then about Alice and Noreen. I wondered whether they were mothers. I wondered whether they were still alive. I knew a lot more then. That was in 1968, when Sally Morgan was seventeen and Jack Davis at fifty-one had yet to publish his first book of poetry and Mudrooroo was still Colin Johnson. I knew then that the bricks we scavenged from the demolition of Colbrook Home to line the pit in my father's garage were shameful bricks. The pit is filled in now, and those bricks are buried. But they will always be there.

His Stories

It is inappropriate, in the space of this brief essay, to enter into the vexing questions that surround David Unaipon's writing – questions of attribution, collaboration and ownership. Any reader ought to be aware, however, that there is a significant amount of David Unaipon's work that has been published without his permission or the permission of his people, and without acknowledgement of Unaipon's authorship.[3] For the purposes of this essay, I shall concentrate on Unaipon's *Native Legends*, published in 1929 under the author's name and with his photograph on the cover.

There are five stories in this booklet, with a brief conclusion under the heading 'Narrinyeri Saying'. The first of the stories is 'Release of the Dragon Flies', which a contemporary reader might be tempted to describe as 'quaint'. Read allegorically, however, this moralising fairy tale becomes politically suggestive.

'Release of the Dragon Flies', narrated by the Fairy, Sun Beam, describes an idyllic pool, surrounded by green grass as neat as lawn and blooming, scented flowers which are 'bewitching in their loveliness'. This 'beautiful spot' is the home of the Dragon Flies, but it has been cunningly designed as a prison by the 'wicked old Froggies':

> Perchance they said some one may enter unknown to us, they shall see no indication of distress, but they shall behold scenery most beautiful and enchanting, which will arouse feelings and emotions of sacred fear, and in reverence retrace their steps, lest they trespass upon holy ground. (1)

The pool, to which the Dragon Flies are confined, is guarded by a 'well equipped' army of 'Bull Froggies', and if this is not sufficient to deter snoopers (and escapees), there is also a band of Frog Ventriloquists producing unearthly noises to scare away the curious.

The various tribes living beyond the confines of the pool gather to discuss the terrible noises. An aged kangaroo addresses the tribes, admitting that 'of all the experiences of my life none is as fearful as this'. Resolutely determined, he leads the Animal, Lizard, Reptile and Insect Tribes to another country, far away from the apparently haunted territory.

After a time, the old Bull Frogs send out scouts to discover whether their plan has been successful. Finding the signs of a grand exodus, the Frogs rejoice and relax their surveillance of the Water Grubs in the Pool. Little Fairy Sun Beams sing the Frogs to sleep, enabling their

Queen to release the spirit of the Dragon Fly, trapped in the water body form of one of the grubs. Witnessing this miracle, all the other Water Grubs come forward and are set free, flying away on silvery wings.

The theme of imprisonment and release has characterised Aboriginal writing since Unaipon. 'Release of the Dragon Flies', however, is less overtly political than much contemporary Aboriginal fiction. Unaipon's 'legend' represents an attempt to fuse the narrative of Aboriginal legend(s) with a Christian message – most particularly the importance of doing good unto others and caring for the 'weaker ones'.

In Unaipon's story, the cruel intention of the furious Frogs to slay the 'harmless', released Dragon Flies is thwarted. The whirlwind, created initially by the millions of Fairy Sun Beams beating their wings and stirring the atmosphere, becomes the wrath of 'a Force and Power greater than [the Frogs] possessed'. This is seen as intervention by a power analogous to a Christian God or 'Designer', whose business is to 'protect the weaker ones'. Furthermore, the Frogs are smitten with a guilty conscience for the wrong they have done to the 'helpless, harmless Water Grubs'. They cower beneath the thunder and lightning of the Great Power and jump into the pool to escape 'the judgement that awaits the Tyrant'. When the storm passes, the Frogs emerge 'repentant' and determined 'not to hinder the harmless Water Grubs from fulfilling their mission', which is transformation and liberation. So doing, they demonstrate the 'greatness and wisdom' of their maker. Thus Unaipon accommodates a Christian cosmology (with its dichotomy of Good and Evil) into an Aboriginal cosmology, while at the same time advocating Aboriginal liberation and harmonious relations based on Christian principles.

Much of Unaipon's work seems to reflect a struggle to reconcile belief systems which Westerners supposed to be irreconcilable. In his short piece 'Totemism', which is neither legend nor short story but something of both, Unaipon acknowledges the conflict between scientific and evolutionary belief systems (about which he was obviously well informed) and the Aboriginal belief system of totemism. In the space of two pages, Unaipon tries to weave these belief systems together, not in order to demonstrate the superiority of one set of beliefs over another, but rather to facilitate the co-existence of different beliefs without discredit or devaluation to either system. He describes Totemism as 'one of the most ancient customs instituted by the Primitive Man', yet is quick to insist that science admits that mythology is functional in that it is an attempt by 'Primitive Man to explain the physical and religious phenomena'.

In 'Totemism', Unaipon attempts to align scientific theories of evolution with the Aboriginal creation story of Spirit Man, who made the 'Great Decision and adventure to be clothed with an earthly body of flesh and blood'. Life, in Unaipon's story, comes 'out of the slimy water overshadowed with dense atmosphere and heat'. Spirit Man observes, however, that through the ages the various creatures with whom he lives side by side (Kangaroo, Emu, Goanna and the Insect Life) all conform to their type and species. Almost immediately, then, the narrative accommodates, into an Aboriginal mythology, a Western scientific theory of evolution and the Biblical creation myth ('And God created great whales, and every living creature that moveth, which the waters brought forth abundantly, after their kind, and every winged fowl after his kind' Genesis 1:21). When Spirit Man decides to take on an earthly body of flesh and blood, he experiences the division between body and soul that is part of Christian teaching; Unaipon differentiates between what he calls 'Spirit Consciousness' and 'Subjective Consciousness, which entirely belongs to the Earth and not to the Sacred Realm of the Spirit'. The Spirit Realm is then described in terms of the Christian concept of a 'Heavenly Home', for which the Spirit Self frets and pines. But it is the Living Creatures of the Earth who take pity on Spirit Man and teach him their lore for survival. 'Thus,' concludes Unaipon, returning to his justification for Totemism, 'the Aborigines of Australia have from time immemorial, either in Central Australia or along the Sea Coast, or living along the banks of the Moo Koolie, River Murray, all tribes have selected these living creatures for companions and guides' (5).

'Pah Kowie – The Creat[ive] Cell of Life and Intelligence' is the third piece in *Native Legends*. It is so brief (just one page) that it confounds expectations of the legend or short story form. Once again, the narrative seeks to justify Aboriginal beliefs. Unaipon seems to be attempting to reconcile the Ngarrindjeri beliefs of his 'ancient fathers' with those of an 'enlightened age'. There is an undertone to the writing that is defensive – a response, perhaps, to knowledge that his readers had been fed on a diet of newspaper articles which freely referred to the inferior mental development of 'the Aboriginal race'. Unaipon concludes 'Pah Kowie' with the suggestion that the Aboriginal ideas he has just outlined, about how Life and Intelligence are sustained, may seem 'fantastic and absurd'. Yet he suggests that the Aboriginal explanation of the origins of human intelligence *can* co-exist with scientific understanding of the Milky Way. The 'cavern of impenetrable darkness' (within the Milky Way) veils the Nawanthee (Home) of Pah Kowie, who gave birth to 'the first female life of flesh and blood, the mould and pattern for all the Mothers of the Earth'. This is described in terms of a 'mental vision' and a 'mind impression'. It is possible, then, for what is known in imaginative or supernatural terms also to be known in scientific terms – one form of knowledge ought not to preclude another. Yet Unaipon's enigmatic conclusion leaves us wondering what he really thought. He writes of ideas which 'are the foundation of a structure and edifice of knowledge under whose shadow we live today'. And as is often the case, we cannot be sure with whom Unaipon is identifying, or whose knowledge casts the shadow.

'Youn Goona the Cockatoo' and 'Hungarrda' are localised legends or 'folklore', as Unaipon described them in the *Observer* (10 October 1925), of the type that he began to collect after an offer from Angus and Robertson to publish a book (which did not appear). Collecting stories like these was not an easy task, given language difficulties, but Unaipon acknowledged that collecting 'folk legends' was for him 'not as difficult as it would be to a European'. Unaipon made use of the totem system. His description of his procedure is a good example of the problems that attach to any assessment of Unaipon's work. While on the one hand he clearly identifies with the Aboriginal race, on the other, his methods *could* be seen as equivalent to the exploitative practices of European anthropologists:

'I have the totem system to help me,' he said. 'The totem binds us together much as Masonry does Europeans. My first duty when I go into a strange tribe is to ask for a totem.

'Then, if they say, for instance, "that man is a swan", I say that my mother was also a swan, and he treats me as a relative, and tells me what I want to know. Or I find a man who is a kangaroo, the totem of my father.' (The *Observer*, 10 October 1925)

'Youn Goona the Cockatoo' seems to be a story from the eastern side of the Parnkalla group, bordering on or even in the country of the Nugunu language group north of Yorke Peninsula.[4] Youn Goona and his wife seat themselves on the bough of a gum tree that is precisely located 'on the east side of the mountain of Gawler Range, where Spencer's Gulf becomes narrow' (9). The vernacular terms used throughout the text are in the Parnkalla language spoken on the eastern side of the Eyre Peninsula. Yet the 'legend' is by no means a straightforward recording of a story told by an informant. Once again, Unaipon incorporates into his narrative ideas from western evolutionary theory and the Genesis creation story. There is a strong parallel between the creation of the male and female cockatoos and the creation of Adam and Eve. Youn Goona, Spirit Cockatoo, is reluctant to taint his Spirit Life by assuming a body of flesh and blood: it is his wife who finally makes the decision and in her new form cries to her husband to join her in the song that becomes the call of the cockatoo as we know it still. Yet, despite the evangelical language of the text ('Choose ye . . . choose ye'), there is no hint of the Christian concept of Original Sin. Youn Goona's reluctance to assume a body of flesh and blood is as much to do with his concern that a body will suffer discomfort and misery as it is with his fear of contamination of the spiritual life. His wife, first to assume physical form, is described as 'intelligent and clever'. It is she who chooses a form that will enable her to enjoy 'all the privileges that the Earth was able to offer', including 'the spirit Love manifested through the emotion of the flesh and blood', without subjecting that form to dangers, such as pursuit by dingoes. In her wisdom, she chooses a body that will survive without slaughtering other bodies for food, but will find 'sustenance in berries, seed and the sweet nectar from Gum blossom' (10). Furthermore, 'although differing from all creatures existing, this body, in her vision, was able to raise offspring like unto themselves, which was a decided privilege and blessing denied them in the Spirit Life and the Spirit Realm'. The legend, therefore, in its telling, celebrates at the same time existence in two realms, the earthly and the spiritual, and serves as another example of Unaipon's synthesising vision.

In 'Hungarrda', for the first time in *Native Legends*, Unaipon preserves the sense of an original narrator, who tells his story in the first person: 'Thus and thus spake Nha Teeyouwa (blackfellow). Nhan-Garra Doctor: Children, I have many strange stories to tell you. All came to me whilst I slumbered in deep sleep' (12). The story, however, is clearly not a transcription of an oral narrative, but Unaipon's interpretation of a Central Australian legend about a spirit ancestor in language appropriate to a stirring Christian sermon.

> Thine anger and thy power thou revealest to us . . . Thus in wonder am I lost. No mortal mind can conceive. No mortal tongue express in language intelligible. Heaven-born Spark, I cannot see nor feel thee . . . My soul is filled with gratitude and love for thee. And conscious, too, of thine all pervading spirit presence. It seems so strange that thou wilt not hear or reveal thyself nor bestow a blessing unless I pray. (14)

This narrative clearly conveys the power of the Dreaming, yet its flavour is Christian evangelical. Whereas this may seem bizarre to Western readers, studies of Aboriginal religions in recent years[5] increasingly suggest that, in Aboriginal societies, ideas which Westerners would define as being different from each other are accommodated 'by establishing relationships of interdependence such that each contains a portion of the other without being subsumed' (Rose 365). This pluralist system depends on the 'recognition of numerous ultimate principles' (Rose 365) and requires us to reassess what we might have thought about the incompatibility of Christian and Aboriginal explanations for the origins and purposes of life. Christian missionaries may have rejected Aboriginal cosmologies, but Aboriginal converts to Christianity, like James Unaipon and his son David, did not necessarily acknowledge the incompatibility of different belief systems. David Unaipon's narratives seem to provide evidence to this effect.

The Reverend Gordon Rowe, secretary of the Aborigines' Friends Association in 1959, commented to a *News* staff reporter that 'David loves to be enigmatic' (*News*, 22 July 1959). The conclusion to *Native Legends* is nothing if not enigmatic. The brief 'Narrinyeri Saying' allegorises life as a journey, just like the journey of Ngurunderi, the Ngarrindjeri ancestral figure, who travelled down the River Murray from its origins in the 'snow-capped Mountain' to the 'Great Ocean'. In Unaipon's allegory, however, after three score years and ten, having been 'baffled and tossed by the angry waves', we are 'cast forlorn and ship-wrecked upon the shore of a strange land'. From neither the Christian nor the Ngarrindjeri perspective should death present such a dismal prospect. Perhaps this puzzle is the closest David Unaipon came to expressing the paradox of his own life and the discrepancy between his desire for racial harmony and the reality of his lowly position among colonial mentors.

WORKS CITED

'An Aboriginal Intellectual'. *The Observer*. Adelaide Saturday 10 October 1925. 46.

Beston, John. 'David Unaipon: The First Aboriginal Writer (1873–1967)'. *Southerly* 39.3 (1979).

Davis, Jack, Stephen Muecke, Mudrooroo Narogin and Adam Shoemaker. *Paperbark*. St. Lucia: University of Queensland Press, 1990.

Muecke, Stephen. *Textual Spaces: Aboriginality and Cultural Studies*. Sydney: New South Wales UP, 1992.

Narogin, Mudrooroo. *Writing From the Fringe*. Melbourne: Hyland House, 1990.

Pratt, Mary Louise. *Imperial Eyes*. London: Routledge, 1992.

Ramsay Smith, William. *Myths and Legends of the Australian Aboriginals*. London: Harrap, 1930.

Shoemaker, Adam. *Black Words, White Page*. St. Lucia: University of Queensland Press, 1989.

Swain, Tony and Deborah Bird Rose (eds.). *Aboriginal Australians and Christian Missions, Ethnographic and Historical Studies*. Bedford Park: Australian Association for the Study of Religions, 1988.

Swain, Tony. *A Place for Strangers*. Melbourne: Cambridge UP, 1993.

Unaipon, David. *Native Legends*. Adelaide: Aborigines' Friends Association, [1929].

_____. 'My Life Story'. *The AFA Annual Report*, 1951. 10–14.

_____. 'Leaves of Memory'. *The AFA Annual Report*, 1953. 6–9.

NOTES

1. See Adam Shoemaker, *Black Words White Page*, 42–50, where Shoemaker contests John Beston's assertion (in 'David Unaipon: The First Aboriginal Writer, [1873–1967]', that Unaipon was 'by no means a white man's puppet' (345).

2. This is the way in which Mary Louise Pratt describes the space in which two races 'previously separated by geographic and historical disjunctures' found themselves in contact, interacting and 'interlocking understandings and practices, often within asymmetrical relations of power' (7).

3. Unaipon's stories 'Narroondarie's Wives' and 'Wondangar, Goon na Ghun (Whale and Star Fish)' were (re)published in *Paperbark*. This is the first time that editors had sought and been provided by the Point McLeay (Raukkan) Community Council with authorised publication rights to David Unaipon's work.

4. I am indebted to Mary-Anne Gale for her unpublished research in this area.

5. See, for example, Tony Swain, *A Place for Strangers*, and Tony Swain and Deborah Bird Rose (eds.), *Aboriginal Australians and Christian Missions, Ethnographic and Historical Studies*.

THE JINDYWOROBAKS
AND ABORIGINALITY

Robert Sellick

The notion of Australian 'regional' literature is a problematic one. Until recently attention has focused on 'national' traits, a concept (measured especially against the competing claims of universalism) that has been remarkably productive of energetic and at times acrimonious debate. Nevertheless, some regional areas have emerged: Western Australia, assisted by a lively press at both the University of Western Australia and the Fremantle Arts Centre, has been able to lay claims to serious attention. Queensland, too, has established a clear regional voice, again through a strong University Press. What of South Australia? There was a time when it was reasonably represented by publishers of some significance but that representation has sadly diminished over recent years. None of the three universities possesses a press (although Flinders University, through its Centre for Research in the New Literatures in English has made a significant contribution, as has the Friendly Street poetry group) and commercial publishing for adult readers has been reduced to one press only, Wakefield Press.

There was a time when South Australia exercised a greater influence on and played a more significant part in the literary affairs of the nation. In particular, South Australia is remembered for three 'events' which attracted considerable attention both at the time and subsequently: the *Angry Penguins* publication, its related 'Ern Malley' hoax and the Jindyworobak 'movement'. The first two of these have continued to excite curiosity; Ern's poems are still in print and interest in the hoax has recently been reactivated through the publication of Michael Heyward's *The Ern Malley Affair* and the celebration of the hoax's fiftieth anniversary. Interest in the Jindyworobaks, on the other hand, seems to have stalled. It is now fifteen years since Brian Elliott's reassessment of the Jindyworobaks appeared. One suspects that the name itself has caused difficulties for many people. Its outlandish ring and slightly raffish connotations can't have helped – Alec Hope's coining of the term 'Jindyworobaksheesh' certainly didn't – and may well account for the lack of interest in both the movement's originator and its theories. Apart from a general concern for the development of Australian litera- ture, the current intellectual and cultural climate with its interest in Mabo and reconciliation should provide sufficient justification for a re-examination of the movement and its contribution.

When Rex Ingamells first published his *Conditional Culture* in 1938, his personal response to a particular discovery of 'Aboriginality' was also the latest manifestation of white Australia's fascination with its Aboriginal past. After all, on a particular literary level, 1940 saw the issue of the first *Meanjin Papers* and it is worth recalling that the title chosen by its editor, Clem Christesen, acknowledged the Aboriginal name for a par- ticular spot on the Brisbane River. Also, since the late 1920s there had been a number of publications, such as *Coonardoo* and *Capricornia*, which focused on Aboriginal subjects and characters.

Interest had been growing since the publication of a revised edition of Baldwin Spencer's and Francis Gillen's *The Native Tribes of Central Australia*, which first appeared in 1899. This condensation, under the title *The Arunta*, appeared in 1927 and Rex Ingamells acknowledged the significance to him of this publication. Brian Elliott has pointed out that Ingamells was born at Ororoo, 'one of the far limits of the Arunta tribe', and suggested that this may have played a part. Rex Ingamells apparently discovered *The Arunta* while he was a student at Adelaide University. It may also be the case that the work being done at that time by T.G.H. Strehlow at the University exercised an influence as well (Strehlow later occupied a personal chair in Australian linguistics).

Even though the revised edition of Spencer's and Gillen's work is more accessible than the original publication, *The Arunta* remains a difficult book. It was the first detailed statement of the complexity of Aboriginal culture, but this is not what attracted Ingamells's attention. There is no evidence to suggest that he had a particular interest in ethnography as such, but whatever the book suggested to him became the point of departure for the Jindyworobaks. He seems to have been more concerned with or attracted by the notion of *Alchera* or *Alcheringa* (as it is rendered in the Aranda language) – which is usually translated as the Dreamtime or the Dreaming:

> In effect [Alchera] is a myth of a time outside the limits of history in which whatever exists has the reality of myth, not of fact. It exists in eternal terms as 'then' or 'now' or 'in the future' or 'always'; it is the time to which all other time goes back, in which the first things were done, the first creatures came to life, the creation-time. The first men and the first plants and animals came together then and were, not physically but totemistically, identified and (as the legends relate) interchangeable. It is a vision of the world so like a dream that it is also called the 'Dreaming' (a more accurate expression than 'Dreamtime'). All men of today belong to their proper totems and are reincarnations of the creatures (animals, human heroes, spirits, wanderers) of the original creation-time. (Elliott xxiv)

The concept of Alchera is central to all aspects of Aranda life and a similar concept exists in other Aboriginal groups: 'For aboriginal minds it is not merely a plausible image, the philosophical-intellectual-religious-ethical medium in which all their myths, legends, ceremonies, institutions and even their very thoughts cohere, it is the very basis of their faith; it is at the root of their concept of reality' (Elliott xxv). But it would be wrong to suggest that Ingamells and the Jindyworobaks generally were interested solely in Alchera. In conformity with other leaders of significant movements, Ingamells drew up and published a manifesto.

The Jindyworobak manifesto appeared in printed form as *Conditional Culture* in 1938. Both the meaning of the word Jindyworobak itself and the movement's broad aims were set out there:

> 'Jindyworobak' is an aboriginal word meaning 'to annex, to join', and I propose to coin it for a particular use. The Jindyworobaks, I say, are those individuals who are endeavouring to free Australian art from whatever alien influences trammel it, that is, bring it into proper contact with its material. They are the few who seriously realise that an Australian culture depends on the fulfilment and sublimation of certain definite conditions, namely:
> 1. A clear recognition of environmental values.
> 2. The debunking of much nonsense.
> 3. An understanding of Australia's history and traditions, primaeval, colonial and modern. (Quoted in Elliott xxvii)

One would have to agree with Brian Elliott that the manifesto, as a manifesto, 'might have been more precise and lucid', especially in relation to exactly how the annexation or joining was to occur. There remains the feeling that the phrase 'to annex or to join' carries with it the sense of appropriation – the taking over, by the descendants of the original white settlers, of Aboriginal language, culture and history. This possibility is to some extent supported, although in a relatively mild way, by the third point: 'An understanding of Australia's history and traditions, primaeval, colonial and modern'. And what exactly is one to make of the second point: 'The debunking of much nonsense'? Is Elliott correct when he interprets this as a reference to 'proprieties of local diction'? (Elliott xxvii). For Ingamells to propose that these 'proprieties of local diction' be discarded in favour of a greater incorporation of Aboriginal vocabulary into Australian writing was interesting. It is almost as though the Jindyworobaks were prepared to undertake the specifically post-colonial tasks of abrogation and appropriation as they are defined by the authors of the recent study, *The Empire Writes Back*:

> The crucial function of language as a medium of power demands that post-colonial writing define itself by seizing the language of the centre and re-placing it in a discourse fully adapted to the colonised

place. There are two distinct processes by which it does this. The first, the abrogation or denial of the privilege of 'English' involves a rejection of the metropolitan power over the means of communication. The second, the appropriation and reconstitution of the language of the centre, the process of capturing and remoulding the language to new usages, marks a separation from the site of colonial privilege. (38)

Although it is possible to dismiss such a program as overly ambitious as far as the Jindyworobaks are concerned – it would for example require a vision of a cohesive multi-racial Australian society that would have been well in advance of its time – nevertheless, there is some justice in accepting that it was at least part of what Ingamells has in mind when he talks of 'debunking'. It is, of course, possible to read almost anything into a statement as vague and imprecise as this.

Despite this imprecision, it is clear that the document does display two major strands: a strong interest in Aboriginality, however defined, and an even stronger anti-colonial or anti-European attitude. Certainly these were points that were noted in several published responses in both the *Bulletin* and *Southerly* to later publications by the group:

Flaunted Banners and Cultural Cross-Section contain the latest explanations and defence of the Jindyworobak theories. *Flaunted Banners* by Victor Kennedy is a reasoned attempt to explain just what the movement stands for and to clear up some common mistakes about it. It does not, he points out, require us to become Aboriginal, live in a gunyah or eat goannas. It is simply 'an effort to link Australian thought with its own natural background'. We are asked to treat 'as alien everything that owes its being directly to other cultures – English cultures, Irish cultures, German, Dutch or American', and to study and make the basis of our own traditions and vision 'the only true and sincere Australian culture . . . that of the Australian race'. We are told we must adapt ourselves to this country since the country will not adapt itself to us. (Hope 44)

Rightly or wrongly, the Jindyworobaks were seen to have allied themselves to Aboriginality (in whatever form) and a fiercely held

Australian-ness. It is therefore not unreasonable to ask of what does this 'Aboriginality' consist. (And I need, at this point, to register some reservations about my choice of this word; its history is a difficult one, if for no other reason than its use as the title of a regular column in the *Bulletin*.)

The word 'Jindyworobak' was taken by Ingamells from James Devaney's *The Vanished Tribes*, a collection of Aboriginal stories and legends which had been published in 1929. Devaney's preface to the second edition (which also appeared in 1929) is in part an exercise in reclamation – a rejection of current attitudes to Aborigines and a celebration of their particular strengths:

> They were matchless trackers and hunters. They invented the boomerang and the spear-thrower, and even a simple spindle for making string. Their legends and folk-lore were ingenious and often beautiful. They were born humorists and inveterate song-makers. Their marriage laws were intricate and admirable, and their moral code very strict. Their corroborees were really aboriginal dramas or primitive operas, and their message-sticks the rudimentary begin-nings of a written language. They were a happy and a care-free people before we came and civilised them with rum and gun-powder.

It is true that this provides a generally reductive view of the strengths of Aboriginal culture. Nevertheless, it serves as a partial expiation for the involvement of the white race in their fate:

> Their fate has been perhaps the blackest blot on the early pages of our short history; it is a tale of terrorism and reprisal, wholesale shootings, poisonings, opium, the Black Police. These things cannot now be undone, but at least we can be just to the memory of the exterminated tribes.

The title of Devaney's collection is of some significance as it repre-sents what appears to have been a prevailing attitude in Australia to Aborigines in the first decades of this century. A similar attitude is suggested by the title of Daisy Bates's *The Passing of the Aborigines*, which was published in 1938. The various poets who gathered under the

Jindyworobak banner also emphasised the impending disappearance of Aboriginal society and culture, for instance in poems such as Rex Ingamells's 'Forgotten People' or his 'From a Dying People' or Roland Robinson's 'And the Blacks Are Gone' (Elliott 11, 18, 122). And to that belief in the imminent disappearance of an entire race was added a sense of guilt for white complicity in events that had caused it.

Ingamells not only borrowed the word 'Jindyworobak' from Devaney; he also found the meaning set out there. Curiously, Devaney does not identify its precise linguistic origin. Indeed, he doesn't provide sources for any of the words he collects in his glossary and this appears to have been the case for the details of the stories he collects as well. When Ingamells later published a vocabulary of Aboriginal/English and English/Aboriginal correspondences (*Australian Aboriginal Words* 1955) he identifies each word's origin on a broad range only, as his 'Regional Key' indicates. Here his categories can be as broad as 'V.: Victoria' or 'S.A.: South Australia' although there are times when he is more precise: 'S.W.B.: Coastal Region around S.A. and W.A. Border'. It is, in fact, a curious compilation and one that makes no pretence to scientific rigour. It is also the type of glossary that prompts questions about the compiler's intentions. What readership did he have in mind? To what uses would the list be put? There remains a lingering suspicion that it might best serve owners who are seeking an appropriate Aboriginal name for their new suburban house. It is also fascinating to note that Ingamells doesn't include 'Jindyworobak' itself in his listing. (He also omits 'Garchooka' and 'Garrakeen', titles of two of his better-known poems and many of the other words that feature in his poetry.) There is, therefore, considerable doubt about the exact provenance of 'Jindyworobak'. Even the National Australian Dictionary is unable to settle the question of the word's origins. There it is described as 'probably from an Aboriginal language'. While it is true that many of the words Ingamells and the Jindyworobaks adopt can be traced back to Devaney, there are problems there as well. Although Devaney claims to have collected his stories in Queensland, some of the words appear to have a New South Wales origin. It is possible that even the word 'Alchera' itself – a term central to Jindyworobak thought – could have been borrowed from Devaney.

At times the link between Devaney and the Jindyworobaks appears to be almost seamless. I have already referred to the fact that the group's leader found the name itself in Devaney's collection of stories. But the debt is even more extensive. One poem in particular, Rex Ingamells's 'Moorawathimeering', appears to have drawn the ire of the critics – presumably on the basis of its apparently outlandish and impenetrable vocabulary.

> Into moorawathimeering,
> where atninga dare not tread
> leaving wurly for a wilban
> tallabilla, you have fled
>
> Wombalunga curses, waitjurk –
> though we cannot break the ban,
> and follow tchidna any further
> after one-time karaman.
>
> Far in moorawathimeering
> safe from wallan darenderong,
> tallabilla waitjurk, wander
> silently the whole day long.
>
> Go with only lilliri
> to walk along beside you there
> while douran-douran voices wail
> and Karaworo beats the air. (Elliott 11)

The story behind the poem is taken directly from Devaney's 'Sanctuary'. This is the tale of a young Aboriginal warrior, Kewora, who is wrongly accused of stealing the kidney fat of the Mara-karaka's rain man, Warrahul. Kawora is pronounced a tallabilla or outcast and the old man's death is to be punished by Warrahul's sons Kaat and Thundung, who take on the role of avengers or darrenderongs. When Kawora and his father retaliate and spear the brothers, father and son are forced to flee to the sacred sanctuary of Moorawathimeering, the country of the waitjurks, the hunted ones. Not only is the narrative outline borrowed from Devaney's story, much of the poem's vocabulary derives from it as well: *moorawathimeering, tallabilla, waitjurk, darenderong*. The remaining Aboriginal terms employed in the poem are taken from other language areas, although their provenance is not clear. Ingamells identifies only one word as belonging to the Central Australian language area: '*atninga*' (vengeance party); others are not glossed either here or elsewhere.

John Opie also finds the inspiration for his poem 'Talabilla' in Devaney's story – or perhaps in Ingamell's earlier 'Moorawathimeering'.

Far from the tribe look-out
where your claw-arms shout
warning, you will go . . .
        Tallabilla
among the driftsands
and hill-rocks your hands
will squander life . . . Tallabilla
the pursuit song
of age, darrenderong,
will whistle . . . from cave-holes
soon . . . one day
as the clouds pass
like barrarangs
in their grave grey clouds
in the sky
        Tallabilla
        my heart,
you will die. (Elliott 153)

The failure of the Jindyworobaks to identify a precise linguistic origin for their use of Aboriginal vocabulary calls into question the nature of the 'Aboriginality' they are presenting. The language is non-specific, unlocalised; specificity has been replaced by vagueness. It is as though the Aborigines are denied an individual voice. They are given only a collective one, in the same way that the diverse tribal structure is subsumed under the white Australian terms 'Aborigines' and 'Aboriginal'. Such a strategy works to present the original inhabitants as composites, even *idealised* beings, as stereotypes and not individuals. The Jindyworobaks, using limited material taken from *The Arunta* and Devaney in particular, constructed a particular Aboriginal society that appears to have little connection with reality. This construct either glosses over or ignores the variation within Aboriginal society and between Aboriginal societies. They may have ignored mythical references drawn from elsewhere and especially from Europe, but the result could be just as alien.

The poetry produced by the Jindyworobaks, taken as a single body of work, seems to bear out this claim. It is difficult to find examples of figures that are other than stereotypes. Or, rather, it is difficult to find figures that are actual and realised. I am not arguing for either autobiographical or biographical authenticity – or even historical accuracy. It is rather the fact that actuality seems to be absent from many of the poems. Look, for example, at the figure of Mary in Rex Ingamells's 'Black Mary':

> Mary, the lubra,
> walks wonderfully.
> She came along the dust-track,
> swinging her body freely, stepping
> lithely with perfect measure.
> The beautiful rhythm of her body
> flooded my heart with joy as do leaf-calls
> in a place of many birdsongs,
> flooded my heart with joy
> such as must be
> to apprehend perfection. (Elliott 17)

This is a description of an encounter with the ideal, rather than an experience founded in reality, as the repeated emphasis on 'perfect' and 'perfection' and the apprehension of it in the final line suggests. Mary's particular attraction seems to reside in her unity with nature rather than in any present reality. Even the title seems to separate the poet and his subject, to set them firmly apart.

One might, with some justification, ask what were the contacts that the Jindyworobak poets had with Aboriginal people. Ingamells was born at Ororoo, in the arid north-east of South Australia, and attended school and university in Adelaide. Much of Ian Mudie's life was also spent in Adelaide, where he was born and educated. William Hart-Smith was born in England and later divided his time between New Zealand and Australia. Roland Robinson was brought to Australia as a child but was later to have first-hand experience of detribalised Aboriginal life. Flexmore Hudson was born in Queensland and moved as a child to Adelaide. The biographies of these writers indicate minimal contact with actual Aboriginal peoples. They were essentially urban writers and there are suggestions that their construction of an Australia and an Aboriginal society within it was the product of an urban need. Useful comparisons might in fact be made between the program of the Jindyworobaks with its emphasis on the Aborigines and the earlier mythologising of the Australian bush and bush values by the writers of the 1890s.

It is hardly surprising, therefore, that together with a tendency to create idealised figures went a conviction of a lost or vanished people. This results in the creation of an *idealised* past, as, for example, in Ingamells's 'Forgotten People':

Before white men made wurlies out of stone
　　To loom like tnatantjas against the sky,
The wandering black, in bushlands all his own,
　　Rubbed fire, speared fish, and watched the eagle fly.

After the white man came, the black man lost
　　His hunting-grounds and camping-grounds. He went
Lonelier and lonelier, pitilessly tossed,
　　By fates he knew not, into banishment.

His waterholes were stolen or defiled,
　　And all his sacred tjurungas were tainted:
He went not stalking when the wan dawn smiled
　　And came not to corroboree, weird-painted.

He lived not in reality, but dreams,
A stranger to his tribal lands and streams. (Elliott 12)

This section of the poem records, even if in a limited way, the cost to the Aborigines of the white invasion. No longer are the 'bushlands all his own'. The full measure of a people's deprivation is to be reckoned only by absence or loss: not only the 'hunting-grounds and camping-grounds' but also their daily activities, ceremonies, and culture. In the section of the poem that immediately precedes the one quoted here, the poet recalls what has been lost through a vision of an earlier time.

Ian Mudie's 'Intruder' makes a similar point, although here the emphasis is more on guilt than on a recreated or recalled idealised past:

> When I walk
> I do not know
> what ancient sacred place
> my foot may desecrate
> or if my tread shall fall
> where some cult-hero bled,
> or shed blood,
> or gave fire to man
> in the far dreamtime.
>
> Vanished elders
> of the long-dead tribe
> forgive
> my taboo-breaking,
> my uncicatrised intrusion
> and do not send
> kadaitcha men
> to haunt my dreams.
>
> Surely you can guess
> my conscience
> is uneasy enough
> already. (Elliott 95)

It is an idealised, heroic past from which the white race is excluded and for which he mourns.

It is evident that the Jindyworobaks saw the Dreaming as a lost heroic age. Hence the attraction of James Devaney's stories, since he set them in an already vanished past, as he acknowledges in the preface to the second edition: 'I have tried to go back to the tribes as they were before the coming of the whites.' In constructing that vanished past, the Jindyworobaks also constructed an idealised Aboriginal society in which all individual differences were subsumed. The most important of those differences were located in language, and by eliminating all sense of actual language the movement effectively rendered the Aborigines silent. The language itself was 'annexed' and an artificial one created. It is for this reason that the 'Aboriginality' that they created is a fragile one with only a contingent relationship to the reality of both past and present Aboriginality and its relationship to actuality. This is not to say that the movement ignored the condition of those Aborigines who were forced to eke out a pitiful existence on the margins of white society, although one has little sense of the movement as one with a firmly held social agenda. It is a truism that for much of its short history Australia has been a land in search of heroes, of a method of establishing unequivocal links with what was frequently seen as a hostile land. It is therefore worth noting the frequency with which the Jindyworobaks turned to other European lands in a quest for suitable candidates. Columbus and Balboa are the subjects of Ingamells' epic poem 'The Great South Land', while Columbus also features in William Hart-Smith's 'Prologue to Christopher Columbus'. This is by no means an exhaustive list and there are also occasions when local possibilities are explored. This is certainly suggested by Ken Barratt's use of the Burke and Wills story in his 'Burke and Wills', and even Ian Mudie's attempt at creating a popular mythology in 'They'll Tell You About Me' is an example of such a preoccupation. The Jindyworobak movement's interest in a lost Aboriginal culture could therefore be seen as yet another attempt to construct a local pantheon.

Although, in the end, the Jindyworobaks' search for a suitable and accessible Aboriginality achieved only limited success, it is still possible to see it as a forerunner of other worthwhile attempts at 'annexation'. Despite the fact that there have been recent announcements of a projected Aboriginal dictionary, the languages of the original inhabitants of this country will continue to elude even the best intentioned of non-Aboriginal writers. At the very least, the halting attempts at introducing an Aboriginal vocabulary into Australian poetry brought the Jindyworobak poets – and those who followed them – into closer contact with their Australian environment. As Arthur Phillips notes, the Jindyworobak movement

> does, however, truthfully record a changing attitude towards our physical environment. It expresses a feeling of the period that the Australian spirit was rooted in a land no less than in a people. If the men of the nineties had felt this influence, they had felt it very differently. The land was still mainly for them a hostile force; if they drew a strength from it, it lay mainly in the confidence springing from the sense of victory over an unrelenting foe, rather than in any feeling of affectionate unity with the soil. (Phillips 83)

In this way Ingamells's third condition was after all fulfilled. There is an additional hope, however: the growing awareness of the complexity and subtlety of Aboriginal poetic forms – an awareness fostered by the work of people such as Catherine and Ronald Berndt – might enable Australia's white writers to move to a fully realised annexation or joining.

WORKS CITED

Ashcroft, B., G. Griffiths and H. Tiffin. *The Empire Writes Back*. London & New York: Routledge, 1989.

Bates, Daisy. *The Passing of the Aborigines*. London: Murray, 1938.

Devaney, James. *The Vanished Tribes*. Sydney: Cornstalk, 1929.

Elliott, Brian. *The Jindyworobaks*. St Lucia: University of Queensland Press, 1979.

Hayward, Michael. *The Ern Malley Affair*. St Lucia: University of Queensland Press, 1993.

Hope, A.D. *Native Companions: Essays and Comments on Australian Literature 1936–1966*. Sydney Angus and Robertson, 1974.

Ingamells, Rex. *Conditional Culture*. Adelaide: F.W. Preece, 1938.

———— (comp.). *Australian Aboriginal Words*. Melbourne: Hallcraft, 1955.

Phillips, A.A. *The Australian Tradition*. Melbourne: Cheshire, 1958.

Spencer, W.B. and F.J. Gillen. *The Arunta*. London: Macmillan, 1927.

CHAPTER

8

BEAT NOT THE BONES

HEART OF DARKNESS RE-VISITED

David Smith

'You knew him well', she murmured, after a moment of mourning silence.

'Intimacy grows quickly out there', I said. 'I knew him as well as it is possible for one man to know another'.

'And you admired him', she said. 'It was impossible to know him and not to admire him. Was it?'

'He was a remarkable man', I said unsteadily. Then before the appealing fixity of her gaze, that seemed to watch for more words on my lips, I went on. 'It was impossible not to – '

'Love him', she finished eagerly, silencing me into an appalled dumbness. 'How true! how true! But when you think that no one knew him so well as I! I had all his noble confidence. I knew him best'.

'You knew him best', I repeated. And perhaps she did. But with every word spoken the room was growing darker, and only her forehead, smooth and white, remained illumined by the unextinguishable light of belief and love'. (*Heart of Darkness* 118)

The cover of the Wakefield Crime Classics re-issue of Charlotte Jay's 1952 novel *Beat Not the Bones* is almost a parody of its contents. 'A tale of terror in the tropics' the publisher's subtitle promises us, while the colouring and contents of its linocut illustration suggest imperial tales of derring-do in far-off places. Any readers who pick up the novel expecting precisely that, however, will surely soon find themselves as disoriented as those late Victorians who started reading the serial version of Joseph Conrad's *Heart of Darkness* expecting it to be another 'Tale from the Outposts'.

Indeed they are very likely to be plunged into as much sense of disorientation as the novel's Australian heroine, Stella, suffers as she makes her bewildered journey into Papua New Guinea, beginning at one of its 'tamed' outposts, Marapai (Port Moresby), and then venturing into its succulent clutching jungles. Throughout the novel the cockroaches, flying ants, geckoes, and jungle rats accumulate, while the environment bears down so forcibly on Stella that at one point she muses, even 'the garden was not behaving according to laws known to her . . . It struck her that this country had passed the limits of richness and beauty and dived off into some sort of inferno' (37).

But let me return to that analogy with Conrad's novella, an analogy particularly appropriate here. Appropriate because, like Jay's *A Hank of Hair* (also reissued by Wakefield Press) with its teasing interconnections with another classic Victorian text, Robert Browning's dramatic monologue 'Porphyria's Lover', *Beat Not the Bones* sets up a haunting and often provocative interaction with *Heart of Darkness*. The structural and thematic similarities between the two books are obvious enough: the protagonist of Jay's novel, Stella Warwick, comes from the centre to a colonial outpost where she finds herself obsessively pursuing a 'pilgrimage' in search of the 'truth', a pilgrimage which takes her up a river to the very heart of darkness where she confronts a final 'horror'. However, as in *Wide Sargasso Sea*, Jean Rhys's 're-writing' of *Jane Eyre*, it is an exploration of the 'revisions' rather than the correspondences that reveals why the interaction is such a memorable one.

Revised echoes of and allusions to *Heart of Darkness* start early. In the very first chapter, for example, we encounter in Trevor Nyall a figure reminiscent of Conrad's laundered 'miracle' of a Chief Accountant: 'He might [muses Alfred Jobe] have been a dummy in a Sydney shop window. There was no speck or crease in his shirt or white trousers, and he had not taken off his coat and tie, which was absurd' (7). It is the same Nyall who later in the novel is seen by Stella Warwick in terms which this time recall the inner emptiness of Conrad's Station Manager: 'She had, now that the moment of contact was over, a peculiar impression of having looked into nothing, of having turned her gaze, not upon a man's face, not upon eyes and lips, but upon a kind of void' (93). A cluster of such revised allusions and images – revised here in the sense that Nyall, with his capacity for keeping himself at a distance from the evil he instigates, records and profits from, *is* both the Chief Accountant and the Company Manager – occurs when Stella Warwick enters her late husband's workplace:

> Stella stood in the doorway and looked around at the office where her husband had worked. It was little different from the Department of Survey. Seven foot walls partitioned it off like a milking shed. There was office paraphernalia – tables, desks, typewriters and filing cabinets. The strange, long, animal body of Papua and New Guinea and a map of the world with the British Empire marked in red were pinned on the wall. An oil painting of a native in a feather head-dress was propped up on top of the bookcase, and there was another drawing, which might have been done by a child, pinned on the opposite wall. Littered about the table among the files and wire baskets were half a dozen tins of bully beef, a round, yellow gourd with a boar's tusk stopper, three little wooden figures and a human skull. Down in one of the smaller offices somebody was using a typewriter (74).

Readers familiar with *Heart of Darkness* will almost certainly be aware of shifting fragments of images from Conrad's novel in this passage: namely the map with its 'vast amount of red' (*Heart of Darkness* 36) that Conrad's narrator, Marlow, sees in the Trading Offices in Brussels, the oil-painting of the woman with the beacon making her way through the darkness encountered by Marlow at the Central Station, the native hangings on the walls and even perhaps (with the mention of the 'human skull') the doctor-cum-alienist who wants to measure Marlow's skull before he leaves for his trip into the darkness: 'I always . . . measure the crania of those going out there' (*Heart of Darkness* 39). However, the images have been re-oriented, in detail and context. There are other confusing signs present which have their origins in the novel's ostensible placing in the genre of crime (it won the first Edgar Allan Poe Award of the Mystery Writers of America): the 'tins of bully beef', for example, which reappear intermittently throughout the novel and which prove to be a crucial factor in the final unravelling of the murder mystery. Geography of course has been radically transformed and with it the nature of the imperial relations; we are now in Papua New Guinea rather than the Congo, and so the colonisers are not the British Empire builders but members of that empire, the colonials, the Australians. The disturbingly ambivalent attitude (on the part of characters and narrator) towards native culture remains – is the horror brought by the white people or are they corrupted by the black culture? – but the perspectives now have added irony.

However, what is surely most striking in the context of the novel as a whole is that the person observing these objects is not a male Marlow, but a female, Stella Warwick. Early on, it is true, she does not make a great deal of what she sees. Moreover, hers is not the dominating perspective; she is indeed no single first person narrator but one of several third person narrators. But she grows and matures during the course of the novel, so much so in fact that in certain crucial sections she wrests the narrative from the male characters. It is Stella who has, at the end of her 'pilgrimage', the courage to face the 'horror' that lies at the heart of this story. But if, as this account implies, Stella is in a sense a female version of Marlow, she is even more crucially Conrad's de-civilised white man, Kurtz's 'Intended', come from the colonising power (Australia) to redeem the name of her Kurtz (Warwick). She is, however, an Intended who breaks loose from the patriarchal clutch of Kurtz, Marlow and Conrad and acquires a narrative voice of her own, a voice which is virtually denied her by this trilogy of men.

Stella's first appearance in the narrative – in the first chapter – could not be more inauspicious. She is no more than a ghostly presence in a letter her husband of a few months, David Warwick, is writing to her back in Australia, rebuking her for having dismissed her sick father's nurse.

It is a first appearance as marginal perhaps as that of the 'Intended' in Marlow's 'Girl? What? Did I mention a girl?' (*Heart of Darkness* 84). The other characters in this chapter – which is set in Marapai several months before the main events of the novel – have no consciousness of Stella at all. Certainly the seedy and shady Jobe isn't aware of her as he tells the apparently unresponsive Trevor Nyall, the Director of Survey, and David Warwick, an anthropologist from the Department of Cultural Development, how he has unexpectedly found gold (the ivory of this narrative) in the jungle village of Eola. Between this chapter and the next there intervenes a gap of several months: it is this gap which Stella – and the reader – have to fill in the remainder of the narrative.

When Stella does finally make an appearance in her own right in the second chapter, she is at first quiet and disoriented, her identity barely acknowledged by those around her. Even her secondary identity as the now late Warwick's wife is questioned. She is either too old (to be his daughter) or too young (to be his wife). She might well be one of those anonymous women condescendingly described by Marlow as best kept 'out of it' 'in a world of their own . . . out of touch with truth' (*Heart of Darkness* 39). When she speaks, however, we learn that it is precisely the 'truth' that she is seeking – just as Marlow, who 'hates and detests' lies (57), seeks truth in *Heart of Darkness*. She has come on a 'pilgrimage' (39) to find out the 'truth' about her late husband's reported suicide. But as her 'large, fanatical eyes' (22) might suggest, she seeks this truth with the obsession, presumptions and naivety of the Intended, the Intended who in the closing pages of *Heart of Darkness* sees her late fiancé, Kurtz, who had lived out his final days in darkness and horror, as morally immaculate, his 'goodness' shining 'in every act' (*Heart of Darkness* 120).

It is soon apparent that for Stella, initially at least, the 'truth', as for the Intended, is only what is an acceptable or bearable truth, a truth that will not shatter the fragile illusion she has about her husband. She may assert, when one of the characters cynically proclaims the unimportance of truth, that 'Truth and justice are the only things that matter' (35), but it is clear that one thing she is not prepared to accept is that her husband *has* committed suicide. There must be a crime; after all, her sick father, having received a letter from Warwick, cried out 'Murder! Murder!' as he died. But the crime, she has resolved, is that her husband has been murdered. That he might not only have taken his own life but also someone else's is not a thought she is prepared to entertain. She knows that he went on an expedition to Eola with an assistant and returned; Jobe, she has decided, is the 'villain' who killed him on his return.

In her early relationships with the two men she has initially to deal with – Trevor and Anthony Nyall, both of whom in their different ways patronise her – she is either submissive, trusting to the 'wide, dependent, childlike gaze that had so endeared her to her father and husband' (61), or simplistic, seeing things in black and white. Convent-educated (where her father had hoped she would be turned into someone 'gracious, submissive and womanly' 40), Stella indeed 'had had no time or opportunity to formulate any complicated notions of wickedness. Wickedness, she believed, was a quality you recognised in the faces of disreputable strangers' (40). Certainly she is unable to cope when Anthony Nyall questions both the nature of her love and the idealised picture she has of her late husband. In a conversation which is both an echo and a revision of that final conversation between Marlow and the Intended in *Heart of Darkness,* she insists '*Everyone* loved him!' (78). When Nyall calmly retorts, abandoning Marlow's script, 'I forget . . . that you're so young' (78), Stella is devastated:

> They were the most terrible words that anyone had ever spoken to her. She felt instinctively that they threatened the whole basis of her faith . . . I forget you are so deluded. This is what people meant when they said, 'I forget you are so young' . . . His quiet, ruthless voice went on. 'You expect the best of him. If you loved him you would accept the worst. You never knew him – how could you? He had no choice but to hide from you what he was.' (79)

It is from this position of naivety, dependence and innocence that Stella breaks free in the course of the narrative, as she gradually discovers first who actually went to the village of Eola and then what actually happened there. The process of her growth is certainly no straightforward one. Even, for example, after she has had the Marlovian revelation of looking into Trevor Nyall's eyes and seeing there 'a kind of void' (93), she still responds to him as she has been conditioned to respond to men, although her response is now mixed:

It was hard to suspect a man who looked straight into your eyes. She was reminded of her father, of the nuns, of her husband, of the procession of adults who had all directed and guided her, who had put their hands on her shoulders and said, 'Now, listen to me, Stella, now tell me, Stella, now, Stella, it's not like that . . .' and had died and left her alone. (116)

It is not until she has started to put together a picture of what happened at Eola which is not simply a reflection of what the men choose to tell her that her development and – the formal recognition of this – her seizure of the narrative from the males really gathers momentum. More specifically, it is once she realises that accompanying her husband on his expedition to Eola were not only such Papuans as Hitola but also another civil servant, Philip Washington.

Washington, the aspiring poet, forms – together with Warwick, the anthropologist – the composite Kurtz of this story. A misogynist who sees women only in general terms ('*Women* must always be making situations' 48), or as beings to be abused and used, Philip Washington is given in the first part of the novel several lengthy sections of narrative from which Stella in the main is conspicuously absent. He is vaguely and patronisingly aware of her existence: aware, for example, of 'a girl with a pale face' (46) in the background (even after he has met her he is still contemptuously thinking of her in terms of 'Miranda' 147). Stella on her part has no knowledge of him at all. Like Kurtz, Washington 'yearns for success' (50) and recognition. Like Kurtz too, it is clear that some disintegration in his personality has taken place:

In the tropics decay is as swift and violent as growth. Overnight mould will bristle up on a hat or shoe; in a few hours a body will rot, in a few weeks a personality will crumble. It was generally said that over the past few months Washington had gone to pieces. He was aware himself of some sort of internal disintegration. (47)

He is consumed by fear – fear of certain Papuans, fear of the dark, fear of magic – although the precise nature and source of that fear is kept from the reader.

Unlikely catalyst though he may be, with the introduction into her consciousness of this misogynistic man, weak and aggressive by turns, Stella, for the first time in her life it would seem, starts to exert her will and gain some control over her destiny. As she questions him, as she forms a clear impression that he is lying to her, so her sense of control increases: 'She had a feeling of power that she had never known in her life. She saw the situation as important and dangerous, and she was dealing with it herself. No one was telling her what to do. She was actually pitting her wits against an older, and more experienced, man' (130).

Stella's development, too, can be measured against Washington's attitude towards the Papuans. For all his avowed interest in their way of life, Washington, along with the other white males in the narrative – and including too, it must be said, a disturbing narrative voice of uncertain origins – displays a complex mixture of patronage, mystification and contempt for the natives of Marapai. Stella, in contrast, after her initial disorientation and ignorance (the 'inferno' image quoted earlier is relevant here), is notably more restrained in her views, and less eager to generalise. She recognises that Papuan culture is not something easily accessible to her, and is ready to respect the Papuans as individuals. It is indeed to Hitola that, at a time of crisis, she looks instinctively for support. Thus the reader is prepared for that strangely moving moment later in the narrative when she and Hitola, the latter now dressed in full tribal costume and daubed with war paint, stand wordlessly side by side over the dead body of Washington.

At the same time as there is an intellectual growth, so there is an emotional growth, as Stella probes more clearly into the nature of her relationship with Warwick and realises that: 'She had been able to transfer to him quite naturally the attitude and behaviour that had belonged to her father' (141). Her concept of love also changes, from the simple idealistic devotion to a man she barely knows to the recognition that there is a depth of love which a badly flawed man like Washington may inspire or a Papuan like Hitola may feel of which she knows nothing – that this was 'a world which she had never entered' (152).

And if it still is of truth and goodness that she is talking the day before she leaves for her journey to Eola ('"I have to find out," said Stella in a voice that she did not recognise as her own. "I have to find out the truth"' 152), her concept of that truth has changed, both in her awareness of the difficulty of finding it and the recognition that it may not be what she wants to find: 'She had come to realise that people lied to her more often than they did not' (142). She has also learnt to lie herself and significantly suffers no Marlovian introspective agonies: 'How easy it is to lie, she thought, and sometimes how necessary' (161). If she is still 'almost powerless in the grip of an old dream', she recognises that it is 'almost meaningless now' (152).

Stella's emotional and intellectual growth is shown most clearly with the departure from 'civilisation', as we become aware of the full extent to which she has gained control of the narrative. It is, for example, through her eyes that we first see the jungle, with its 'succulent trunks and . . . gigantic blades of leaves' (79), and even when we return nominally to the narrative perspective of Washington in the next chapter, many of his most important thoughts are dominated by his reflections of her: 'Stella gave him confidence . . . The irony of this – that Stella should inspire him with confidence' (171). During the course of this chapter Washington's disintegration becomes even more pronounced, his abandonment to fear more grotesque. It is to Stella that he now looks for support, though he seeks mystical explanations: 'the jungle that had robbed him of reason and strength had given these very qualities to her. He had been rejected and she had been chosen' (177). Stella is much more matter-of-fact about why she is now in control:

> Freed from the illusion of having loved David, she was free from those opinions and attitudes of his that she had worn as her own . . . people had always come to her second hand, stamped with the insignia of someone else's approval . . . She felt that everyone she had known had hidden from her, had protected her from the dangers of discovery because they had enjoyed in her a condition of innocence . . . (181)

Stella it is who now makes the decisions, 'her large eyes, once so wild and fanatic, [now] clear and determined' (189). She it is who leads, while Washington follows; she who 'commands', while he stumbles on 'obediently' (190). Even when the narrative switches to Washington, his dependency upon her strips him of all authority as he weakly pleads for her not to leave him alone. As they near the village of Eola, so his fear and panic increases, and it is in this fear and panic that he confirms her growing suspicions of how he and her late husband came to Eola and robbed the villagers of their gold. But he still withholds the last vital piece of information.

Stella now moves forward alone, the narrative hers entirely, the plaintive cries of Washington retreating into silence. The village ahead of her seems strangely, ominously deserted, devoid at first of any sign of human or indeed animal life. Then something moves, a 'gross, obese' jungle rat and, as she watches it scuttle confidently up the steps of the long house – that male preserve where, we have been told in the first chapter, most of the gold had been stored – so she suddenly realises what has happened at Eola, why Philip Washington so dreads to return and what had led her husband to take his own life:

> She was calm. She knew now that there was nothing to fear, and walked confidently. The only danger was in allowing the horror that was in Eola, that draped the village and inhabited the huts, that crawled and rotted on the ground, to invade her own body and mind. But some protective force that guards human beings at such times paralysed her senses and held her mind at a dumb, frozen level of consciousness. (199)

In *Heart of Darkness* Marlow, having brought aspects of the 'horror' into momentary close focus, chooses from then on to obscure his account with abstractions. Stella, on the other hand, significantly chooses to unveil all. Her choice is partly dictated by the fact that the genre in which she is the protagonist is a crime novel: the crime must be revealed. But it is also the case that she is still intent upon pursuing the truth, whatever that truth may prove to be. It will not be found, she now feels, amongst abstractions like 'justice' and 'goodness'. So, unlike Marlow (and Conrad) who lowers his telescope when the horror looms too closely ('I put down the glass and the head that had appeared near enough to be spoken to seemed at once to have leaped away from me into the inaccessible distance' [*Heart of Darkness* 97]), Stella does 'not shirk her inspection. She [makes] sure' (199). She moves, a careful observer, through the 'rotting' village amongst the scattered, ant-infested skeletons of men, women, and children. And as she moves, past the pathetic bones of a child, hearing the rustling of the swollen rat, the feeding noises of insects, so 'the horror around her slide[s] slowly nearer' (207). Once again the mundane image of the tins of bully beef appears and the reader is left in no doubt that Washington and Warwick – with their superior Trevor Nyall manipulating them from behind his desk – have, for the sake of gold, murdered an entire village.

Washington's subsequent death is almost an afterthought to this story. Stella now returns and faces variants of Conrad's Company Manager with his bland, obscene talk about Kurtz's 'Unsound Methods'. First there is the comparatively harmless 'methodical' (156) District Officer Thomas Seaton:

> 'Bad show. Funny how people break up here. Never know what they'll do next . . . Bad for the Territory . . . bad for the administration.'
> 'Bad for the Eolans', said Stella, and started to laugh. (207)

But above all there is Trevor Nyall, who meticulously writes for the official records a 'detailed report of the whole thing' (213). In a passionate attack which returns to the laundered image of the Chief Accountant, Stella accuses him of being a 'monster':

> He sits behind his desk and thinks up monstrosities, keeps his hands clean and sleeps at night without dreaming. I'm not afraid of him, though he knows I know. He wouldn't dirty himself with hurting me. He's so clean. (213)

Despite Stella's recognition that the narrative she is in has changed irrevocably – 'there is no murderer to chase, no Jobe to hate, no justice to pursue' (202) – the last few pages of *Beat Not the Bones* do return somewhat glibly to the safe haven of the genre of the crime story – with Jobe and Nyall tying up the loose ends and a criminal recognised and punished. Appropriately, because this is no longer her story, Stella appears no more, marginalised into Jobe's patronising comment: 'nice little thing, pretty as paint' (216). However, the reader is unlikely to forget how, against all the masculine power bearing down on her, this 'nice little thing' has managed to refocus the narrative, wrenching it away from the Nyalls and Washington, in the process giving the Intended an adult voice so long denied her.

BIOGRAPHICAL NOTE

Charlotte Jay was born Geraldine Mary Jay in 1919 in Adelaide, where she works under her married name, Geraldine Halls, as a writer and oriental art dealer. She grew up in Adelaide, and worked as a secretary in Adelaide, Sydney, Melbourne and London during the 1940s and as a court stenographer for the (Australian) Court of Papua New Guinea during 1949. Between the 1950s and 1970s she and her husband, John, who worked for UNESCO, travelled and lived in Lebanon, Pakistan, Thailand, India, France and England.

Charlotte Jay was the name Geraldine Halls used to publish most of her mystery novels, which were first published in London and New York between 1951 and 1964, and which are listed by title in Michael J. Tolley's essay in this book. They reflect a life spent travelling and her fascination with ethnological questions, as do her seven 'straight' novels published as Geraldine Halls between 1956 and 1995. As Geraldine Halls, she was one of the first post-war Australian novelists to 'engage' with Asia, notably in her trilogy set in Thailand and India, *The Cats of Benares*, *The Silk Project* and *The Cobra Kite*. Her latest novel, *This is My Friend's Chair* (Wakefield, 1995), is set mainly in Adelaide.

WORKS CITED

Conrad, Joseph. *Heart of Darkness*. 1902. Harmondsworth: Penguin, 1973.

Jay, Charlotte. *Beat Not the Bones*. 1952. Kent Town, S. Aust.: Wakefield, 1992.

CHAPTER

9

RECENT SOUTH AUSTRALIAN POETRY

Andrew Taylor

The recent publication of an anthology of South Australian poetry is a convenient occasion on which to look at what has been occurring in poetry in this state over the last decade and a half. For this is no ordinary anthology. There have been a number of anthologies produced over the years, such as *The Orange Tree* and *Dots over Lines*, not to mention the annual *Friendly Street Readers*.[1] They have met with modest success, although the annual *Readers*, forming a record of what has been read at the monthly Friendly Street readings, are keenly awaited each year. But the new anthology is something different. *Tuesday Night Live: Fifteen Years of Friendly Street* provides us with an opportunity to see just what has been occurring in poetry in South Australia since the beginning of those readings on the evening of 11 November 1975.

Of course, no anthology by itself will be adequate to reflect fully all that has been occurring in South Australian poetry over the last fifteen or more years. The contents of *Tuesday Night Live* have been drawn only from the annual anthologies, and many poets have published significant work over the period covered which has not been included in them. But it is hard to think of any poet of any stature writing in South Australia – with the exception of Ken Bolton – who does not have work included in *Tuesday Night Live*, a fact that indicates something of the centrality of the Friendly Street readings for poetry in Adelaide, and possibly even in the state as a whole. *Tuesday Night Live* is thus a convenient sampler of the work of almost every published South Australian poet, including some who have moved interstate and several who are now dead.

Given the centrality of Friendly Street, it is perhaps pertinent to say a little about the readings, and what has grown from them, before turning to the poetry itself. Jeri Kroll and Barry Westburg give an excellent account of the history of Friendly Street in the anthology, and anyone interested in more detail than I can provide here should refer to their essay, 'A History in Progress'.

Friendly Street

The Friendly Street Readings were set up by Ian Reid, Andrew Taylor and Richard Tipping, all of whom had recently returned to Adelaide from overseas. While in the United States they had attended, and participated in, public poetry readings held, usually, in bars, coffee shops and similar informal, public venues. In early November 1975 there was a meeting in Taylor's cottage in North Adelaide, which included five other poets as well as the original three, and a time, a date and a format for regular poetry readings were agreed on. Taylor had drawn up a list of over twenty well-known, published poets living in Adelaide who, to the best of his knowledge, had never all been in the one room together. It seemed time to remedy that situation and to create more of a sense of community among the city's poets. The readings would provide an outlet for new work, feedback from the audience and other poets, and a point of contact among those who shared an interest in poetry.

All of these intentions, and more, were eventually fulfilled. The first reading, held on the day of the Whitlam Labor government dismissal, has prompted a wry comparison between the fortunes of parliamentarians and that of Shelley's 'unacknowledged legislators'. Although initially held each fortnight, the readings eventually became monthly, and the venue changed from the Media Resource Centre to the Federal Box Factory. But the basic format remains much as at first. Originally one, and later two, guest or main readers read. After a break for announcements and advertisements, there would be an open reading on a first come, first served basis. This mixture enabled more established poets to read for a substantial amount of time, and others to try out new work in the open reading. When a newer poet had accumulated enough material of quality to occupy one of the main spots, he or she was normally put on the program.

A major development, central to Friendly Street's ongoing significance, was Richard Tipping's idea of bringing out an anthology of the best work read during the first year. This was the beginning of the annual anthologies. To be included, poems had actually to be read at one of the readings. This, as much as anything else the readings provided, served as a strong incentive to attend and participate. Without it, it could be argued that Friendly Street would not have become, and remained, so central to poetry in Adelaide. The publishing aspect was expanded in 1982, when Friendly Street became the publisher of five individual collections of poems, and it has continued to be the major publisher of poetry in the state, recently in collaboration with the Wakefield Press.

One other aspect of the readings that requires mention is that they also provided a venue for writers from interstate or even from overseas. They have thus become a place where a wide-ranging interchange can occur, and because of the offer of publication – either in the Readers or in a book of one's own – they have remained a strong attraction to Adelaide's poets.

South Australian Poetry

Because of the central role of Friendly Street, it is tempting to try to find something of a South Australian style, or even a common set of pre-occupations which could be considered as distinctly South Australian. Such a search would be misleading, however. Poetry occupies a more complex, intertextual space than a single, regular poetry reading, and South Australian poets are as alert to developments in other parts of the country and of the world as their counterparts elsewhere. It is not even true that performance poetry predominates, which might have been expected. It seems that the readings have accommodated poems which would normally be read silently just as readily as pieces for performance, some of which would not translate happily into printed form anyway. However, it is noticeable that all the poems in the anthology, of whatever kind, are capable of effective oral presentation. Some of the more complex language games and visual tricks found elsewhere are absent, and if one wants to find them in South Australia one needs to turn to Ken Bolton's *Selected Poems, 1975–1990*.

Bolton has been a challenge to poetry in South Australia. Oriented towards contemporary visual arts and popular culture, his self-conscious postmodernism, with its slangy irreverence, its recurrent citations of other people's work and names, and its typographical complexities, is unrepresented in *Tuesday Night Live*. This brief excerpt from 'poem (Day & Night)' (49) is taken from his *Selected Poems*:

night

II

the lovely benevolence in the look
of the last of the dregs of the flagon

the electric light , the dead flies , our company,
the Rolling Stones coming from blocks away,
postponing our departures

as in prayer to the flagon

o, flagon, you have stayed!
& it did too – we didn't throw it out

the light , the stones , the cool warm nights.

the terrific
days
of summer

Bolton's poetry has a visual dimension which a reading situation would hardly do justice to. On the other hand, it also has a chatty breeziness, an irreverent willingness to dart off at tangents, to leave the unfinished phrase hanging, which give the poems a complex, engaging and always interesting voice. The debt is to Frank O'Hara, who is mentioned in 'Lines for the New Year' (134):

> The man of 38, say, looks back
> on the young man of 21. Thirty Eight.
> *Still young!* Younger than Frank O'Hara was –
> when *he* died. Younger of course
> than Rimbaud, when he quit. (?) Frank O'Hara died
> almost before he heard the Beatles.
> *I* heard the Beatles.
> But I don't know if it helped.

This has rarely been the tone of poetry in South Australia, and is perhaps most associated in Australia with such poets as John Forbes and John Jenkins, with whom Bolton has collaborated.

Two poets whose work has a particularly strong performance element are Rory Harris and Geoff Goodfellow. Harris claims that his poem 'Dialogue Poem/Between the Butchers' (Kroll and Westburg 139–40) was actually overheard in the meat section of the Central Market, so that it is both a performance piece and a found poem:

> 1   very clean/
>   killing/lady
>   jus was walkin
>   in paddock
>
>   few days ago
>   lady
>
> 2   yeh/lady
>   i got his sister
>   here too/lady
>   she's fresher/got killed
>   after him
>   veryfresh/lady

Humour of this kind is not all-pervasive, but is an effective element in performance poetry, where the aim, of course, is to produce the greatest impact on the audience in the brief duration of the poem's reading: there is no opportunity for a second or third browse through, as with other poetry.

A tougher note is sounded in Geoff Goodfellow's poetry. Defiantly working-class, Goodfellow has taken his poetry to prisons, construction sites and schools, and is able to shock those normally unsympathetic to poetry into rapt attention. His poetry often deals with the outcasts or the overlooked, those on drugs or ruined by alcohol, and displays a passionate sense of social justice and a hard-hitting command of idiom and the rhythms of speech:

> *Don't call me lad*
>
> > *dad*
>
> *just don't call me lad*
> *got more hair on my balls dad*
> *than y'v got*
>
> > *or had*
>
> *i'm eighteen years old man*
> *& i'll sink or i'll swim*
> *just don't call me lad*
>
> > *dad*
>
> *my name is James*
>
> > *or just Jim*
> > (174)

In fact poetry about young people is a characteristic of much South Australian writing. This is possibly due to the fact that a number of the poets are, or have been, teachers. It also reflects the renewed popularity of poetry in schools, which has resulted in a number of poets serving as writers-in-residence in schools and universities, where they encounter young people and gain some first hand acquaintance with their problems. Harris in particular has done this, and has edited anthologies of poems produced by his students during such periods. John Griffin's wryly understated 'February Poem' (173) tells on the other hand of the problems facing the school teacher:

> The lady in green
> is here to enrol
> her current de facto's
> first wife's
> step-daughter
>
> for three weeks
> or four, until they all
> move to Townsville
>
> and would we please
> teach Julie to read.

Not a prolific poet, Griffin has nonetheless produced a body of poetry which is sound rather than spectacular, firmly grounded on observation and displaying an often ironic awareness, whether it be of the classroom and schoolyard situation, or of the Great Themes such as History, Sex and Death.

If young people and their problems and opportunities are a frequent concern of South Australian poetry, so too are children and, by extension, parents. This seems to reflect the lives of many of the poets – a fair number of whom are baby-boomers – who, over the last decade or so, have had children of their own and, at the same time, have had to cope with their own ageing relatives. Jeri Kroll's 'Bathtime' (161) details the delights of admiring her infant in the bath:

> Everything about him's edible,
> unpredictable.
>
> Curls bloom red-gold over a forehead
> clear as a myth,
> smooth as a magic stone.
> I kiss it and wish.

Graham Rowlands's 'Who's Who' (160) is one of a number of poems which explore the emergence of a new life within that of the writer. 'Who's Who' looks at the kind of confusion of identities that results when someone is trying to teach a child to talk by teaching the child by example to say hello to the speaker by name. Quirky as much of Rowlands's poetry is, the result of this confusion is not distress, but a comic liveliness and a sense that the coming of the son into the father's life introduces a strangeness which both invigorates and amuses. It also marks a move away from the engagement with politics and questions of public morality which had characterised many of his earlier poems.

Others who have written about children are Jeff Guess, Rory Harris (on the birth of his daughter), Peter MacFarlane and Jan Owen. Jeff Guess's 'David' (158) is particularly touching in its exploration of the way a child's crying at night wakes within the father some long-forgotten memory of the desolation and loneliness of infancy:

> Connecting the ends of a long forgotten
> > twisting and turning – knotted
> in a night-cry we both know, outside the
> > comfort and the cradle of any arms.

It may be a metaphysical loneliness that the cry awakes, 'somewhere older / than the blood's fine-point / that lurches in its chrysalis / of skin and bone'.

By contrast, it is the excitement of watching the ice being delivered in summer during her own childhood that is conveyed in Jan Owen's 'Ice-Oh!' (167). Poems which recall childhood with a mixture of nostalgia and amusement appear also in Owen's *Fingerprints on Light* and in particular in her most recent collection, *Blackberry Season*. The latter collection is, in fact, wholly devoted to this, and provides a warm portrait of childhood, and of Adelaide in the 1940s and 1950s. On the other hand, 'Boy with Telescope' (176), the title poem of Owen's first book, is a kind of reworking of Yeats's 'A Prayer for My Daughter'. Observing the boy observing distant constellations, the parent thinks:

. . . may he always stand so –
a little to one side of what he loves;
earn a clear view
through delicate adjustments,
steady care.

And the poem ends with the wish: 'May his mind reach out, tactile as fingertips, / to the sharp braille of the skies'.

Poems about ageing, or about the aged, also occur. Looking back from later life, John Bray wrote a witty poem, 'Crested Pigeon' (168), in which the analogy is drawn between the departure of a hand-reared pigeon to the vet, and his own cruel loss of childhood security when he was first driven off to boarding school. And in 'My Mother and the Trees' (169) Christine Churches recalls how her mother, in her passion for 'a dwelling place of shade', made reluctant slaves of her children 'as she / marshalled [them] with iron buckets / to carry rations to the trees'. But the result of all this reluctant industry was that while the children hid, 'she / filled the sky to the brim with trees'. The poem is a delicate balance of the children's resentment at, and the adult poet's love and admiration for, the mother's vision and persistence.

If the older generation can seem suddenly cruel to children, they can also seem frail and pathetic when those children are in middle age themselves. Richard Tipping's 'What Happens Then?' (184) is a sensitive portrait of an old lady, while Kate Llewellyn's 'The Aunts' (182) observes the 'bones / in the tissue paper / parcels of their hands' and thinks of the time they would 'toss their heads / at cheeky boys' so many years before. Both poems approach the question of ageing and death by means of the family, giving to the theme a personal note and a gentleness lacking in an earlier age's more abstract approach. John Bray's 'Tobacco: A Valedictory' (185) cheerfully and defiantly farewells his smoking days after being advised to quit by his doctor. And a doctor, Peter Goldsworthy, in his 'Mass for the Middle-Aged' both wittily and painfully liturgises the ageing process as he 'awakes, alarmed. / For the first time / regrets outnumber dreams'. Just as Bray lovingly recalls his various brands of cigarettes and the occasions for smoking them, Goldsworthy cleaves to the world he will inevitably lose, despite its imperfections. Rejecting the idea of becoming an angel after death, he prays to the Lord that he may 'wear bikie colours in heaven', as he 'would rather / be nothing / than improved'. Both poets bring a sharp intelligence to the theme of ageing and death which serves not to diminish the subject, but to focus it in intricate balance with the pleasures of a flawed world.

These qualities are also prominent in Bray's contrast of two attitudes towards love and sex, 'Non Event' (24):

> You can't say I deceived you.
> I never promised rings.
> You want Tristan and Isolde.
> I want a twang on the strings.

In fact sexuality, the body and love are major themes, and the editors of *Tuesday Night Live* have devoted two sections to it: 'Love's Body' (in contrast to 'The Body Politic', another section) and 'Sexual Politics'. Donna McSkimming has two powerful poems in the former section: 'Ululation for a Red Headed Woman' (15) and 'The Wait' (11). 'Ululation' is a physically energetic celebration of lesbian love, a theme which has emerged in South Australia, as elsewhere, over the last decade or two. McSkimming is an assured young poet whose firm rhythmic energy and concreteness of language make her a significant contributor to this field. Her other poem, 'The Wait', brings the same qualities to the subject of PMT and menstruation, and draws on that alternative, age-old tradition of women's folklore in a powerful and imaginative way:

> If I walked the earth
> I'd blight the crops,
> cause cattle to abort
> the fruit trees to die.

Another poet capable of genuine eroticism is Steve Evans. 'The Invention of Fire' (1) is enraptured by the transfiguring flash of sunlight on a girl's red hair as she alights from a bus, 'a torch in the suburbs'. In 'Hunger' (12) he celebrates lovemaking and love, a passion that renews itself by satiation:

My opium
my love
with you
always
the hunger.

This poem has the delicate suggestiveness of good contemporary film dealing with the physicalities of lovemaking, including a capacity to make the physical surroundings (the bedroom) and the light (in this case the onset of evening) serve to give it focus and define its meaning.

A similar quality is found in Beate Josephi's 'Tuscan Dream' (215). Originally from Germany, Josephi brings a familiarity with non-Anglophone culture to Adelaide's poetry. 'Tuscan Dream' makes allusion to Italian late Medieval and early Renaissance painting and architecture in a surreal blending of the ancient and the modern, in the midst of which an unnamed 'they' 'read books whose expansive style embraced whole worlds and / particularly their uncertainties'. Mysteriously roused from their absorption, they create in painting and then in masonry an 'inner courtyard' which is both fruitful and 'A revelation of the beauty of inner wounds' – 'their Courtyard of Lions, their cloister, their / passion'. Opulently allusive, 'Tuscan Dreams' is a poem in which artifact and sexuality speak, it seems, with a single, yet double-tongued voice that is quite original.

A very different voice is heard in Jenny Boult, a poet who has worked extensively with community groups and other organisations as a writer-in-residence. Something of a performance quality is apparent in most of her work, expecially in 'I'd Like to Know about the Fruit Bowl' (28) in which the speaking woman muses on whether her lover is moving in or moving out:

Because you lived here
but didn't live here . . .
It's difficult to know whether or not
you still don't live here.

Addressed to the man who has left his shaving gear but 'taken the nail clippers', the poem hinges on a state of uncertainty which is not unlike

Keats's 'Negative Capability, that is, when a man is capable of being in uncertainties, Mysteries, doubts, without any irritable reaching after fact and reason'.[2] Although the effect of Boult's poetry is hardly Keatsean, the way this poem explores a liminal situation without the drive for resolution and outcome gives it both an enigmatic and a humorous edge. The same could be said of her poem 'Electric' (22), in which desert and urban knowingness, electrical storm and hailstones intermingle.

Diane Fahey's 'Andromeda' (38) is concerned not so much with sexuality as with the politics of sexuality and the power relations between gender and sex. One of a number of Fahey's recasting of Greek myths, 'Andromeda' speaks the woman's part in what has been traditionally a patriarchal discourse. Chained sacrificially to her rock as appeasement of the dragon, 'she was a whirlpool / of rage and terror and shame' when Perseus arrives to rescue her. Naked and bruised, 'She waits for the moment / when he will meet her eyes'. Fahey is a poet whose steady development ranges, like Josephi's, over European culture, though with very different results. In 'Sacred Conversations' (192) Fahey muses on a Titian painting of St Sebastian she saw in Venice. If Andromeda was 'The First pin-up. / Naked and bejewelled', this St Sebastian is one too: 'he imagines being gazed at by each woman who enters / the church' who realises that 'the knots in that white cloth / can be undone'. The contrast of male and female roles is striking.

Two poems by Kate Llewellyn confuse this contrast. 'Sassy' (51) shows how aggressive and apparently casual, confident behaviour on the woman's part is a mask for insecurity and fear. On the other hand, so to speak, 'Breasts' (44) muses on the curiosity, in all senses, of breasts. 'These breasts always want to know everything', and poke their way into all sorts of places, 'always getting there first', even if they are 'more of a nuisance than anything else'. Still, 'some men seem to think highly of them / peering and staring', unaware that they are 'not glamorous / merely dangerous'. None the less, the 'bosom by Rubens under the shirt by Sportsgirl' of Jan Owen's Mona Lisa-like 'Swimming Instructor' (53) lures her pupils' middle-aged fathers with a 'half-innocent' eroticism still uncaring of cancer. She is a world away from the hard-bitten barmaid in Geoff Goodfellow's 'Tailor Made' who, when a customer says to her 'i'd love to get into y'r pants' replies, 'i'm sorry but i've got / one cunt in there already / I DON'T need another'.

Goodfellow also has a characteristically tough piece on Anzac Day Marches, deploring the alcoholism afflicting his father, an ex-soldier, and the family misery that results ('Marching Orders' 65). Graham Rowlands, who has written frequently on political themes, is deftly ironic in 'The Confidence Man' (70): 'Knowing your confidence man through & through / gives you confidence in being honest – / even as you lose your life savings'. The confidence man is your plausible businessman or politician who 'makes fraud look like incompetence'. With South Australia still suffering from the losses of the State Bank, Rowlands's poem has no lack of ready targets. But two of the best poems dealing with politics or social issues have a consciously less local point of reference.

Rob Johnson's 'The Falklands' (73) is not so much about the Falklands War as about the tug of his English upbringing as he feels 'the sympa-thetic pang / as the flag's pulled out of the map'. A subtle poet, Johnson explores the intertwining of the political and the personal. A similar complexity is found in Beate Josephi's 'Working on a German-English Dictionary' (68). During this apparently mundane task, two 'odd bedfellows' appear: '*Kesselschlacht, Kristallnacht*', and the Nazi atroci-ties against the Jews come back, frighteningly, into mind. 'The words stop dancing / freeze on the page in their threadbare lettering / fearful of their own fate'. Although both poems are anchored in the personal, they are a timely reminder that not all politics is local. They also demon-strate how poets not born in Australia have enriched South Australian poetry with their complex experiences.

Not surprisingly, the Australian landscape can seem strange to Rob Johnson. In 'Crossing the Mallee' (99) he is struck by the blankness of it, where names on the map turn out to be not towns but silos, 'grey / featureless cathedrals' against which 'imagination beats its head'. A locally born poet, Peter MacFarlane, in 'Ash Wednesday' (94), can make a powerful metaphor for the end of the world out of the disastrous bushfires:

If the world is going to end
it will end on a day like today

a pungent smell
and a thinning cloud of dead ash.

On the other hand, Geoffrey Dutton claims, in 'Grevillia and Firetail Finches' (92), that 'Red is the conscience of our country' and 'the firetails are a reminder / That passion may dance as well as sigh'. And in 'The Dam in February' (97) he speaks as a country-man and a farmer, observing his dry dam, musing on what is now found in it and what has been lost forever, and denying himself the sentimentality of despair: 'Only the city-dweller can afford despair, / The luxuries of pessimism, safe by the twist of a tap'. A prolific writer in many forms, Dutton is one of a number of poets in *Tuesday Night Live* who no longer lives in South Australia.

Christine Churches also seems to have been lost to South Australian poetry, as she has published little since her booklet, *My Mother and the Trees*, in 1977. 'Being Neighbours' (106) and 'Night Vision, Yarrawonga' (89) are both excellent examples of her clear vision, precise language and subtle love of the Australian countryside.

A similar clarity is found in 'Carpentaria' (108) by Louise Crisp. The poem deals with the women working on the fishing trawlers in the Gulf of Carpentaria where, 'on the dogwatch / all the boats are steered by women'. A contrast is then made between the obsessions of men, and the accomplishments of women:

. . . obsessed men spent lifetimes
with trails of camels
specimen cases and typewriters
in search of the inland sea . . .

while the boatwomen
spend each dawn watching
as the gulf shifts and swells
and all the waters run under our feet.

Like McSkimming, Crisp is one of a younger group of women poets who could make a major contribution to South Australian poetry.

Strangely for a city which, according to visitors, is quite distinctive in character and style, Adelaide seems to have provoked little poetry focusing on what makes it different. Poems about it could really be about any other large Australian city. It may be that Adelaide's poets are wary of sounding parochial, or it may simply be that residents are less conscious than visitors of how Adelaide differs from other places. Also, although there is much Australian poetry about the country, and more recently about city life, there is little of that fascination with place that characterises American poetry and popular culture. Whereas an American musical can be called *Oklahoma*, one would be surprised to hear of an Australian one called *South Australia*. The map of the Australian countryside may be dotted with names (even if they turn out, as Rob Johnson notices, to be nothing but silos), but they rarely figure in Australian poetry. Adelaide, with its old stone buildings, its rings of parkland, its encroaching hills and its distinctive climate, as well as its convict-free past, is still waiting for a poet to capture its qualities in the way that Barbara Hanrahan did for it in prose.

On the other hand, Adelaide's poets seem happy enough to write about other cities: Panama City, Kyoto, Melbourne, Sydney, Malucca, New York. Like other Australian poets, South Australia's may not necessarily be cosmopolitan, but they have travelled, both physically and imaginatively. It is a far cry today from the situation described in Shirley Hazzard's novel, *Transit to Venus*, where 'going to Europe . . . was about as final as going to heaven. A mystical passage to another life, from which no one returned the same' (37).

Conclusions

It is not possible to draw any firm conclusions about the poetry of a whole state over recent years. Poets do not necessarily stay in the one place. All three founders of Friendly Street have moved interstate; older poets such as Geoffrey Dutton, and younger ones such as Larry Buttrose and Anne Brewster, have too. Several, such as Nancy Gordon and Flexmore Hudson, have died. Some poets, on the other hand, have come to live in South Australia from other states or other countries.

What is clear, however, is that the number of poets producing publishable work, some of it of the highest quality, has expanded dramatically since that first Friendly Street reading in 1975. Friendly Street, both as a reading place and as a publishing venture, undoubtedly has something to do with this. So has the funding – too little though it always is – made available to writers by the Literature Board of the Australia Council and by the South Australian Government's Department for the Arts. Another fact, related to this one, is the renaissance that has taken place in Australian poetry generally since the late 1960s. Some South Australian poets (for example, Bolton, Dutton, Fahey, Goldsworthy, Kroll, Llewellyn, Josephi, Owen, Taylor and Tipping) have been published by major interstate publishers. But that the majority have been published locally by Friendly Street should not obscure the fact that a large number of South Australian poets have shared in, and significantly contributed to, that renaissance.

WORKS CITED

Bolton, Ken. *Selected Poems, 1975–1990*. Ringwood: Penguin, 1992.

Churches, Christine. *My Mother and the Trees*. Sydney: Angus & Robertson, Poets of the Month Series, 1977.

Shirley Hazzard. *Transit of Venus*. Harmondsworth: Penguin, 1991.

Kroll, Jeri and Westburg, Barry, eds. *Tuesday Night Live: Fifteen Years of Friendly Street*. Adelaide: Wakefield in association with Friendly Street Poets, 1993.

Owen, Jan. *Fingerprints on Light*. Sydney: Angus & Robertson, 1990.

_____. *Blackberry Season*. Canberra: Molonglo, 1993.

Pearson, K.F. and Churches, Christine, eds. *The Orange Tree: South Australian Poetry to the Present Day*. Adelaide: Wakefield, 1986.

Rollins, Hyder, ed. *The Letters of John Keats*. Oxford: Oxford UP, 1958.

Rowlands, Graham, ed. *Dots over Lines: Recent Poetry in South Australia*. Adelaide: Adelaide U Union P, 1980.

NOTES

1. The *Friendly Street Readers* are edited by two different people each year, and are published by Friendly Street Poets and Wakefield Press.
2. From a letter to George and Thomas Keats, 21 December 1817 in Hyder Rollins, ed., *The Letters of John Keats*.

'Your only entry into the world'

Barbara Hanrahan's Adelaide

Kerryn Goldsworthy

My purpose tonight is to look at the only place in Australia that I know well, the only place I know from inside, from my body outwards, and to offer my understanding of it as an example of how we might begin to speak accurately of where and what we are. What I will be after is not facts – or not only facts, but a description of how the elements of a place and our inner lives cross and illuminate one another, how we interpret space, and in doing so make our first maps of reality, how we mythologise spaces and through that mythology (a good deal of it inherited) find our way into a culture. You will see, I hope, how a writer might be particularly engaged by all this, and especially a writer of fiction; and you will see too why any one man might have only a single place he can speak of, the place of his earliest experience. For me that was Brisbane. It has always seemed to me to be a fortunate choice – except that I didn't make it. But then the place you get is always, in the real sense of the word, fortunate, in that it constitutes your fortune, your fate, and is your only entry into the world.

(David Malouf, 'A First Place: The Mapping of a World' 3)

The way that 'the elements of a place and our inner lives cross and illu-minate one another' is at the heart of Barbara Hanrahan's Adelaide. In much of Hanrahan's work, the self and the city exist in a symbiotic rela-tionship: the process of self-construction, not just as remembered and described but as actually enacted in the writing, is mutually interde-pendent with a particular vision of the city. If Adelaide made Hanrahan, so too does Hanrahan make a very particular Adelaide, working in her writing back and forth along a continuum with memory as the middle point between history and imagination.

Most of her writing is 'Adelaide' writing, mapping the city with a web of names – Houghton, Appleton, Cudlee Creek; Bowden, Thebarton, Mile End; Rose Street, North Terrace, Victoria Square. But, while much of her work is hard to define generically, this essay concen-trates on demonstrably autobiographical texts – interviews, articles, essays, *The Scent of Eucalyptus* and *Kewpie Doll* – because its argu-ment is largely about the process of self-fashioning.

'Recent theories of autobiography', as Paul Salzman points out in his study of Elizabeth Jolley's fictions, 'have taken us past earlier, crude for-mulations about the dichotomy between truth and fiction. Now, the autobiographer is seen as constructing a self actively during the process of writing' (57). In Hanrahan's case, this 'self' is very specific to its city; she represents herself as having been fashioned in and by the Adelaide of her childhood. But the converse is also true – if the city fashions the written self, the writing self also fashions the city. Hanrahan's Adelaide is a unique personal vision, an element in her own life story, full of private landmarks, and represented – often quite literally – from her personal point of view. When asked to contribute to Drusilla Modjeska's *Inner Cities*, subtitled 'Australian Women's Memory of Place', Hanrahan responded with a piece about the Adelaide of her childhood and ado-lescence, entitled 'Earthworm Small':

> I wrote down the lectures, I passed the exams; I painted the University Bridge and the lily pond in the Botanic Gardens . . . I should be dreaming of a Snow Queen refrigerator, frilled cross-over curtains. Instead, I wanted to be like my dead father who'd played billiards and drank at the Wheatsheaf and walked with his hands in his pockets. Somehow art seemed something to do with

that – it had got away from the palette knives and artists' smocks and the art lecturer's careful words about shading and perspective. I didn't want to paint gum-tree landscapes in dust-storm shades; the little view of the grass at my feet was more interesting. I wanted to get earthworm small, to creep with the ant. (151)

The subject position she establishes here, as rebellious spectator of the microscopic, is essentially about a process of rejection that needs to be energised by disgust: her resistance to Adelaide is precisely what gives her a position from which to represent it, but at the same time she is constructing an Adelaide that demands to be resisted. Hanrahan's Adelaide of the 1950s is remarkably consistent across a range of texts, as is the narrative of personal resistance: city and reacting self are instantly recognisable in other autobiographical essays like 'Beginnings' and 'Weird Adelaide', in interviews, and in *Kewpie Doll*, where the city is a place the narrator needs to reject violently in order to define herself against it. In 'Earthworm Small', the lectures, exams, dull realist pictures, protective smocks and careful words are all represented as part of an (implicitly gendered) attitude to art that goes with desirable items of kitchen decor ('Instead, I wanted to be like my dead father'), and all of this is closely identified with 'Adelaide':

The 50s were over. I went on pretending to believe in the pattern, and taught art to girls like I'd been once. At night I went back to the art school on North Terrace and started to make prints. At home, behind the berry bush, I unlabelled myself . . . 1950s Adelaide, that closed repressive decade with its savage rules of conformity, gave me the aloneness, the intensity to create my own private world . . . (152)

Adelaide 226/Rose Street Trees

On the Duke's Highway just northwest of Keith, there's a sign saying 'Adelaide 226'. Two hundred and twenty-six kilometres later, the bemused motorist will find herself somewhere between the Strathalbyn and Mount Barker exits on the South-East Freeway. And in the back of my car there's a copy of *Gregory's Adelaide Street Directory* (42nd edition) which – though Barbara Hanrahan lists her childhood address as '58a Rose Street, Thebarton' – firmly maintains that Rose Street is in Mile End (Carroll 103). Even on such innocent and literal sites of writing as directories and signs, where accuracy is the whole point of the exercise, the relationship between words and the city has become problematic and untrustworthy.

What, then, are we to make of Hanrahan's 1982 screenprint 'My Family – My Australia' (Carroll 90)? Behind a lineup of children and adults, some recognisable from Hanrahan's descriptions or from other prints, a map of Australia is divided into patchwork-like squares, each with its own design incorporating drawings, numbers and/or words. One of these squares contains the words 'Adelaide Adelaide', written in curly cursive and standing on end, approximately in the location of Perth.

One of the many things this joke conveys to me is the idea of a portable, 'written' Adelaide, detached from its geographical moorings. Hanrahan has a strong sense of the ways in which a place can exist as a literary construct. She describes *The Albatross Muff* as being set 'in a Dickensian London' ('Beginnings' 85); in *Kewpie Doll* the narrator says, 'I can't imagine London, but I think it's a place shut away in one of my grandfather's books' (152–53); and when asked by Rosemary Sorensen in an interview about *Flawless Jade* whether she's ever visited China, Hanrahan replies: 'Oh no. I don't think that's necessary. In fact, for me and my sort of writing the reality of China would probably be a barrier. *The Peach Groves*, which is set in NZ, got its impetus from Katherine Mansfield, not from any real country – though I try to get the details right' (8).

But Hanrahan's Adelaide is not merely a construct of language and memory, any more than it is merely the material fact of the square mile inside the four Terraces on any given day, with 'the details right'. It is, rather, a constant movement between the two: her writing sets up a kind of dynamic, an ongoing process of interaction between the Adelaide that is a matter of public record – social history, geography, town planning, architecture, old families – and the Adelaide of her own personal mythology, the one whose epicentre is the memory of her childhood home in Rose Street. 'History and memory', argues Chris Healy:

refer to different orders of activities constituted in different forms in different sites. Memory is dream-like; it is private, imaginative, particular and saturated with sensation; it does not obey chronology, it is hard to discipline and document; it is rarely evidential and tends to be determined by its moments of enunciation. Memories possess and articulate some of the anti-historical qualities which we require to inhabit space and time through our bodies. History is realist and rational, public and prosaic; it consists of disciplinary chronicles which aim to certify . . . (74–75)

Hanrahan uses history as a kind of scaffolding for memory, interleaving – and rearranging, from one text to the next – the private and the chronologically unlocatable with the comforting linearity of public record. In an interview with Candida Baker, she tells how, while writing *The Scent of Eucalyptus* in London, she used to write to her mother 'and get her to check up on things in Adelaide – the sorts of trees on Rose Street, the order of the statues along North Terrace; it was like being a detective' (78). Yet despite this stickling for material detail, she adds a few sentences later: 'All that way from Australia the memories grew sharper, there were none of the everyday annoyances of the real Adelaide to get in the way of my imaginative recreation of the past.'

Hanrahan lived in several places as an infant, but 58a Rose Street is, in the David Malouf sense, her 'first place'. Her formative years, between the ages of one and fifteen, were spent in 'the pebbledash house with the slippery red veranda, the fig tree, the quince tree, the lavatory creeper and the corrugated iron fence', a house with a women-only household, 'the three who were important': Ronda, Reece and Iris Pearl, mother, great-aunt and grandmother, adult figures which recur frequently in her books and prints ('Beginnings' 81; *Scent of Eucalyptus* 12).

Chapter five of *The Scent of Eucalyptus* details the Rose Street house room by room, using a mixture of tenses to effect the collapse of past into present which is such a consistent feature of Hanrahan's representations of Adelaide. At every stage of this guided tour – escaping the heat in the cool front bedroom; looking out from a photograph on the mantelpiece of the sitting-room; lying on a rug in front of the dining-room fire; sharing a brass bed in the sleepout with her mother – the child-narrator's body is placed with precision as both the source and the object of memory:

> The front bedroom, shadowed by the verandah, was the coolest place in the house. In summer I escaped to it in my petticoat – soothed myself amongst its chilly lino daisies, lost myself in its crocheted quilt, breathed in fluff and darkness from under the bed. It was a silent room, a repository for best clothes and half-forgotten dreams . . . (33)

This chapter ends with a blunt, prosaic, oddly cheerful and demystified description of the mother's body – as though that were at the centre around which the detailed account of the house has been circling closer and closer:

> When my mother came I was asleep; woke, to see the eye of her cigarette blinking, finally disappearing in the dark. Then I curved leech-like to her body, lost myself in the pillow of hen's feathers . . . Then I am older . . . The brass bed disappears; I watch my mother dressing when she tells me to shut my eyes: see India-rubber nipple, frizz between her legs, arse-hole dot – and am surprised. (36–37)

The repetition of the phrase 'lost myself' in these two passages is suggestive. The bed-sharing memories are those of a very small child still able to recapture pre-Oedipal sensations of oneness with the maternal body; the 'older' child's response to a clear (and forbidden) vision of her mother as both other and visibly different is one of surprise, as though the conscious realisation of this difference and separateness were new: 'the brass bed disappears'. But that phrase 'lost myself' suggests that the child's relationship to the house is to some degree homologous with that to the maternal body: something from which separation, however painful, is necessary to the formation of the self.

There's an interesting sequel in *Kewpie Doll* to this first surprised vision of the mother's body, an image which suggests a further stage of separation. In the throes of her own adolescence, battling with bodily changes and allotted gender roles, the narrator is confronted by her mother's remarriage and its consequences:

> Then it was a day when they carried in my mother. She was home
> early from the Advertising Department, plastic wrapped round her
> below the waist. She didn't see me, her eyes were closed. My
> grandmother was running, the bedroom door slammed. Uncle Bill
> was in there, I was shut out. She had the baby clothes knitted but
> the baby bled away. (42)

'She didn't see me', 'her eyes were closed', 'I was shut out' – the narrator is confronted by an overdetermined message. And she is separated from her mother not just by her mother's unawareness, but by a
layer of transparent yet impermeable plastic, a bedroom door (the
bedroom where she once 'lost herself'), a stepfather, and finally a
ghostly sibling. The mother's body, bleeding into its plastic, is figured as
both too contained and not contained enough, simultaneously inaccessible and leaking. Not even this episode, reworked from the mother's
point of view in the story 'Rambling Rose', is safe from the deathly-polite
reactions and denials of Hanrahan's Adelaide: 'When I went back to
work after a fortnight there were still blood spots all down the stairs. But
nobody ever said anything to me about what had happened. They
knew, but they didn't say anything – they had manners' (154).

That house-mapping chapter of *The Scent of Eucalyptus*, dealing
with the pre-adolescent childhood before the advent of the stepfather
'Uncle Bill', charts the complex associations between the household and
the house: traces of 'the three who were important' appear as features
and fixtures from room to room, generating meaning and memory. In
one bedroom there is the wardrobe full of her mother's clothes, in
another her grandmother's cupboard-drawer full of jujubes, chocolate
and liquorice allsorts, and, in the dining-room ('I was happy in the
dining-room'), the bodily presence of grandmother and great-aunt
themselves: 'we turned the light off and there was just the fire . . . I lay
on the rug – lulled by Reece's knitting, Nan's newspaper, the murmuring
wireless' (35).

'We comfort ourselves', says Gaston Bachelard:

> by reliving memories of protection. Something closed must retain
> our memories, while leaving them their original value as images.

Memories of the outside world will never have the same tonality as those of home and, by recalling these memories, we add to our store of dreams; we are never real historians, but always near poets, and our emotion is perhaps nothing but an expression of a poetry that was lost.

Thus, by approaching the house images with care not to break up the solidarity of memory and imagination, we may hope to make others feel all the psychological elasticity of an image that moves us at an unimaginable depth . . . the house is one of the greatest powers of integration for the thoughts, memories and dreams of mankind. (6)

The address, the house, the women, the child self and the 'murmuring wireless', bringing the city's localised public culture into the room by the fire, are fused in the image from *The Scent of Eucalyptus* by the 'solidarity of memory and imagination'; and what they add up to is a private 'integration [of] thoughts, memories and dreams', a mythos of Adelaide and, simultaneously, of the self.

Hanrahan left her grandmother's house at fifteen to live with her mother and new stepfather in the Adelaide suburb of Oaklands Park in 1955. But it was not until she heard of her grandmother's death in 1968 that 'history' and its strict facts and chronologies could give way in writing to the greater elasticity of memory; she refers several times in interviews and essays to the causal relationship – sometimes as a catalyst, sometimes as more of a liberation – between her writing and her grandmother's death. 'I was in London,' she recalls in 'Beginnings':

and she was in Adelaide . . . I started keeping a diary again . . . The past was mixed up with the present; sometimes it seemed I was writing a letter to my grandmother . . . The old world was gone from me physically, yet it was inside my body, hurting so much it had to get out . . . for the next six months I sat down every day and wrote about my childhood in Adelaide . . . Dead, my grandmother set me free to write . . . (82–84)

The Grave of the Father and the Gown of the Queen

In interviews, as well as in her more directly autobiographical writing, Hanrahan structures her own subject formation as a sequence of separations: from her mother's body, from the Rose Street house, from a childhood innocent of class and gender inequities, from her public identity as an Adelaide 'proper person', from Adelaide itself and, finally, from her grandmother. The teleology of this sequence is her identity as an artist and, more specifically, as a writer; its geography is an Adelaide (and beyond that a world) concentric to the mother's body, expanding in widening circles: bed, room, house, suburb, metropolis, 'the city is an island, surrounded by hills and sea' (*Scent of Eucalyptus* 79).

But the place, the art, the tale and the teller are all haunted by the ghost of the lost father. William Maurice 'Bob' Hanrahan died at twenty-six of tuberculosis, the day after his only child Barbara's first birthday. The first chapter of *The Scent of Eucalyptus* ends with a cleverly disorienting account, again conflating past and present, of a visit to the cemetery where her maternal great-grandparents and her father are all buried, given from the point of view of the semi-comprehending child:

> Elizabeth was my great-grandmother.
>
> She went, vanished utterly – leaving behind four children that do not exist.
>
> Once I clasped the fingers of one of them and walked to a cemetery . . . When we reached the baker and his Stella, they were further from us than ever. There were no eyes to see, no ears to hear, not even a mouth – just silence . . . And there was another plot . . . But it hurt more this time, for it was my father . . . And the poet that lived on dangerously said things about heedless marble.
>
> I stood before the slab that bore his name – and it was my name. (10–11)

This is one of two images in Hanrahan's writing which seem to me emblematic both of the inseparability of 'place' from 'self' and – to some extent the same thing – of the interdependency of the public and the private. The other is also of an object which, like the grave-stone, bears witness to the connection between a body and a name:

'William IV', reports Hanrahan in 'Weird Adelaide', 'had . . . a German consort whose Honiton lace robe was wreathed round the hem with Amaranth, Daphne, Eglantine, Lilac, Auricula, Ivy, Dahlia, and Eglantine again – the initial letters forming her name, Adelaide . . . It was the King's desire that the new colony's capital should be named after her' (6).

The gown and the gravestone, respectively bearing the words 'Adelaide' and (presumably) 'Hanrahan', are signifiers of public history and private memory – but not in any simply identifiable or mutually exclusive way. In the respective descriptions of gravestone and gown, the father's name is depersonalised – substituted for the body, and applied to more than one person – while the city/queen's is repersonalised, fitted to and wrapped around the body, and 'given back' to the person it originated from. The gravestone marks a private life, but is a public memorial to that life; the gown, with its rebus-acrostic monogram, is an elaborately personalised garment worn by a particular body, but also a relic and emblem of monarchy and empire.

The image of Queen Adelaide also, of course, recalls the place of the British monarchy in the value system of 1950s Adelaide, Playford's Adelaide in Menzies's Australia. The description of her gown suggests by association the embroidered coronation gown of Elizabeth II, with its equally elaborate semiotics and its so much more heavily politicised imagery of Commonwealth emblems and symbols. In the opening paragraph of *Kewpie Doll* the time and place are brilliantly evoked in a welter of consumerism and conservatism involving the incidental torture of small children:

> When it was the Coronation I sat up all night listening to the radio, it wouldn't be patriotic to desert the Queen for bed . . . Then it was the Glorious Year competition in *Woman's Day* when you could win a Holden car or an electric stove, a five-valve mantel model radio, a pair of Springtime crimp crepe stockings by deciding which photo of the Duke you liked best and telling why. When it was the Royal Tour, our school lined up with all the others in King William Street and waited and we each had a flag to wave . . . and barley sugar to suck for exhaustion. We waited for hours. The car went past so fast – I saw a hat, a hand in a glove. I saw the Queen, some girls fainted. (9)

The image of the absent father, in memory of whom the 'poet lived on dangerously' on his gravestone, is one that Hanrahan associates closely with being a 'real' artist, and there is a case to be made for the proposition that he was far more effective in this role dead than he would have been had he remained alive. 'Did you miss the presence of a father in your life?' asks Candida Baker. 'Not really', Hanrahan replies, 'because I felt as if he was still there. I felt I had a hero for a father, because he was so good-looking in his photograph' (91). This, it seems to me, is a version of Freud's 'family romance', the 'common childhood phantasy of replacing one's real parents with ones deemed to be more worthy'. The ironic consequence of this, as Judith Brett explains it, is that 'the powerful parent images of infancy live on in their transformations – the noble, heroic parents who replace them. Seeking to escape the power of their parents, children only fall more heavily under their spell' (212, 215–16).

But Hanrahan's father, safely dead, can simply be transformed into a hero rather than actually rejected for a superior model. 'Heavily under his spell', she identifies with him and then identifies him with art – a chain of association which in turn is connected with the emphatic rejection of Adelaidian values, in the essay 'Earthworm Small' and elsewhere: 'Instead, I wanted to be like my dead father . . . Somehow art seemed something to do with that' (151).

Terrible Silences

> I grew up in Thebarton and I went to school there. I loved Thebarton, but it was only when I got to the tech school that I realised there were girls looking down on me . . . That feeling stayed with me for a long time. I remember once standing outside Liberty's in Regent Street, and thinking, what is a person like me wanting to go into Liberty's for to buy Liberty material? Am I allowed to do this? This is an awful Adelaide thing, all this. (Baker, 85–86)

Towards the end of *Kewpie Doll*, this constellation of associations – art, the dead father, poetry, the past – organises itself around what Sue Thomas calls the narrator's 'night self':

Hanrahan discerns . . . a split self, which I will summarise here as kewpie doll mimicking the conditioned ideal of suburban femininity and the night self, the 'dark' side of herself which is the canker at the heart of her grandmother's and mother's suburban ambitions for her. It is implicitly the night self which will frustrate the suburban ambitions of her maternal figures: it is the creative, coarse, sexual side of her personality. (56)

While I think this is a very useful distinction, I also think that 1950s Adelaide and its particular discourses of class are far more important factors in this fracture than Thomas's article suggests. *Kewpie Doll* tracks a process of identity-splitting which, far from being pathological, is represented as essential to the narrator's sanity and survival inside the restrictions of the city in which she grows up. This process is summarised in 'Earthworm Small':

1950s Adelaide, that closed repressive decade with its savage rules of conformity, gave me the aloneness, the intensity to create my own private world. Though even that wasn't strong enough to break through the pretence . . . It needed my grandmother's death at the end of the 60s to get the fake barriers down. Then, without meaning to, I began to write about my childhood.

But it only happened because I cared enough and hated enough. I had to stay loyal to the old things, I had to keep on feeling them. If I wrote about my beginnings in that working-class suburb of Adelaide caringly enough, I might be writing about a place in a Greek myth. (152)

Like so much of Hanrahan's other writing, 'Earthworm Small' is structured largely by discourses of class; and her 1950s Adelaide is organised around signifiers of class distinction. The progress from primary to secondary school is marked by an abrupt initiation into the knowledge of Adelaide's social structures:

the girls I used to know in Grade Seven who'd gone on to the high school . . . lived at Mile End too, in the same sort of house as mine, but now they learnt Latin and French and could look down on me. And the girls who learnt piano and went to Methodist Ladies' College and Walford House looked down on the high school girls, in turn. I wanted fawn gloves, lisle stockings, silver braces on my teeth, a little enamel flag brooch on my lapel to tell what House I was in. (148)

When Candida Baker asks 'What about Jo [Steele, Hanrahan's companion of many years]? He came from a very different background to you, didn't he?' (87), Hanrahan replies, 'But he was still shown his place. He went to St Peter's College, and one of the rules of his life was that he was never allowed to talk to a high school girl.'

Kewpie Doll outlines another Adelaide class watershed: 'The English lecturer tells a story about looking for the shit house, but the Infant lecturer calls it toilet while others say lavatory, and a terrible silence falls' (135). The reason for the 'terrible silence' is deliberately left unspoken: it could be to do with diction and what it reveals about one's own class origins; or it could be to do with the vulgarity of discussing bodily functions at all ('there were still blood spots all down the stairs . . . but they didn't say anything. They had manners'). This connection between propriety and the denial of the body is made frequently in Hanrahan's work, perhaps most memorably in *The Scent of Eucalyptus* when the narrator realises – amid a savagely funny account of the social page of the *Advertiser* – that her pleasure in her own body and its freedoms, part of the 'night self', is what might liberate her from the city's labels and rules:

And there were other grooves more sticky, more well-oiled that sought to bind: all those things that a little girl who knew her station ought to do . . . Yet I was saved by the crudity that made me pee in the bath, and revel in the tar-black shit that poured out of me and stank. Therefore I was different.

At night, alone, I pulled myself clear of the mediocrities that sought to claim me. I freed my hair of its restricting pins and it shivered like a thistle bush. (158)

Toilets, lavatories and little flag brooches pale into insignificance, however, beside the clearest class test of all:

> My mother grew up in Bowden, which was the poorest Adelaide suburb at that time. She used to draw, and she'd send her drawings to the newspaper's Sunshine Club, and she had a pen-name, Rambling Rose. She'd cut out her drawings that were printed in the paper and stick them in a book. No one ever saw that book but herself. As well as her name, her address was printed underneath each drawing so she had to scrub the address out with her finger or scribble over it in ink. I thought that was terrible – the shame of living in Bowden was even there inside her private book. (Baker 86)

As has already been suggested, it's possible to trace, across a range of texts, a pattern of associations – ideas, things, people – which Hanrahan lines up in opposition to the Adelaide of 'proper people' and 'labelling', as a way of supporting her own resistance. The 'day self' is the one who lives and works within the city's rules: 'I lecture at the Teachers' College in my sheath frock, I am a proper person in high heels . . . it's the person at home who's peculiar. I can only work on my drawings if I feel free. It means not existing in the outside world of proper people' (*Kewpie Doll* 136). The 'night self' becomes increasingly closely identified with everything that is anathema to proper, orderly Adelaide: poetry and the dead father, childhood and art, pleasure in the body and its processes, freedom and escape, working-class culture, the sinister, the fantastic and the weird. In *Kewpie Doll*, the 'night self' is clearly the one privileged by the narrator and destined to dominate in the end – but not without a distressing struggle, articulated in the last few chapters:

> And I didn't want the part of myself that kept on looking back. Or the part of myself that kept looking forward to . . . starting on that journey to aloneness, going off to the legendary land across the sea that offered the only chance of returning: of burrowing back through that aloneness to the childhood I thought I'd lost . . . I didn't even want art . . . I wanted to be modern and hard and in fashion. The past was dead, it didn't mean a thing . . . *Now* was all that meant anything, because it meant nothing . . . (144–45)

'I went to London in 1963,' says Hanrahan in 'Beginnings', 'because I wanted to be an artist, and because it was the easiest way to escape Adelaide and a world where they always asked you what school you'd gone to' (82). She returned to Adelaide with Jo Steele, for good, in 1978; and 'the Adelaide we came back to', she tells Candida Baker, 'was quite different from the one we'd left' (80). They had left Playford's Adelaide and come home to Dunstan's, and the intervening fifteen years had done away, at least to some extent, with the terrible silences: the denial of the body, the muteness of St Peter's College boys in the face of high school girls, the heartbreaking blanked-out spaces in a private book where the word 'Bowden' used to be.

The breaking of more Adelaide silences became for Hanrahan another way of 'burrowing back'. *Annie Magdalene*, published in 1985, was a new departure for her writing in terms of subject matter and, especially, narrative voice; and in 'Beginnings' she explains how this had its origins in her return to Adelaide to live. 'My life had turned full circle', she recalls:

> I was back to my beginnings. And out of that returning grew a sense of solidarity with the generations of working-class women who'd gone before me . . . I wanted to write out of the language of women like my grandmother, to set down a culture that would soon be gone forever . . . I wanted to get behind the silences kept in place by social shame . . . And so my 'I' became Annie's, I was writing *her* language through *her* imagination. (86–87)

Annie Magdalene – and after it *Dream People* and *Good Night, Mr Moon*, both 'Adelaide books' which continue to 'set down a culture that would soon be gone forever' – are enactments of the manifesto at the end of 'Weird Adelaide':

> What we want now in Adelaide are writers and artists who work from the heart of those commonplace suburban streets, who recognise the weirdness of the ordinary, who record it before the version we have now is swept away. We want passion and intensity, an art that comes from places like Port Adelaide and Thebarton and Holden Hill; that stays unofficially weird.

WORKS CITED

Bachelard, Gaston. *The Poetics of Space.* 1958. Trans. Maria Jolas. Boston: Beacon, 1969.

Baker, Candida. *Yacker 2.* Sydney: Pan, 1987.

Brett, Judith. *Robert Menzies' Forgotten People.* Sydney: Pan Macmillan, 1992.

Carroll, Alison. *Barbara Hanrahan, Printmaker.* Netley, S.A.: Wakefield, 1986.

Hanrahan, Barbara. *The Scent of Eucalyptus.* London: Chatto & Windus, 1973.

_____. *Kewpie Doll.* London: Chatto & Windus, 1984.

_____. 'Beginnings'. *Eight Voices of the Eighties.* Ed. Gillian Whitlock. St Lucia: University of Queensland Press, 1988. 81–87.

_____. 'Weird Adelaide'. *The Adelaide Review* March 1988: 6–7.

_____. 'Earthworm Small'. *Inner Cities: Australian Women's Memory of Place.* Ed. Drusilla Modjeska. Ringwood: Penguin, 1989. 143–52.

_____. 'Rambling Rose.' *Heroines.* Ed. Dale Spender. Ringwood: Penguin, 1991. 144–54.

Healy, Christopher Leo. 'The Training of Memory: Moments of Historical Imagination in Australia'. Dissertation. University of Melbourne, 1993.

Malouf, David. 'A First Place: the Mapping of a World'. *Southerly* 45 (1985): 3–10. The fourteenth Herbert Blaicklock Memorial Lecture, delivered 26 September 1984.

Salzman, Paul. *Helplessly Tangled in Female Arms and Legs: Elizabeth Jolley's Fictions.* St Lucia: University of Queensland Press, 1993.

Sorensen, Rosemary. 'Barbara Hanrahan: The Art of Detail'. *Australian Book Review* December 1989: 8–10.

Thomas, Sue. 'Writing the Self: Barbara Hanrahan's *The Scent of Eucalyptus*'. *Kunapipi* 11.3 (1989): 53–66.

Nicholas Jose

'Travellers among mountains and streams'

Lyn Jacobs

She came curiously to examine the token of what they were seeking. It would be pure luck if they found one, as they worked hard sifting the weed in search of a shell that might not exist or might crack in your hands as you reached for it. (*Paper Nautilus* 39)

Wally ran with them. His walking boots gripped the ice. He was running with arms open to grasp something that he knew must be there because its absence hurt so much. Charging forward to grab at its hem before it vanished, Wally was like all the crowd who had a conviction stronger than any dream that what they demanded was real or necessary and kept from them by a curtain only. (*Avenue of Eternal Peace* 287)

Nicholas Jose is a writer consistently engaged in quests for knowledge. In a paradoxical way, however, the value of the acquisition of knowledge is challenged by his texts. His narratives question certainties, rather than confirm them, and his protagonists strive towards realisations of experience rather than achievement. What constitutes desirable know-ledge is also a question Jose investigates.

Jose's early interest in scrutinising the human heart has developed into more complex analyses of cross-cultural relations ('Possibilities of Love' 30). In his more recent writing, Jose reviews the constructed nature of knowledge about national identities and the ways in which people 'script' their readings of each other in order to accommodate and interpret gender or cultural difference.

As the quotations above suggest, Jose uses metaphor, imagery and recurrent motifs (patterns of absence and presence) to consider indi-vidual commitment and social and political ethics. Characters are granted moments of enlightenment as they decide what is real or necessary, but in the process often find that language is both medium and 'veil'. Like the poststructuralists, Jose's fiction considers language as an entity with systems and structures which may or may not provide access via signi-fication; like the postcolonialists, he re-reads both history and signifi-cation; and, like a good novelist, he entertains, educates and provokes.

Jose has an established reputation as a novelist, poet, translator, essayist, critical commentator, academic and cultural emissary to China. His later writing is notable for its balanced and sensitive appraisals of conditions of mind and state and for its informed awareness that: 'know-ledge, belief and social attitude is culturally constructed and mediated by various forms of discourse' (Hamilton 15). This is tempered by recog-nition of the power of the imagination and the human capacity for revelation as a strategy of resistance or survival.

Jose taught Australian Studies in China and his images of both cultures are enhanced by his bilingualism, but he makes the point that to know a language is not necessarily to know the culture. In fact, he suggests that to articulate a knowledge 'perfectly' may incur suspicion ('Non-Chinese Characters' 7). He has consistently outlined the dangers of what Edward Said would describe as an 'orientalist' view of the diverse cultures of Asia and refuted commodified or complacent ideas about our own. He recently claimed that some Australian literature tends to 'exclude the outsider because it is so full of local detail': that we have 'a surface sense of ourselves . . . that another intimate Australia is hidden under the stones' ('Possibilities of Love' 31). With this kind of awareness of the contradictory, ambivalent and often ambiguous nature of representations of our own and other cultures, Jose has generally avoided narratives which attempt to 'dissolve difference and contradiction' – a totalising impulse – and preferred those 'which investigate representations by which we understand our world' (*Avenue of Eternal Peace* 70). In this writing, departures often prove necessary. Unlike the work of some novelists, however, for whom departure means escape, here local and regional identification provide a measure of distance travelled and a valued point of return.

The early work, a novel, *Rowena's Field* (1984), and two collections of short stories, *Possession of Amber* (1980) and *Feathers or Lead* (1986), investigated subjective terrains. In the second collection, the economy of stories like 'Roo Easter' and 'The Chinese Bride' won praise, but discursiveness and over-insistence marred others for critics. His best prose is understated and elegant. 'Roo Easter' affirmed the known world, by depicting recognisable initiation rites, while in 'The Chinese Bride' two lives and two worlds are set in stark juxtaposition. The poignancy of the latter resides in the demonstrated chasm between divergent ways of reading the world (the couple are polarised by race, gender and experience) but ignorance and a lack of sensitivity result in the girl-bride's flight. These narratives implicitly analyse custom and define worth.

Rowena's quest, in *Rowena's Field*, features an escape from Adelaide ('one of the most beautiful Victorian Cities') and an empowering search for self, but the subsequent return to Yorke Peninsula and reconciliation with the past is something of an anticlimax. Here breadth of field results in a loss of focus.

Jose's maturity as a writer was confirmed with the publication of *Paper Nautilus* (1987) and confirmed by *Avenue of Eternal Peace* (1989). These later novels are more carefully structured and controlled. *Paper Nautilus*, which has a South Australian setting, offers a subtle evocation of post-war Australian life. As in David Malouf's *The Great World*, the known world provides essential points of reference:

> The place was its own beginning and ending, and also a place that would be there before and after those points of finitude, when all his

life had encompassed, and would encompass in future, resolved in one story . . . He would live his life, setting it down according to his own drifting words and pattern, like a white unfurling scroll or a paper nautilus edging shorewards one year in seven, seeking completion. Eventually it would be there. He thought of currents. (117)

Jose begins with a wedding, works through 'snapshots' of a family's past, in a manner reminiscent of Thea Astley's *It's Raining in Mango*, and ends with a retrospective which defines the distance between the novel's initial event and the bride's parents' wedding night. The replay also admits aspects of the nation's story. In a recessional flow of memory, Jose 'sifts the weed' to reveal the kinds of 'tokens' that sustain and give meaning to family and national life. Jack Tregenza and his niece/ward Penny's patience, vision and capacity to love is epitomised by the rewarded search for the rare nautilus shells: 'the weed caught the shells unharmed but you had to find them without breaking them yourself.' At the other extreme, is Penny's mother, Vera, the pragmatist, who, having 'made a mess of her life', shocks the selfless Jack with the claim that 'Happiness . . . is all that matters. Why? Because happiness is the easiest thing to lose on account of some imaginary principle' (*Paper Nautilus* 52).

While the 'imaginary principle' and the search for 'the rare and beautiful' provide crucial incentives for the central characters of *Paper Nautilus* and *Avenue of Eternal Peace*, Jose admits antithetical, subversive ideologies – like those of Vera in *Paper Nautilus*, or the influential Professor Hsu in the *Avenue of Eternal Peace* – to weigh the relative truths of a range of propositions and modes of operation.

The temperamentally different Tregenza brothers are reunited in the final days of the Japanese invasion, when Jack escapes from incarceration in Changi and Peter's plane crashes near Balikpapan hospital. Jack – 'bashed, starved, hopeless . . . hanging in life by an obstinate stupid fibre of will, some link or stay he couldn't shake off' – survives the horrors of war-time experience. Peter, who 'expected life to be easy', dies of cholera, but not before handing Jack the responsibility of his child. This inversion of expectation seems futile to Jack but, in the long term, the child's presence replies to Jack's plea for a rationale for the seemingly 'senseless death' of his brother.

Like the nautilus shell and its cyclic inevitability, the woman Vera returns to re-establish contact with Penny. In Jose's fiction people may fail to articulate their love, but moments of shared experience are signified by tokens like a bird's egg, shell or Saint Christopher medal, which remain to remind or redeem. *Paper Nautilus* speaks of luck, but seeks and celebrates order, design and purpose as the novel shapes and echoes the dignity of lives simply lived.

The known world of the South Australian southern peninsula around Wooka, Parawurlie Bay and Gleesons' Landing, has its local dangers (freak waves and sexual adventures) but 'new worlds [come] within reach' throughout the span of the character's lives. Incursions of distance and time re-locate and change the population: for example, the arrival of Stan with his experience of 'poverty desire and oppression' and active service. The full extent of Jack's lost experience and sacrificed youth is defined by antithesis as the next generation lie on the beach, safe in each other's arms: 'She took his hand and he was content, not thinking, but frowning, not looking but dreaming'. There is no recourse to the modernist angst of 'drowning or waving' in this novel but there are quiet and eloquent demonstrations of the costs of war and alienation.

The Karamazov epigram claiming memory as an 'instrument of salvation' is curiously re-contextualised at the end of the novel as Vera revises her prepared script in her need to face Wooka 'ready for the story she would tell'. This tale provides a means of shedding the past and maintaining contiguities, and in this Vera prefigures Wally, the narrator of the next novel, *Avenue of Eternal Peace*, who re-reads the past to accommodate loss in a different way.

Avenue of Eternal Peace is set in China. The novel begins in peacetime, but the title becomes ironic. Generally applauded as a prophetic novel because it prefigured the events in Tiananmen square in 1989 (a postscript comments on the real events which took place after Jose's fictional speculations), its comparison of ways of seeing and being extends beyond the horizons of *Paper Nautilus*. Nicholas Jose has claimed that: 'The image of another country is very much in the eye of the perceiver . . . and this is particularly true of Australia and Asia but distortion or misunderstanding of an alien reality is by no means a simple or one way process' ('Green Oil' 42).

Wally Frith, the narrator of *Avenue of Eternal Peace*, exemplifies this dilemma. Wally, an Australian visiting professor at Peking Union Medical College, arrives in China unsure of Chinese colleagues' expectations of him. Anticipating research and an exchange of ideas with specialists in his field, his foreign affairs guide disconcertingly makes it plain that what is wanted is advice and an opportunity 'to study you'. Faced with a change of pace, an alien climate and environment, a language difficulty and an 'inscrutable' guide, the foundations of his knowledge and authority are progressively undermined. At the outset, incongruous apologies for a delayed welcome banquet serve as an unsettling indication of things to come.

Wally, laden with his Western Eurocentric knowledge and attendant 'cultural baggage', is radically disoriented. He is accustomed to direct answers to questions. In China he feels trapped 'in a situation of infinite deferral' until he recognises that the withholding of information also represents power (18). Initially, his capacity for action diminishes and his inactivity sees him embroiled in a circuitous 'process of opinion-forming' (Jaivin 43). Throughout, the enquiry into the nature of knowledge is offset by the recognition of different kinds of manipulation and control. Alison Broinowski has observed that: 'Some 150 years after the opium wars, the Chinese in Nicholas Jose's *Avenue of Eternal Peace* have turned the tables on the foreign devils and are corrupting Australians with bronzes, porcelain, girls, boys, currency and heroin in a Beijing bar' (186) and that, by now, Australians have been in Asia long enough to be 'sent up'. The sense of China's 'otherness', its distinctiveness and ethnocentricity, prevails, but Jose is aware of the clichés of the mysterious orient, and Wally's dilemma provides him with the means of considering issues inherent in cross-cultural interaction which are not unique to the China–Australia relations:

> The concept of insider and outsider are fundamental at so many levels of life. The language, script and culture are expressions of this separateness, the manifestations of a society that is self-enclosed, centred on itself, hermetic and needing hermeneutic translation before it can be understood by outsiders. The visitor is always the outsider. ('Non-Chinese Characters' 7)

Negotiating the difficult terrain of race, gender, class and diplomacy, *Avenue of Eternal Peace* offers a representative vision of China through sympathetic, foreign, but worldly eyes. Wally is not a raw tourist or a crass Australian abroad in Asia, but an experienced traveller who is accustomed to physical strangeness and the need to improvise and adjust expectation. His earnest engagement is offset by chapter titles which subvert seriousness by suggesting antithetical readings. For example, 'crackers' feature in the celebration of the Chinese New Year but the experience of alienation defined in the initial chapter makes the more colloquial, wry understanding of the term apt. Following chapters also bear labels that promise revelation – like Chinese proverbs – but further chaos ensues and reassuring titles like 'Thorough Democracy' become satiric.

Jose arranges, and then has his narrator deconstruct, composite 'truths'. Desperate for company and armed with 'thermal underwear and a map', Wally experiences the warmth of Chinese hospitality as the uninvited guest at a wedding banquet, where he meets Ying/Eagle, watches a demonstration of *Qigong*, the breathing power – a tech-nique developed from the 'long accumulation of body knowledge' – and drunkenly ponders the meaning of 'The Forbidden City':

> The patched together houses, dwellings of former petitioners to the Emperor, hung over the moat like stalactites. High above their heads a gatehouse loomed. Nothing was as black as the wall.
>
> Could this nocturnal wasteland really be the northern capital, navel of the universe, seat of the Heaven's mandate? Was it from here that astronomers threw nets across the sky, imperial gardeners produced blood-red peonies with golden stamens, hieratic opera singers electrified the air, women grew contorted for beauty, and men cut off their balls for power? Reverberated the gong to the limits of the four seas? Imperial puppets turned to clay . . .
>
> Born again as 'Beijing' in the official romanisation of New China's standard language, a tongue no one spoke, the city of ghosts had been repossessed by peasants, soldiers and officials rising to the surface of the great Chinese ocean. City of devastation, high-rise and infernal dust, trial and error, whims put into praxis, it was a

masterwork in the stripping of human dignity. Yet here at its heart was the other masterwork of Time waiting monumentally in shadow. Time's two masterworks stripping down and building up. (6–7)

The terms of Wally's drunken reverie, a neat summary of Edward Said's 'orientalist' clichés, define him as 'outsider' and this is further confirmed by his need to seek out other expatriates in the 'New Age' bar in Beijing. In complete contrast to the impromptu fellowship experienced between Chinese and Australians, the formality and 'profligate speechifying' of the overdue welcoming banquet fails to generate any warmth at all. Wally decides that 'to talk in riddles was easier than to talk straight' (13) and dutifully repeats after his minder/instructress: 'there is no Professor Hsu' – despite the obvious evidence of his eloquent and learned articles. It is the absence of this man that provides the direction of the quest in the novel.

Wally is a Western oncologist with more than a professional interest in China. He is retracing the path of a loved grandfather (echoing Jose's own experience), who had lived and worked in Peking. He is also seeking a mentor in the elusive Professor Hsu, the focus of his intellectual pilgrimage, but mostly he is evading the pain of his wife's recent death from cancer. These interwoven desires lead to an emotional involvement with Jin Juan, a colleague, but Wally's no-nonsense upbringing and background sees him ill-equipped to comprehend the complexity of Jin Juan's reality:

He came top of the class in his final year at Wollongong High; he worked for it. He was offered his first choice, a place in Medicine at Sydney University.

Wally was a straightforward young man, though neither he nor his mates, who read philosophy and literature and talked politics, self-consciously, and involved themselves in campus activitites, were typical medical students. Wally was secretary of the Student Socialists, an unfrivolous lot regularly assailed by the more numerous Libertarians, a flamboyant anarchic set who were not politicised until Australian boys died in Vietnam. Wally did not need a stinking post-colonial war to establish his convictions. He was a socialist on scientific principles. He believed in the common good being served by common cooperation. Knowledge as much as wealth was power and neither should be the privilege of a few. His views set him at odds with his brothers in the medical school. (37)

Although Wally realises that 'something about Jin Juan invited trouble', she remains a mystery to him (the double fiction of the operatic cousin's presence stretches credibility). He hears of her long engagement and family difficulties but Jin Juan's dealings with her fiancee, Zhang, while familiar at a sexual level, remain culturally foreign:

He turned to face her using the act of taking her hand as a pretext to press her belly. He felt full of himself, a sensation of distinct pride. 'After all these years' he said, grinning at her.

Her narrow eyes bore an expression of dependence stiffened by dignity. He could not fault her. She would not ask directly for the thing she wanted, and now he could not break away from her into indifference.

He laughed bitterly, out loud. 'We'll need to consider the situation', he announced, as at a committee meeting. 'Examine.' He squeezed her hand desirously. 'First you must have an ultrasound test. If it's a boy – '

The shouts and laughter of kids in pleasure boats joined the slapping wavelets, the cicadas and the whispering leaves.

'Sooner rather than later', she said at parting. 'I can't wait too long/' (187)

Wally and Jin Juan are divided by age, race, gender and custom, but they manage to find moments of harmony together. Curiously, their attempts to find a common language are paralleled by the professor's definition of the relationship between eastern and western medical science:

The tragedy, he said, was that, after Liberation, Chinese medicine and Western medicine were severed from each other. What passed for Chinese medicine, though allegedly the great pride of the people, became an ignorant travesty; and what passed for Western medicine was often crude and behind the times, an application of technique without understanding. That had led to the present-day 'reconciliation', where, for instance – he gave a bucktoothed grin – the common cold would be blindly treated with a huge shot of penicillin in the bum and a sack of dirty dandelion roots to be consumed with gallons of bitter tea.

His complaints were not against medicine in China. In many areas skill and progress were great; it was the larger failure, of the creative vision required to understand the wisdom that already was there in the culture and the people that grieved Hsu. (228)

After multiple adventures and intrigue, Wally experiences a comparable 'failure of vision' when he finally finds Professor Hsu. His desire for answers is not met. Professor Hsu is determinedly retired and unmoved by Wally's revelations about Kang's plagiarism and usurpation of his life work. He has no interest in Wally's Western demand for retribution through world recognition of his achievements. His Taoist wisdom sees power as less of an achievement than self-knowledge and he has moved to a point of acceptance further along the way. He replies: 'If the work is true, others will discover it for themselves' (230).

In this context, Wally's knowledge is small beer indeed. His mentor then challenges his Western idea of academic property by revealing the sources of his knowledge:

He chortled. 'Who is the source? Chicago gives Kang a medal for ideas he lifts from me. My ideas cannot exist without my wife. But she records the doings of a shaman. So perhaps he is the source. But he is just a mountain man, one of the masses'. (231)

Hsu's refusal to share Wally's outrage indicates another story or 'way of seeing' to be accommodated, as he claims that he is 'now liberated' by his 'lack of imagination' (230).

There are diverse stories encapsulated within this novel and they are used to facilitate or interrogate Wally's perceptions or to suggest the fabric of life in China over an extended period of time. Wally retrieves Bet's story, reads Peg's narrative and listens to Clarence's, Autumn's or Dulcia's and Jumbo's hopes, desires and fears. A boy named after his

Autumn birthday offers love to a dying Western photographer, and an opportunistic young man uses an ageing Western woman to escape a regime stifling his creativity. For these characters, bound by worldly aspirations, imagination is a driving force. David's, Eagle's and Philosopher Horse's stories indicate the dangers of their chosen paths, but their temporary ties 'unwind', as easily as the winder in Wally's jammed camera, when their significant moment has passed. Like characters in the Peking opera, these players are masked and unmasked by their actions.

The hierarchy of personae also includes caricatures: party greenhorn, Bi the bartender, Mr foreign trader, and Build-the-country. Linda Jaivin observes that Build-the-Country (Jianguao) is 'as common a name as Geoff in Australia' (13), while Broinowski notes that while Jose used Chinese characters for chapter titles, and was the first to take the trouble to explain his use of *pinyin* romanisation, his translation of Chinese names 'conveyed amusement from inside the culture with accuracy and humour, not from outside it with contempt and carelessness' (187).

The other Australian, the thick-skinned and resilient 'Ralph the Rhino', is defined by his acceptance that 'in China anything could happen'. He is affectionately portrayed:

> frankness and ingenuity and sheer sticking power had endeared him to his contacts. A compulsively inquisitive intellectual anarchist, Ralph wasn't trying to get anything out of China, nor concerned with making a 'success' of it. His first and last love was herbal medicine. Originally, back in Sydney, he had trained as a doctor, but he never did things properly. A side track led to pharmacopoeia, the ancient script, and ever more *recherche* explorations of ancient science and philosophy, all pursued with an amateur's passion . . . crazy Ralph was respected. (113)

Build-the-country perches on a ruined column in the Old Summer Palace and incongruously inverts Hsu's wisdom as he shouts to the onlookers that 'When life has no interest, dreams matter', while Jin Juan, who had subjected herself to the foreigner as an act of revenge, gives Wally the gift of a future that he had thought lost. When she deliberately confronts her fiancé Zhang with her 'disgrace' she is liberated as she sees that she no longer 'has to listen to [him] any more' (264).

Wally knows about Taoist thought but pragmatism is 'foreign' to him. In contrast Eagle, who does not 'exactly believe in religion', seems to embody the capacity to 'take the path of least resistance naturally' but he has not yet arrived at Professor Hsu's calm sense of himself (34).

In the chapter entitled 'Extraterritorial' the expatriates are isolated: 'all categories were insulated, all were exposed' (106), but by the end of the evening, when the expatriates are liberated by alcohol, cultural differences seem less significant. Wally observes the action but his sense of being 'extraterritorial' takes place on the bicycle ride home as he 'passes a man keeping guard over a pile of cabbages':

> China this, China that. Ralph the Rino was right. Settle his heart. Put his mind to rest. He could no more understand China than he could understand himself. Journalists, diplomats, photographers, China was too big for their lenses. The Five foreigns met the Three Chineses and had the Four conversations. Was the political line really the Right but pretending to be Left, or really the Left and pretending Right? Was China booming like the new Japan or struggling to hang on? What was the latest absurdity of the currency apartheid that obliged foreigners to use expensive funny money? And there was always so-and-so's claim to have discovered the Real China, where they had 'never seen a foreigner before' as if to see a foreigner rocketed people into a new kind of space-time. All under the same moon, he thought, noticing the sky. (119)

In this novel difference and sameness co-exist and the narrator learns the ways in which easy definition may disguise: an apparent tribute like 'He could not be surpassed', might mean that 'he was in the way' (136). Similarly, a declaration of love might mask a whole range of contrary emotions. Song has a child who can recite the capital cities of the world in alphabetic order but what does one do with such knowledge in a closed society? At the other end of the continuum, Waldemar's cross-cultural experience teaches him that 'there are no final solutions. What passed for forgiveness was often stored away to be remembered another time' (121).

Hsu's resistance to Wally's request for information echoes Mrs Gu's withholding techniques, but now Wally has the wisdom to define this as a 'back current against the merry chortling of the stream'. Wally discovers that he must find his own answers:

he had come grieving to China, and through all its layers – his searching for a treatment, a past, a lost old man, a lover – had been a quest for Bets, for a body to wear her shadow. What Jin Juan had done was refuse his offer. She had profited from his kindness only so far as suited her independence and dignity . . . There were political struggles and human struggles and a compulsive groping for sense. People were running forward with their arms open. (291)

When Wally's thirst for intellectual guidance is unappeased he, somewhat reluctantly, takes up his family's narrative:

Half-heartedly Wally returned to his quest. Was it not already an achievement to have come so far? Quest was simply a sluggish flow of the current. He had reached the town where his grandfather had built the mission hospital, where his father had been conceived and learned to toddle; the place that had been reconstituted in family lore and a young boy's myth of China. (241)

Wally's journey is cyclical, 'a matter of gravitational force', Hsu observes, but he has travelled further than his parents (232). The experiences, knowledge and empathy accumulated by Wally and Jin Juan's grandparents was subsequently lost to their children, demonstrating that understanding must be learned by each generation. Western attitudes to China are satirised by Jose as Wally recounts his parent's views:

Wally's people were creating a blockade of incineration and carnage in Vietnam to stop the Yellow Peril. His mother said that she didn't want to break her back in a rice paddy and eat stones for bread. His father said that if the Chinese stood in a line holding hands they would ring the globe. (39)

In a reversal of the impromptu banquet when cultural difference is ameliorated by goodwill, Wally, dining with Chinese friends, is accosted by a Chinese version of his mother's cultural xenophobia:

'Throw the foreigners out' he ordered the boss. 'We don't want foreigners with our women. We are China. My father was skewered to death trying to keep the little Japanese out of our town. My Uncle joined the Red Army to throw off foreign oppression. My grandfather was a Boxer for the Emperor. Am I not a Chinese man? Kill the foreigners!' (289)

Jose's fiction dispels some of the myths which have resulted in unproductive interchanges between East and West. It also indicates the changing face of imperialist prejudice. It is Clarence who voices this shrewd assessment of the nature of the history of cultural relations, and locates Wally, and perhaps Jose, in the historical process: 'Liberate the Chinese? Change China? That's the oldest con in the book. Merchants, diplomats, missionaries, generals. They've all tried, all been gobbled up. Now from their citadels of enlightenment come the kids of the 1980s' (23).

Jose has said that 'fiction is a kind of licensed lie' that may reveal a considerable amount about the expectations and practices of viewer and subject. He observes that:

> I was pleased to see a translation of my novel *Avenue of Eternal Peace* published in China with a warning that allowances should be made for the distortion in the foreign writer's account of contemporary China. It might have been more effective to say that any resemblance to actual places and persons was purely co-incidental. ('Green Oil' 43)

The question of the relationship between history and fiction is currently under scrutiny. 'Positivist and empiricist assumptions' have seen historians distancing themselves from 'anything that smacks of the merely literary', while writers of fiction have increasingly ignored arbitrary boundaries between the narratives of history and fiction (Hutcheon 95). The congruence of the real and the imaginary is highlighted by the novel's postscript. It is a final irony that a fictional search for truth should end with an authorial condemnation of power held 'by the only means at its disposal – violence and lies' in a medium which Jose has defined as 'a licensed lie' ('Green Oil' 43).

The title of *Avenue of Eternal Peace* reminds us that even the naming of a street or a city can be read variously and that there is a distance between the idealistic semiotics of the original Chinese nomenclature and this narrator's re-reading of perceived actuality in what he calls 'the megalomaniac thoroughfare of Changau' (5). Jose has observed that: 'The Chinese may challenge the notion of individual autonomy, finding selfhood constituted by the groups to which they belong: family, locality, workplace, class, race. The kind of stories they live out may have a different teleology' ('Non-Chinese Characters' 8).

Jose varies his narrative structures to meet the story-telling criteria of his settings. *Paper Nautilus* and *Avenue of Eternal Peace* are worlds apart in this respect and the latter's synthesis of memoir, reportage, essay and fable illustrates some of the difficulties of translation. We glimpse 'the foreign writer's reflection in the mirror', as language is seen to be volatile: a communicating tool, a disguise, a weapon or defence or merely sounds that substitute for silence. John McLaren observed that:

> Language plays a critical role in this book. Jose has a keen ear for the deadly excuses of bureaucracy, the brave proclamations of protest and the fumbling words with which people try to overcome barriers of culture and suspicion as they try to enter honest rela-tionships. He also recognises the use of words as a defence, a Taoist tactic for bending to the wind. (3)

In time, the narrator learns to question the validity of his own reportage and experience:

> Why do we always end up talking of them as 'the Chinese', 'they', 'them' as if they're a different species? As individuals they're as different as chalk and cheese. But it's the larger organism that fascinates us, the group thing, the nation, the race . . . They slide past us, round us, through us . . . but afterwards you feel there's been no contact at all. Wally was thinking of Jin Juan. (*Avenue of Eternal Peace* 117)

The practise of defining oneself against 'the other' is a human preoccupation but the interrogation of the construction of 'otherness' is also imperative if the nature of our discourses (among them the fictions which illustrate history) is to be understood. Jose's narratives engage with linguistic and cultural phenomena as an imperative. Through his oncologist's eyes the 'larger organism' of Chinese society is uniquely perceived as capable of exerting influence by joining together 'like cells metastasing, a concentration of force' (*Avenue of Eternal Peace* 286). There is no underestimation of the collective people's will in this fiction and this insight remains to disturb or reassure, post Tiananmen.

This writing negotiates sites of difference and charts the route recommended by the Chinese painting – 'between mountains and streams' – to share discoveries, principles or things of beauty. In an era where the people of the world are struggling to overcome the bonds of economic rationalism and political suspicion, this is significant fiction.

The final poem of a series entitled 'Friendship Packing Company' from Jose's *Cities of China, 1989–1990* provides a poignant postscript:

I had no time to see the persimmons.
In late October the imperial orchard
hangs with fat, waxy fruit, swelling lanterns
that hover before they plop to grassy earth,
golden melons too heavy for gaunt limbs.

The packers have come on cue to despatch me.
China is wrapped and luggage carted away.
Last-minute gifts arrive, awkward, unwanted,
and farewell parties offer their embrace.
Deserving better, these people are driven.

At last there's one suitcase and my old bike
which I ride through the fog in search of home. (78)

Biographical Note:

Nicholas Jose was born in London of Australian parents in 1952 and grew up mainly in South Australia. He took an Arts degree at the Australian National University, then a DPhil at Magdelen College, Oxford, on a Rhodes scholarship. He became a language teacher at

Milan and Bergamo, part-time tutor at Merton College, Oxford, lecturer at ANU and took study leave at Oxford, Rome and Harvard. He studied Chinese at Canberra College of Advanced Education and visited China in 1983 for the first time (his grandfather was born there). In 1987 he went to China as cultural counsellor at the Australian Embassy in Beijing. He taught Australian studies in China. He has published four novels, two collections of short fiction, and a book of essays. He has recently released *The Rose Crossing* (Penguin, 1994), a further cross-cultural fable investigating contrasting wisdom and 'cross-pollination', and *Chinese Whispers: Cultural Essays* (Wakefield, 1995), which includes revised versions of some of the articles cited.

The title of my article echoes a chapter heading of *Avenue of Eternal Peace* which took its name from the Yuan painter Fan Kuan's painting in the Taipei Palace Museum ('Non-Chinese Characters' 10).

WORKS CITED

Broinowski, Alison. *The Yellow Lady: Australian Impressions of Asia* Melbourne: Oxford,1992.

Hamilton, Annette. 'Fear and Desire: Aborigines and Asians and the National Imaginary', *Australian Cultural History* 9 (1990): 14–35.

Hutcheon, Linda. *A Poetics of Postmodernism: History, Theory, Fiction.* New York: Routledge, 1988.

Jaivin, Linda. 'Romancing the Lotus'. *Editions* June 1993: 13–15.

Jose, Nicholas. *The Possession of Amber.* St Lucia: University of Queensland Press, 1980.

———. 'Possibilities of Love in Recent Australian Short Stories'. *Island Magazine* 20 (1984): 30.

———. *Rowena's Field.* Adelaide: Rigby, 1984.

———. *Feathers or Lead.* Adelaide: Rigby, 1986.

———. *Paper Nautilus.* Ringwood: Penguin, 1987.

———. *Avenue of Eternal Peace.* Ringwood: Penguin, 1989.

———. 'Screen Dreams and Nightmares' *Modern Times* March 1992: 22–24.

———. 'Non-Chinese Characters: Translating China'. *Southerly* 52.2 (1992): 3–11.

———. 'Cities of China, 1989–1990'. *Southerly* 52.3 (1992): 75–78.

———. 'Green Oil and Tall Puppies', *ABC Radio 24 Hours*, April 1993, 42–43.

Leys, Simon. *The Burning Forest: Essays on Chinese Culture and Politics*. New York: Holt, Rinehart, and Winston, 1986.

McLaren, John. 'Courage against Lies'. *Overland* 116 (1989): 23.

Pearson, M.N. 'Pilgrims, Travellers, Tourists: The Meanings of Journeys', *Australian Cultural History* 10 (1991): 125–34.

Said, Edward. *Orientalism*. New York: Pantheon, 1978.

CHAPTER

THE LIST OF NO ANSWERS

IN THE MATTER OF P. GOLDSWORTHY

Brian Matthews

I   Peter Goldsworthy's Almanac

almanac [ɔlmənæk] *n.* (also almanack) an astronomical calendar of months and days, usu. with listings of astronomical data, weather and other information. [ME f. med.L *almanac(h)* f. Gk *almenikhiaka*]

Meteorologically, Peter Goldsworthy can be quixotic: heat and humidity often stifle his suburban villas and the summer evening gloom of his city streets. The weather of his fiction is somehow warm, gusty – changeable yet invigorating. Nature though is no more than an amiable background rustle: reality lies not in the fluidity of water or the rush of winds or the pathetically fallacious cradling or promise or threat of this-goes-with-that natural ambience, but in the crosscurrents of words and conversations and silences, always running at an angle to the emotional truths they so desperately want to impart and examine:

Terry had a kind of Daffy Duck voice that he often slipped into, especially late at night, or when drunk: a voice that let things slip

that were too embarrassing or too serious to speak of in normal conversation; a voice that could say things from behind a duck-mask
with a fool's frankness. The voice had quacked out its lust for Jenny –
his wife's friend, his friend's wife – once too often, the truth half-
hidden under cover of banter, but this time not sufficiently. The
silence that followed revealed something about themselves to each
of the four.

That silence seemed to last for minutes. Finally one of two things
had to happen: someone had to say, yes, let's do it, let's swap,
or someone had to say, I think that's enough, you've spoilt the
evening . . . ('The Death of Daffy Duck')

If you want to cool off (though it won't always be pleasant) you need
the Goldsworthy poems. Where bleak, icy splinters of only-too-true
flick casually at your senses and sensitivities; where an iron honesty
stares straight back at you out of a hard reflecting winter light till you try
to look away; where trying to look away reveals to you, in other equally
intransigent mirrors of trembling pools or the irrelevant sheen of green
leaves, the catastrophic rightness of this or that word, the destabilising
oddity of image that goes on haunting . . . This is serious weather, light
not of the sun, air sinister, mirages collapsing and reassembling, relent-
lessly revealing.

After the doctor, the steam-cleaners,
more usefully. I drive home to bed
through intersections sequinned with glass:
it's Christmas Eve, season of donor organs.

What is the meaning of life? I shake you
gently awake. What answer would satisfy?
you mumble, yawning, from Your Side.
To understand is to be bored, you say,
practising, perhaps, for Speech Night.
Knowledge is a kind of exhaustion, you say.

A child enters our room: is it morning yet?
Not Yet. In another room the lights of the Tree
wink colourfully, and when the telephone rings
again, it is almost, but not quite, in time.

('Suicide On Christmas Eve')

In Goldsworthy's Almanac there are – properly, and in the nature of Almanacs, Atlases, Gazettes, Yearbooks, Cartularies, Files, Gazetteers, Rotas, Canons, Hagiologies, Rosters, Indices, Empanelments, Inventories and Directories – many kinds of lists: of diseases (for he is hypochondriacal); of symptoms (for he is hypochondriacal and curious); composers (for he loves music and is a musician); authors (for he loves books and is a writer); oddities of science and behaviour (for he is a medic); foods (for he loves food and is an eater); words (for he is wordsmith, jotter, garreteer, stylist, portrayer, librettist, scriptwriter, co-author, composer, inditer . . .); lists within lists (for he is arguably and on occasion postmodern and loves lists).

II   The Cosmology of Peter Goldsworthy

cosmology [kɒzmɒləʤi] n. science or theory of the universe [ME f. F cosmographie or mod. L cosmologia]

No benign God, nor for that matter a malign one, presides in Goldsworthy's Cosmology. The fates of his characters are, though the author seems often to regret it, in their own hands. Shaping and rough hewing, they obey forces and pressures they are scarcely aware of. Indeed, they are rarely aware enough until it's too late for them to do anything but lament the lack of awareness which has become their greatest yet bitterest insight. Maestro's Paul Crabbe is one of many Goldsworthy creations to have this experience:

As I rose from the bed, the sun broke below the heaving clouds: a rare, golden light drenching, saturating the town. Always these deft, elemental touches move me: light breaking through clouds, rain spattering on roofs, pink sunsets [note I above, Peter Goldsworthy's Almanac: 'Nature though is no more than an amiable background rustle . . .'] As I gazed across the town I was overcome with nostalgia . . . and regret that I had not taken more notice, kept a better *record* of those beautiful years [emphasis added: note I above, re the keeping of lists/records]. Never again will time move as slowly as it did then, and never again would there be so much to be discovered, to be touched and tasted for the first time.

And now it was too late: once we begin to sense our childhoods, we are no longer children. And decisions have been made – by omission, neglect, inertia – that cannot be unmade.

Goldsworthy's bleak rooms are not only in the various suburban and city buildings his characters inhabit but also in their hearts: despite all their brushes with spiritual possibilities they inhabit a world which insists, constantly and roughly, on the secular. For Goldsworthy's various young-to middle-aged medicos, lawyers, family people, home-makers and -breakers, death is their reminder of the spiritual; brushes with death (sinister diagnoses; accidents; oesophogeal spasms; the loss of relatives, friends and acquaintances) are occult warnings against the determined secularity of their materialist lives. Once again, the poetry offers a chillier, more precise insight: the nameless, imperturbable and inde-fatigable speaker of so many of the poems does not need morbidity to enforce a realisation of what life might be about, or why it isn't about anything. The world of even the most benign of Goldsworthy's poems is at heart threatening: in that world, not even words behave.

I read once of a valley
where men and women spoke
a different tongue.

I know that any uncooked theory
can find its tribe,
but this might just be true:

for us there are three languages,
yours, mine, and the English between,
a wall of noises.

At times our children interpret,
or music connects our moods.
There are also monosyllables,

the deeper grammar of fucking,
a language too subjective
for nouns.

But even after conjugation
the tense remains the same:
present imperfect.

We take our mouths from each other,
we carry away our tongues,
and the separate dictionaries in our heads.

('After Babel')

III Peter Goldsworthy's Separate Dictionary

It's not a matter of odd or even idiosyncratic vocabulary. He's capable of that, of course. But his natural tendency is, as he might or might not say depending on mood, to brachylogy not epexegesis. His method is to write spare then pare. Not much is left: either it works at a level of amazing density, evocative flickers; or it zips by like vagrant newspaper sucked off a stormy street and tossed forever beyond random conventional roofs. In Goldsworthy's stories, much has happened before anything happens. Some of them start late: 'You've ruined it! *Ruined* it!' (first sentence of 'Tuxedo Junction'). Others seem to implode, to roll the carpet up, taking the world with them, leaving nothing: 'even as she shouted she knew the threat was empty; knew that the boy was safe, that he would hear no voice from beyond the grave' (last sentence of 'A Nice Surprise'). Some do both:

Again the child plucked at his mother's sleeve.

He ruled a thick line across the page beneath his words. If nothing else, there would, surely, be no need for further entries.

(first and last sentences of 'A List of All Answers')

But there is a need of course. It is Goldsworthy's need. The dictionary in his head has plenty of words but the meanings are elusive – he strains after the further entries, the what-comes-next. As always, it's in the poetry that a destabilisingly rational, expect-nothing voice conjures with the next move, the one you never make because you don't know what it is, the one that nobody else, not even Shakespeare, tells you about . . .

ACT SIX
Act six begins
when the curtain falls,
the corpses awake,
the daggers are cleaned.

Act six
is Juliet in the supermarket,
Mr Macbeth on the 8.15.

In act six
Hamlet sucks a tranquilliser,
Romeo washes up

and death
is gentle and anonymous:
Lear's life-support
switched discreetly off.

WHAT COMES NEXT
There is nothing as empty as the future,
or as bleached and pale blue: a type of summer
a long school holiday, unpunctuated even
by our little lives, rounded with brackets.

Outside those brackets, what? Or – far worse – why?
Don't ask so many questions, wise adults
repeated, often, when I was young –
but each year I push an extra candle

through the crust and panic:
another pilot-flame to extinguish, quickly,
lest something uncontrollable ignites,
or I find myself breaking through the icing

into the molten stuff beneath, suddenly
reduced to composite materials.
Perhaps this is the final homecoming:
a fair and even redistribution of matter;

my atoms permitted to cease their restless
jiggling, at peace among the other particles;
my bits and pieces returned to where
I sprang from – or less I, than me;

and less me, than him: his handful of carbon
returned to that topsoil, his water-quota – fifty litres –
to those streams and clouds, his ash to that ash;
his dust to *that* dust, there, no longer mine.

In his essay on Charles Dickens, George Orwell quotes a description of a meal ('the family were at dinner – baked shoulder of mutton and potatoes under it'), and remarks that 'the unmistakable Dickens touch [about this], the thing nobody else would have thought of', is the detail of the potatoes under the mutton. 'It is something totally unnecessary, a florid little squiggle on the edge of the page; only, it is by just these squiggles that the special Dickens atmosphere is created' (451).

In 'What Comes Next' there is a Goldsworthian equivalent to this Dickensian trademark that is as certain a signature as his name at the bottom of the poem: it is the 'fifty litres' quota of body water. His insatiable curiosity about detail (*'Men kill women in bedrooms, usually / by hand or gun'*), fuelled by knowledge and terminologies drawn from several disciplines (*'here is always logic in this world / And neatness. And the comfort / of fact'*), fills his separate dictionary so full of the arcane, the heteroclite, the freakish and the aberrant that it becomes dictionary, almanac, necronomicon, atlas, directory, encyclopaedia

(*Don't be alarmed, there is understanding / to be sucked from all such hard / and bony facts, or at least a sense / of symmetry*) – a huge and elaborate distraction, a dynamic muddle from which, however, there emerges on to the page a fabulous pointedness.

But 'squiggle' is not the word for Goldsworthy's laconic, knowledge-able glimpsings always just to one side of your concentration ('After the doctor, the steam cleaners / *more usefully*'); it's more like a marginal doodling (remembering how revealing is doodling to those willing to see – or invent); and it's not 'florid', but mordant, saturnine. Yet it is by just these page edge twitches, hints and glimpses that the special Goldsworthy atmosphere is created: in the fiction, a sense of doom always avoided or postponed; joking in the lifeboat. In the poetry: a calm voice rehearsing and squarely facing up to the fact of essential and ineluctable loneliness. In his poetry, Goldsworthy is artist and intellec-tual; in his fiction he is artist and conjuror, brilliant but not *quite* prepared to accept the responsibilities of brilliance. He comes nearest to this acceptance, as far as the fiction is concerned, in *Maestro*, but even there, Paul Crabbe's final emotional insight has more of confusion than resolution about it. But it is an honourable confusion, since Goldsworthy himself remains anxious and uncertain about the burdensome inextri-cability of past, present and future in individual lives, as his many pronouncements on the subject, marginal and otherwise, reveal; not to mention his fascination with that theme in, among other works, *Flaubert's Parrot*.

IV Goldsworthy's Adelaide

. . . ripping down from Prospect with a dust-caked windscreen, parking up an alley or at No Standing Anytime or where it says Loading Zone but never Medical Staff Only, who needs medical staff at the Lannathai in Pulteney Street anyway? Well, Goldsworthy for one, as he swallows a whole chilli and suffers oesophageal spasm, hacking and gasping while delivering as clear a medical description of what's actually happening to him as one could expect under the circumstances but our amusement turns to concern (he really *is* choking) and the Thai waitress who must be new here laughs and laughs (what wonders is he spitting on over there?) apparently not knowing Goldsworthy as an *aficionado* of Tom Yum which he certainly is and it's just like 'The Death of Daffy Duck' the real facts behind which, recovering with water and Singha Beer, he now wheezingly tells us; will his own spasm become another story ('The Near Death Experience of PG Watched By . . .'); 'story' he prefers not that 'short fiction' bullshit; out now anyway with cauterised throat into the honest light of hot Adelaide with sun-cracked upholstery burning the bum ignition brings engine and 'The Trout' to simultaneous life Brrrm Brrrm Brrrm Da dum dee dum dum daa daa dum dee dum dee dum dee daa the well known bit and a quick trip to the *Adelaide Review* for some goss which he files in his separate dictionary for reference but always leaks *can't help myself* before a rush down Anzac Highway to his Plympton surgery to do a stint of doctoring 'how did you injure your cartilege?' he asks, 'fucking' she replies, he remains impassive: a Hippocratic matter, this, but storing it for stories and then off to soccer where his reconstructed knee offers no twinge of cartilege or any fucking thing and his scintillating form against age and odds convinces him of certain cosmic truths hard to specify, slipping his mind, C'arn the Crows was probably what it was *In South Australia I Was Born* then back to Prospect with a Bangkok take-away and his big house bursting with laughter, music, children and phone messages: will he read at this Festival and chair that session and what is this new novel he's working at (is it really called *Jesus You Honk*?) got to keep it quiet he says but it's about gene transfer anyway, make a mint if no one gets in first, time out to ripple a bit now at this keyboard Da dum dee dum dum daa daa now at that *Later, Barbara remembered a platitude she had read somewhere: an orgasm was a kind of death, a little death* lately taking to hanging out round the 'shoot' on location with the stars who are throwing around his excellent script (no irony intended he is a brilliant script writer, its minimalism suits him, he works well in a team no irony intended he has been known to co-author) getting into film, he says, twiddling the still hot steering wheel ripping in to Elder Hall for a concert, film's the answer – brevity, glance, flicks, lights camera wow stick with me baby and I'll *the person to avoid, alone, is mostly you yourself*

V Goldsworthy His Books/The Goldsworthy Variations

Readings From Ecclesiastes
This Goes With This
This Goes With That: Selected Poems 1970–1990
Archipelagoes
Zooing
Bleak Rooms
Maestro
Magpie (jointly with Brian Matthews)
Honk If You Are Jesus
Little Deaths

For he and all his tribe are very tall
For he lives in a house pitched for tallness
For he has a dog that goes close to the ground and is paranoid
For he is a devotee of 'wogball' and The Crows
For he has in this way a serious division of his personality
For he is given to gloom
For he is suspicious of the Academy
For he nevertheless willingly and generously gives his time
    to students
For he knows the Staff Clubs and the lecture rooms
For he affects ignorance of Literary Theory
For he is by and large actually ignorant of Literary Theory
For he does not consider himself thereby disadvantaged as
    a writer
For he is in this almost certainly right
For he understands intertextuality
For he is not intimidated thereby
For he would likely appreciate a serious critique of his work
For he pines for a real critic
For he secretly wonders what a true theorist would make of
    his work
For he longs after deconstruction
For he lusts to know his characteristic discourse

For he will shrug and accept as always lacunae
For he will say what else can you expect
For he will begin a novel or a story or a libretto or a script or
    a poem
For he will say what the hell
For he will be content
For he will be as content as someone of his temperament is
    capable of being

VI Little Deaths in Venice

Here is Goldsworthy in the writer's studio in Venice, crippled with hypochondria. There is not enough light in the Northern hemisphere, he will later explain, and this leads to depression and inertia. He has crash-coursed his way into Italian: *Buona sera*, says a passing Venetian. *Buon giorno*, responds Goldsworthy smoothly, spotting the trap; *mantenete allacciata la cintura di sicurezza* he continues by way of small talk; and: *È pericoloso sporgersi* he adds, feeling confident. But he is not himself. Travel fills him with medical possibilities and he succumbs, at least in imagination, to most of them. He is an anxious man and it is all he can do to force down the pasta and the rosso and dream of home . . . Adelaide, South Australia: where only parochialism can deny him his true stature as one of Australia's very best poets, one of its finest prose writers, one of its most interesting, original and intriguing intellectuals.

WORKS CITED

Orwell, Sonia and Ian Angus, ed. *The Collected Essays, Journalism and Letters of George Orwell*. Vol. I. 1945. London: Secker & Warburg, 1969.

CHAPTER

CRIME FICTION IN SOUTH AUSTRALIA

Michael J. Tolley

That the majority of titles in the first dozen Wakefield Crime Classics, a series of reprinted Australian mystery novels, are from South Australian writers is not sheer parochialism on the part of the series editors. In the perspective of time it appears that South Australia has contributed more than its fair share of good Australian mystery writers, particularly if one ignores the last decade (which, in the wake of Peter Corris, has been dominated by New South Wales productions). Although Adelaide, the City of Weird Murders, has often provided copy for the gutter press recently, novelists have mostly refrained from capitalising on this. The local writers chosen by the Wakefield editors are Charlotte Jay, Arthur Gask, and A.E. Martin. All of these writers have an international reputation – but then so do others, notably Max Afford, Guy Boothby, Carlton Dawe, A.G. Hales, Gavin Holt, Edward Lindall, Paul McGuire and Elizabeth Salter. This survey will present a brief chronological account of the work of these major figures; minor ones are grouped partly by period, partly by theme (historical), partly by origin (if outside the state). For reasons of space only, several authors and many titles are omitted.

William Carlton Lanyon Dawe (1865–1935) was born in Adelaide but went with his parents to Melbourne ca. 1880 and thereafter to England, settling in London after travelling widely, and becoming a prolific fiction writer. His series detective, Colonel Gantian, figures in at least ten novels, the first of which, *Leathermouth* (London: Ward, Lock, 1931), set in London, presents him as a private investigator with a background of wartime employment in the Secret Service. He is approached by Scotland Yard regarding a missing millionaire and proceeds to check-mate a mysterious Arab involved in an international conspiracy. Thereafter followed such titles as *Fifteen Keys* (London: Ward, Lock, 1932), *Leathermouth's Luck* (London: Ward, Lock, 1934), *The Green Killer* (London: Ward, Lock, 1936: the green killer is a lorry), and *Live Cartridge* (London: Ward, Lock, 1937). However, his novel-writing career began much earlier than this; his output shows his taste for exotic sub-jects as well as his ability to change with fashion. One of his more popular novels, *The Emu's Head: A Chronicle of Dead Man's Flat* (London: Ward & Downey, 1893, 2 vols), is a gold-rush thriller.

Guy Newell Boothby (1867–1905), was born in Adelaide, the son of a member of the House of Assembly; he was educated in Australia and England and became private secretary to the mayor of Adelaide, where he wrote unsuccessful plays, before returning to live in England in 1894. He made such an impact in England that his friend Rudyard Kipling wrote, 'Mr Guy Boothby has come to great honours now. His name is large upon the hoardings, his books sell like hot cakes.' His swindler-hero, Simon Carne, who appears in *A Prince of Swindlers* (London: Ward Lock, 1900), a.k.a. *The Viceroy's Protege*, is the first gentleman crook in literature, anticipating Raffles by a couple of years and Grant Allen's *An African Millionaire* (London: George Bell, 1897) by a month or so. Dr. Nikola was expert in hocus-pocus; Boothby himself was a stage magician. He favoured exotic locations and these include (for his London readers) Australia; his book *On the Wallaby* (London: Longmans, 1894) describes a journey he made from Cairns to Adelaide. Paul Depasquale has made a study of his work,[1] but it is so extensive that he is known today mainly for the highly collectable decorated bindings in which such works as *Doctor Nikola* (London: Ward, Lock, 1896) appeared. Representative titles include the very popular *A Bid for*

Fortune or Dr. Nikola's Vendetta (London: Ward, Lock & Bowden, 1895); *Across the World for a Wife* (London: Ward, Lock, 1898), a blend of thriller and detective story; *The Lust of Hate* (London: Ward, Lock, 1898), another Dr. Nikola novel, set partly in the Victorian goldfields; *The Mystery of the Clasped Hands* (London: F.V. White, 1901), set in England, where series detective Jacob Burrell investigates the fatal stabbing of a woman; *My Strangest Case* (Boston: L.C. Page, 1901), which features the private detective George Fairfax, whose investigation of a bank fraud takes the reader to Singapore and Burma, as well as Queensland; *The Childerbridge Mystery* (London: F.V. White, 1902), set partly in Queensland, as are *Connie Burt* (London: Ward, Lock, 1903) and several others.

A(lfred Arthur) G(reenwood) Hales (1870–1936) was born at Kent Town, Adelaide. He had scanty formal education but travelled widely in Australia, working as a journalist and dabbling in mining. He was war correspondent for the *Daily News* in World War I. John Long advertised his work as 'Adventure' and this puts his output in a genre which fits rather awkwardly into the crime fiction slot, although most adventures include at least one villain. Depasquale's *Critical History* should be consulted for the work of this prolific author. His series hero, an Australian of Scottish descent called McGlusky, is the less likely to be found amusing today because of his outrageous Scots lingo: he was subject to extraordinary vicissitudes, as the titles suggest, for instance *McGlusky, Empire Builder*, *McGlusky in India*, *McGlusky o' the Legion*, *McGlusky the Mormon*, and *McGlusky the Seal Poacher* (a novel which includes Jack London among its characters). *A Lindsay o' the Dale* (Sydney: T. Fisher Unwin, 1907) is unique, apparently, in being set in South Australia: it features bushrangers. *McGlusky the Gold-seeker* (London: Hodder & Stoughton, 1920) is also set in Australia and deals with claim-jumping, and *The Mystery of Wo-Sing* (London: John Long, 1924) is set in the Northern Territory. *The Wanderings of a Simple Child*, as 'by an Australian "Smiler"' (Sydney: Gibbs, Shellard, 1890), presents various crimes set in the Australian outback or Broken Hill.

Arthur Cecil Gask (1872–1951) was born in London and was a dentist for over forty years. He settled in Adelaide in 1920 and had a practice on North Terrace. He wrote his novels principally for recreation, but after

the success of his first effort, *The Secret of the Sandhills*, first published locally by Rigby in 1921, he established relations with Herbert
Jenkins in London, and they became his regular publishers. His novels
were highly regarded and widely translated: Clement Atlee, Bertrand
Russell and H.G. Wells (with whom he corresponded) were among his
admirers. His series detective is Gilbert Larose, who has been described
by Depasquale as 'a ruthless destroyer of the criminal classes, a master
of disguises, and the possessor of a trained mind and alert instincts'.
He first appeared in *Cloud the Smiter* (London: Herbert Jenkins, 1926),
which is set in Adelaide. Typically, his mystery thrillers are mixed with
romance; the latter can drag on sometimes too long for modern tastes,
but on other occasions Gask provides a piquant mix of humorous
roguery with suspense, as in *The Secret of the Garden* (London: Herbert
Jenkins, 1924), also set in Adelaide, now in the Wakefield Crime
Classics. Most Gask titles are set in England or Europe: the South
Australian ones are listed here. They include, besides those already
mentioned, *The Dark Highway* (London: Herbert Jenkins, 1928), in
which Larose investigates a double crime, perpetrated at midnight
among the sand-dunes of the Coorong; *The Lonely House* (London:
Herbert Jenkins, 1929), set in the Cape Jervis area, where Larose, who
is on holiday after an attack of typhoid, decides to live off the land and
tangles with an arch-criminal; *The Red Paste Murders* (London: Herbert
Jenkins, 1924), a.k.a. *Murder in the Night*, in which Adelaide suffers
eight night murders in a fortnight; and *The Shadow of Larose* (London:
Herbert Jenkins, 1930), in which an Adelaide bank clerk is involved
in murder.

A(rchibald) E(dward) Martin (1885–1955), was born in Adelaide and
grew up in Orroroo, where his father had the Imperial Hotel. In early
youth he rambled around the fairgrounds of Europe with the great
Houdini as his mentor and guide. He worked for a time on the *Adelaide
Critic*, where he met C.J. Dennis, who employed him as a full-time
journalist with *The Gadfly* till its demise in 1909. He travelled widely,
'managed prize fighters, freaks and great stars', bought documentary
films in Europe and exhibited them there and in Australia, then established a travel agency before the war put an end to its activities. He
moved to Roseville, NSW in the late 1940s and was by then a full-time

author, sometimes writing radio plays and serials. Martin used his carnival background in his novels, for instance *Common People* (Sydney: distributed by Consolidated Press, 1944), also known, rewritten for Simon and Schuster, as *The Outsiders*, and filmed as *The Glass Cage* (US title *The Glass Tomb*) in 1955. Martin won £1,000 in 1942 for this novel from *The Australian Women's Weekly*. He also submitted an even better novel, *Sinners Never Die* (New York: Simon & Schuster, 1944), using a small town based on Orroroo in the 1890s, as he and his son Jim did again in *The Hive of Glass*, posthumously published (Adelaide: Rigby, 1962). Martin's other novels are *The Misplaced Corpse* (Sydney: NSW Bookstall, 1944); *Death in the Limelight* (New York: Simon & Schuster, 1946); *The Curious Crime* (Sydney: Doubleday, 1952); *The Bridal Bed Murders* (New York: Simon & Schuster, 1953), a.k.a. *The Chinese Bed Mysteries*; and he also contributed some excellent short stories to the genre. *Common People* and *Sinners Never Die* are in Wakefield Crime Classics.

Gavin Holt is a pseudonym of **Percival Charles Rodda**, who was born in Port Augusta in 1891, and educated in Adelaide. He worked as a journalist for *The Age* before working for *Musical America*: several of his novels have a musical background. In 1926 he went from America to London, lived in France and England thereafter and established his reputation as a crime-writer with about forty titles under the 'Holt' pseudonym. His major series hero is Professor Luther Bastion, as in *Six Minutes Past Twelve* (London: Hodder & Stoughton, 1928) and *Steel Shutters* (London: Hodder & Stoughton, 1936). 'The Aztec Skull', which features Bastion, appears in the Odhams collection, *Fifty Famous Detectives of Fiction* [ca. 1948], in which Holt is the only Australian representative. Another series detective, Inspector Joel Saber, first appears in *The Theme Is Murder* (London: Gollancz, 1938). Holt's settings are usually English or European, but one or two are partly Australian, as with *The Garden of Silent Beasts* and *Storm* (both London: Hodder & Stoughton, 1931). Rodda also published under his own name, as with two bushranger novels, *The Fortunes of Geoffrey Mayne* (Sydney: NSW Bookstall, 1919), and *The Scarlet Mask* (London: Thomas Nelson & Sons, 1926), the story of 'Captain Scarlet'. As Gardner Low, he wrote *Invitation to Kill*, set in New York; it appeared in Australia in 1956 as one of the Phantom series. Rodda also had the distinction of colla-borating with Eric Ambler, using the pseudonym of Eliot Reed, though it seems that Ambler was not always involved with the six Reed titles.

Paul Dominic McGuire (1903–1978), was born in Peterborough and educated at Christian Brothers' College, Adelaide and the University of Adelaide, where he read history. He was a lecturer, a Commander in the Navy Reserve and a career diplomat, but nevertheless found time to write mystery fiction, verse and non-fiction, including several books on travel and on world order. He and his wife, Frances Margaret McGuire (see below), with Betty Arnott, wrote a study of *The Australian Theatre* (Oxford: Oxford University Press, 1948). The State Library of South Australia includes the Paul McGuire Maritime Library, established in 1979. His novels were decidedly popular, and the murder mystery thriller *Burial Service* (London: Heinemann, 1938), a.k.a. *A Funeral in Eden*, was included in the Garland series, 'Fifty Classics of Crime Fiction 1900–1950'. It is set on the South Sea island of 'Kaitai' and features Sultan George Buchanan as detective. However, McGuire tended mostly to use English settings for his novels. *Murder by the Law* (London: Skeffington [1932]) introduced a series detective, Inspector Fillinger, to deal with the case of a murdered novelist; and *Murder in Bostall* (London: Skeffington, [1931]), a.k.a. *The Black Rose Murder*, introduced another, Chief Inspector Cummings; the two detectives come together in *Murder in Haste* (London: Skeffington, [1934]), which employs an unusual murder weapon: a bus-ticket puncher. McGuire has a fine humorous touch, as in *There Sits Death* (London: Skeffington, [1933]).

Max Afford (1906–1954), was born in Parkside, Adelaide. He was a reporter and feature writer with the *Adelaide News* (1929–1934), when he joined the staff of radio station 5DN as Production Manager and play-wright before moving in 1936 permanently to Sydney, where he worked as a playwright for the ABC. In 1938 he married Thelma Thomas of Broken Hill, who designed costumes for his stage plays. He wrote more than sixty radio and stage plays and radio serials, many of them crimi-nous, won several awards and achieved the notable coup of a Broadway production for the comedy-thriller *Lady in Danger*. Several radio series featured Jeffery Blackburn, English professor of Higher Mathematics, who also figures in most of the novels; in *The Sheep and the Wolves* it is revealed that he once worked as a PI with Moratti's agency in New York and that his wife, Elizabeth, was in charge of the cipher department, British Intelligence. Tracking Afford's output is rendered less easy by the use of multiple titles for the same novel. His output includes: *Death's Mannikins* (London: John Long, [1937]), a.k.a. *The Dolls of Death* (probably), set in Devonshire; *Blood on his Hands!* (London: John Long [1936]), a.k.a. *An Ear For Murder*, set in Melbourne; *The Dead are Blind* (London: John Long, 1937), which deals with murder in the BBC; *Fly by Night* (London, John Long, [1942]), a.k.a. *Owl of Darkness* (Sydney: Collins, 1949), an English country-house mystery; *The Sheep and the Wolves* and *Sinners in Paradise* (Sydney: Frank Johnson, n.d.).

Edward Lindall, the pseudonym of **Edward Ernest Smith**, was born in 1915 in Adelaide and spent most of his life there, though he once described his spiritual home as London. His fiction has been published in at least ten languages. His thrillers are set in Australia, especially the north, and Papua New Guinea, but some of his titles belong to the mainstream. For instance, *No Place to Hide* (London: Hutchinson, 1959), a.k.a. *The Paper Ghost*, has on its blurb the comment: 'could be classed as a mystery story, or even a spy thriller. But the important thing about it is that it is a contemporary novel'; its plot includes blackmail and spies. Other titles include *A Lively Form of Death* (London: Constable, 1972), wherein croc-hunter Gregory Lander's peace is ruined by drug-runners; *Death and the Maiden* (London: Constable, 1973), in which a half-wit rapes a newly-married woman in the Northern Territory then is hunted down and killed by her husband and other station hands; *A Day for Angels* (London: Constable, 1975), a thriller set in the Australian bush, in which two international mining moguls are kidnapped by terrorists; and *The Last Refuge* (Melbourne: Gold Star Publications, 1972), which features Americans who wish to buy out the Northern Territory and Maoist Australian guerrillas who try to stop the deal.

Elizabeth Fulton Salter (1918?–1981?), was born at Angaston, and left in 1952 for London. She began writing novels when secretary to Dame Edith Sitwell. As a biographer she has written on Sitwell and also on Daisy Bates. Her popular five novels are *Death in a Mist* (London: Geoffrey Bles, 1957), which is set in the New Zealand thermal region, and is the first title to feature her series detective Inspector

Michael Hornsley, who figures in all the stories; *Will to Survive* (London: Geoffrey Bles, 1958), about cyanide poisoning in the outback; *There Was a Witness* (London: Geoffrey Bles, 1960), set in Sydney; *The Voice of the Peacock* (London: Geoffrey Bles, 1962), where Hornsley investigates two murders at a NSW radio station; *Once Upon a Tombstone* (London: Hutchinson, 1965), which is set in Austria, Sydney and southwest Queensland and is initiated by a frightening déjà vu experience.

Geraldine Mary Halls, better-known as **Charlotte Jay**, was born in Adelaide in 1919. She left Australia at the age of 21 for England and thereafter travelled extensively. She says her most interesting job was as court stenographer for the Supreme Court at Port Moresby. She has also lived in Asia and the Middle East and has used such exotic locations in her novels. She settled in Somerset near Bath, where her husband had an antiques business. A widow, she is now again resident in Adelaide and is delighted by the new lease of life she has obtained as a consequence of being rediscovered by the series editors of Wakefield Crime Classics. As Geraldine Halls, she has written mainstream fiction, although *The Voice of the Crab* (London: Constable, 1974), set in Papua-New Guinea, presents an island in the thrall of a man who murdered his wife. As Charlotte Jay, she was once among the most highly esteemed crime fiction writers in the USA, and is one of the only two Australians to have received the prestigious Edgar Allan Poe Award from Mystery Writers of America for best crime novel (Jon Cleary's *Peter's Pence* has also had this distinction). *Beat Not the Bones* (London: Collins, 1952), won the Edgar in 1953, on its first American publication. Her other crime titles are *The Knife is Feminine* (London: Collins, 1951), set in New South Wales; *Arms for Adonis* (London: Collins, 1960), set in Lebanon; *The Fugitive Eye* (London: Collins, 1953), set in London, as is *A Hank of Hair* (London: Harper & Row, 1954); *The Man Who Walked Away* (London: Collins, 1958), a.k.a. *The Stepfather*; and *The Yellow Turban* (London: Collins, 1955), an exciting thriller set in Pakistan. Under the pseudonym G.M. Jay, she has published *The Feast of the Dead* (London: Robert Hale, 1956), a.k.a. *The Brink of Silence*; it too has a New Guinean setting.

The first novel printed in Adelaide had strong elements of crime in it: this was a work by **George Isaacs**, who was born in London and died in Adelaide in 1876: *The Queen of the South: A Colonial Romance* (Gawler: W. Barret, 1858). Isaacs also wrote *The Burlesque of Frankenstein*, which was written for production in 1863, but apparently never performed; it was rescued from obscurity (a miscellany called *Rhyme and Prose*, published in Melbourne in 1865), by the Sydney bibliophile, Graham Stone (1989). Adelaide-born **James W(illiam) Hay**'s *Mysie's Pardon* (London?: Blackwood, 1873), includes forgery. Perhaps he was the father of **William Gosse Hay** (1875–1945), also born in Adelaide, then educated at Cambridge. He returned to the vicinity of Adelaide in 1901, then settled in Tasmania, the setting for his novels. His work includes *Captain Quadring* (Sydney: T. Fisher Unwin, 1912), which involves a mutiny of convicts; *The Escape of the Notorious Sir William Heans (And the Mystery of Mr Daunt)* (Sydney: George Allen & Unwin, 1918); *The Mystery of Alfred Doubt* (Sydney: George Allen & Unwin, 1937); and *Strabane of the Mulberry Hills* (Sydney: Allen & Unwin, 1929), which includes the notorious bushranger, Martin Cash. **Patrick Eiffe** published anonymously an early mystery, *The Three L's: or, Lawyers, Land-Jobbers, and Lovers: A Tale of South Australia Twenty Years Ago* (Adelaide: Webb, Vardon, & Pritchard, 1882). It begins at Emu Flat, four miles south-west of Clare and features detective John Wolf, searching for a missing heiress, Louisa Ford, who has apparently been robbed and murdered. Paul Depasquale considers this to be 'the first introduction of a credibly methodical detective (that is to say, of a detective who "detects") into a novel set in South Australia'.[2] **Simpson Newland** (1835–1925), was born in England; his family settled at Encounter Bay in 1839. He was MP for Encounter Bay 1881–1887 and State Treasurer 1885–1886. *Blood Tracks of the Bush: An Australian Romance* (London: Gay & Bird, 1900), set in western NSW, includes several murders by what Stephen Knight has described as an Australian Jekyll and Hyde. Better known is *Paving the Way* (London: Gay & Bird, 1893), which is set in South Australia, although it includes the famous NSW bushranger, Captain Thunderbolt. **S.J. Stutley** and **A.E. Copp** were South Australian writers who co-authored two novels, *The Melbourne Mystery* (London: John Lane, 1929), which is notable for its presentation of the labyrinthine Chinatown district, and *The Poisoned Glass* (London: John Lane, 1930), set in north-eastern Australia, in the town of 'Sexton'.

Ken(neth Andrew) Attiwill (1906–1960), was born in Adelaide, and worked as a journalist there, as well as in Melbourne and London. He was a Japanese prisoner of war in the second world war, and was resident in England for most of the latter part of his life. Notable are *Reporter!* (London: John Long, 1933) and *Sky Steward* (London: John Long, 1936), which features an airline steward called Kneebone as the detective. **Dorothy M. Langsford**, born in 1896 at Mintaro, and educated at the Methodist Ladies' College, Adelaide, wrote three Australian stories, *The Outlaw* (London: Epworth Press, 1925), *Sun-Chased Shadows* (London: Epworth Press, 1927), set in the Mount Lofty Ranges, and *Dan of the Ridge* (London: Epworth Press, 1928). *The Outlaw*, set in the north-west of the State, is, according to Depasquale, a 'melodramatic romance': in it, a bush parson befriends a local robber, who is his look-alike, and at one stage is arrested in mistake for him. **H(arold) A(rthur) Lindsay**, born in Adelaide in 1900, includes in his output *And Gifts Misspent* (London: Hale, 1964), set partly in South Australia, which features George Sebastian, a young man who has a mind-reading gift and mis-uses it, partly for criminal purposes; it is based on a police dossier. It is pleasant to record that **Brian Elliott** (1910–1991), an Adelaidean by birth and education, who taught at The University of Adelaide from 1940–1975, where he pioneered the teaching of Australian literary studies, is allowed into this survey: his novel, *Leviathan's Inch* (Sydney, London: Angus & Robertson, 1946), which is set in and around Victor Harbor, ends with a murder and suicide. **Frances Margaret McGuire**, (née Cheadle), was born at Glenelg, c. 1900, and studied biochemistry at The University of Adelaide. An author and freelance journalist, she was a member of the Australian Delegation to the League of Nations in 1939 and a member of the Federal Board of the National Council of Women of Australia, 1936–1942. The widow of Paul McGuire, she lives in North Adelaide. She has published one thriller and three other novels. *Time in the End* (London: Heinemann, 1963), features Jack Apsley, whose wife remained on a small Pacific island when he was captured by the Japanese on another island in 1942; he survives prison camp but it is only when, twenty years later, a man is strangled and dumped in Sydney Harbour and a witness is throttled, that Apsley learns what happened to her.

Bernard Cyril Boucher, born in England (1934), moved to Australia in 1965; he settled in Adelaide and became a journalist, being deputy chief of staff for *The Advertiser* (1968–1973), and a full-time writer since 1978. His books include *The Megawind Cancellation: A Suspense Novel of the Great Darwin Disaster* [Cyclone Tracy] (S. Melbourne, N. Sydney: Macmillan, 1979), and *Opalesque* (S. Melbourne: Melbourne House, 1982), set partly in the Australian opal fields, partly in Hong Kong. **Alison Elizabeth Broinowski,** born 25 October 1941, took a degree from The University of Adelaide, then worked as an Australian foreign service officer and a journalist. She lived in Tokyo for three years, travelled extensively in Asian countries and, at last hearing, now lives in Surrey Hills, Victoria. Her novel, *Take One Ambassador* (S. Melbourne, N. Sydney: Macmillan, 1973), set partly in Tokyo, partly in Canberra, is about the abduction of an Australian ambassador and a race against time to free him from a right-wing Japanese secret society. **Jennifer Ann Burley**, born in 1938 in Adelaide wrote the novel *Stop Press* (Collingwood, Vic.: Greenhouse Publications, 1982), about an Adelaide woman and her three daughters who shoot their husband and father who has subjected them to domestic violence. **A.E. Farrell**'s *The Vengeance* (London: Hale, 1963), is set on the Nullarbor Plain, and includes cattle stealing, murder, and a black tracker.

Michael Innes, the pseudonym of **J.I.M. Stewart,** is a somewhat anomalous figure for the bibliographer, because although he was not born in Adelaide, but just outside Edinburgh (1906), it was while he was Jury Professor of English at The University of Adelaide (1935–1945) that he made his reputation as a writer of elegant mystery fiction and so was, for a few years, regarded as an Australian writer. He hardly ever uses Australia in his highly popular books. However, in *The Gay Phoenix* (London: Gollancz, 1976), Appleby visits Adelaide and hears the story of two English brothers who were sailing across the Pacific: when one is accidentally killed, the other assumes his brother's identity, and blackmail follows, as well as attempted murder.

Madelyn Palmer was born in South Australia in 1910 and later moved to England. Under her own name she has written *Dead Fellah!* (London: Jonathan Cape, 1961), which is set in the Northern Territory and features Sergeant Dooley as investigator of the case of a speared man found in the bush, and *Fareham Creek* (Bath: Cedric Chivers, 1974). Under the pseudonym **Geoffrey Peters**, she wrote a series of seven novels featuring Detective Inspector Trevor Nichols and his assistant Sergeant Tom Burton. Among them is *The Eye Of A Serpent* (London: Ward, Lock, 1964), which presents a murder in central Australia. **Barbara Tarlton Jefferis** (born in Adelaide, 1917) has worked as a journalist and TV writer. At least half of her eight novels are set in Australia, among them the psychological thriller, *One Black Summer* (London: Morrow, 1967), and *The Wild Grapes* (New York: Sloane, 1963), which is set locally. **Peter L(aurence) Lyons**, was brought up in Adelaide and is a successful journalist and businessman; he has won the Ian Mudie Prize from the Fellowship of Australian Writers for short story writing. His work includes a thriller, *The China Tape* (Cammeray, NSW: Horwitz, 1981), which is about a plot by China to take over Australia. **Neil Thompson**, born in South Australia in 1929, has written thrillers and adventure novels, one of which, *The Elliston Incident* (London: Hale, 1969), is set in the Elliston region in the west of the State: it presents racial conflict, ending in a massacre. **Wal Watkins**, born in South Australia in 1922, has written a number of thrillers, some for juveniles. His work includes such titles as *Soliloquy in the Simpson* (London: Hale, 1965), set in central Australia; *The Wayward Gang* (Adelaide: Rigby, 1965), set in a fettlers' camp on the Nullarbor Plain; *Andamooka* (London: Hale, 1967), which features Lex and Ivor Durgan, murderous twins; and *Shadow of the Whip* (London: Robert Hale, 1967), set in Adelaide, which includes confidence tricks, larrikins, and problems with police.

Although the history of South Australia has not been sullied so much by convicts and bushrangers as that of most other States, some works manage to feature them, for instance **Mrs John Immyns Waterhouse**'s *Bowled Out: A Story of Bushranging in South Australia* (Adelaide: Vardon & Pritchard, 1891): Depasquale points out that this 'sensational fiction' draws on John Wrathall Bull's *Early Experiences of Colonial Life in South Australia* (Adelaide: Advertiser, Chronicle and Express Offices, 1878). **Robert Bruce**'s *Benbonuna: A Tale of the Fifties* (Adelaide: W.K. Thomas, 1900) is set in the northern part of South Australia in the 1850s and includes affrays with bushrangers. The popular writer of historical fiction, **Nancy Fotheringham Cato**, who was born in Adelaide in 1917 and educated at The University of Adelaide, includes various crimes in her novels; of South Australian interest are those collected in *All the Rivers Run* (London: Heinemann, 1958), set largely on the Murray River. **Rex Grayson**'s story, 'The Pirates of Kangaroo Island' was published in the collection of Australian Journal Bushranger Stories, *The Night Raiders* (Melbourne: Massina, n.d.). **Nara Lake** was born in Adelaide and lives in Victoria. In the 1970s and 1980s she produced about fifteen novels mingling mystery, suspense, history and romance. They include *Man From Kanpur* (London: Hale, 1983) and *The Painted Girl* (London: Hale, 1984), both set in Victoria in the last century; *The Running Girl* (London: Milton House, 1973), is set partly in Adelaide, partly in Melbourne, in the 1850s. The historical novelist, **Patricia Ainsworth**, alias of **Patricia Nina Bigg**, is an Adelaidean, born in 1932. Both *The Devil's Hole* and *Portrait in Gold* (London: Robert Hale, 1971), combine mystery fiction with informative history: the former is set in Victoria in 1877, the latter in the Victorian goldfields in the 1850s. **Kay Brownbill**'s *Blow the Wind Southerly* (Adelaide: Rigby, 1962), is a mystery novel set partly in Adelaide (1842, 1890–1891), partly in England (1961), as 'colonial shadows fall across modern lovers'. Interstate writer **Will(iam) Lawson**'s work includes stories set on the Murray River, notably *Old Man Murray* (Sydney: Angus & Robertson, 1937), and *Paddle-Wheels Away* (Sydney: F.J. Thwaites, 1947). **Michael F. Page**'s *Magpie's Island* (London: Hale, 1964), is set on an island off South Australia in 1856.

Current writers of note include **Rory Barnes**, who was born in 1946 in London and spent his childhood in various places: England, Africa, Norway and Australia. He studied philosophy at Monash University, and has worked as an academic and in pig-farming in Gippsland. Although he is a local writer principally by virtue of being currently resident in Adelaide, he may receive mention, particularly for his unconventional thriller, *The Bomb-Monger's Daughter* (Adelaide: Rigby, 1984). The more recent *Water from the Moon* (with James Birrell) (Ringwood: Penguin, 1989) is set in Indonesia. **Tess Brady**, born in Adelaide on 20 June 1948, among whose writings are *Paint Me a Murder* (Hawthorn, Vic.: Hudson, 1989), which is set in Adelaide, and features a female police detective, Senior Sergeant Kristina Petersen, who investigates the murder of a well-known painter, Benjamin Pake. **Garry Donald Disher** was born 15 August 1949 and moved to Melbourne in 1974. He was a teacher before becoming a full-time writer. After his crime story, 'Cody's Art', was included in Stephen Knight's anthology, *Crimes for a Summer Christmas* (Sydney: Allen & Unwin, 1990), he developed the popular series anti-hero, Wyatt (modelled upon Richard Stark's tough professional criminal Parker), who has appeared so far in *Kickback* (Sydney: Allen & Unwin, 1991), set in Victoria, and *Paydirt* (Sydney: Allen & Unwin, 1992), which opens in the mid-north of South Australia. **John Emery**, who was born in Cairns in 1947, then educated in South Australia (where he continues to live and work), incorporates crime into his novels, short stories and filmscripts (e.g. the 1977 production, *Backroads*). One of his short stories, 'Rape', won the 1974 Commonwealth Bank National Short Story of the Year Award. He has also published *Freedom* (Adelaide: Rigby, 1982), based on his own screenplay, which is set in Adelaide and on the Duke's Highway; *The Sky People* (Adelaide: Rigby, 1984), set in New Guinea in 1937; and the story collection, *Summer Ends Now* (St Lucia, Qld.: University of Queensland Press, 1980). **Kurt von Trojan**, born in Vienna in 1937, reflects in his fiction early experiences of life in an authoritarian state; he has settled near Adelaide. *The Transing Syndrome* (Adelaide: Rigby, 1985), a dystopian novel set in the near future, was a notable success; *Mars in Scorpio* (Adelaide: Wakefield Press, 1990), based on a prize-winning radio play, features an immigrant who wants to murder the man having an affair with his girl friend. **Jan McKemmish** was educated at The University of Adelaide; her experimental novel, *A Gap in the Records* (Melbourne: Sybylla, 1985), has been highly praised by some. It features a group of women who set up a world-wide spy ring. Her second novel, *Only Lawyers Dancing* (Sydney: Angus & Robertson, 1992), a murder mystery, is apparently derived from the real-life case of the serial rapist and murderer, 'Mr Stinky'.

Barry Westburg, born in the USA, did not begin his career as a creative writer until after he had settled in Australia, as a Senior Lecturer in English Literature at The University of Adelaide. *The Progress of Moonlight* (Sydney: Angus & Robertson, 1990), set in Chicago, is a humorous novel which includes private detection and the police violence in 1968 at the Democratic Convention.

Arthur Upfield moves Inspector Napoleon Bonaparte around the country; the early *Bushranger of the Skies* (Sydney: Angus & Robertson, 1940), a.k.a. *No Footprints in the Bush*, is set near Diamantina in the far north of South Australia; *The Battling Prophet* (London: Heinemann, 1956), is set in the south-east; *Man of Two Tribes* (Garden City, N.Y.: Doubleday, 1956), runner-up for the Crime Writers' Association award and enshrined in Geoffrey Dutton's *The Australian Collection – Australia's Greatest Books* (North Ryde, NSW: Angus & Robertson, 1985), is set on the Nullarbor Plain; and *Bony Buys a Woman* (London: Heinemann, 1957), which was chosen as Book of the Year by *Ellery Queen's Mystery Magazine*, in the Lake Eyre region; *The Lake Frome Monster* (London: Heinemann, 1966), left unfinished by the author when he died in 1964, was completed and revised by **J.L. Price** and **Mrs Dorothy Strange** (Lake Frome is fictitious). Also posthumous is *Breakaway House* (Sydney: Angus & Robertson, 1987), a romantic thriller featuring policeman Harry Tremayne. *The House of Cain* (London: Hutchinson, 1928), another invertebrate novel, is a thriller set partly in the north of the State; it features a millionaire who runs a haven for murderers. Most of the popular Carter Brown series novels are set in America but *Caress Before Killing* (Sydney: Horwitz, 1956) includes Woomera and Adelaide amongst its locations. The principal writer of the series, **Alan Geoffrey Yates** (1923–1985), has also written a spy story set in Adelaide under the pseudonym Dennis Sinclair: *The Blood Brothers* (London: Corfi, 1977).

Other novels in the group of those which are not written by South Australians but have the state as their setting include **John Clive**'s thriller about Nazis who survived the war, *Barossa* (New York: Delacorte, 1981), which is set partly in the Barossa Valley and Adelaide, in the 1970s, partly in Europe, in the 1940s. Clive was born in London in 1933 and now lives in Ireland. The lively American writer **Richard Condon** has written an international thriller, *Bandicoot* (New York: Dial Press, 1978), which includes Adelaide and Coober Pedy amongst its locations. (**Andrew Garve**'s 1969 Collins novel *Boomerang* includes Adelaide in its chase narrative, but this is only a step on the way to a nickel mine farther north.) **Jack Danvers**'s *The Living Come First* (London: Heinemann, 1961) is a thriller set in the far north, which deals with the murder of an 18–year-old girl found shot in a car and includes a black tracker. **Elizabeth Ferrars**, the prolific writer of detective stories, who was born in Rangoon (as Morna Doris MacTaggart), sets both *The Crime and the Crystal* (Sydney: Collins, 1985), and *Come and Be Killed* (Sydney: Collins, 1987), in Adelaide. Also her *The Small World of Murder* (Sydney: Collins, 1973), a suspense mystery which has amateur detective Bill Lyndon making the return air trip, London-Adelaide-London, includes the drowning of a man in the Murray on Christmas Day. One supposes she must have toured Australia more than once. **Frederick Gestäcker** (1817?–1872), whose name is variously spelt, was born in Munich and came to Australia for a year in 1851. His novel, translated as *The Two Convicts* (London: Routledge, 1857), is set on a station on the Murray River and in Adelaide. **Max Gill**, a West Australian who has lived at Woomera and Coober Pedy, is the author of *Count Down for Murder* (Sydney: Danger House, 1991), which is set in South Australia; it won first prize in the inaugural Tom Howard Mystery Novel Contest, for which there were 467 entries. **W.A. Harbinson**'s *The Gentlemen Rogues* (Sydney: Scripts, 1967) is a humorous novel which includes Adelaide, as well as Sydney, Melbourne and Wagga Wagga. **Robertson Hobart**, a pseudonym of **Norman Lee** (1905–1962), sets *Blood on the Lake* (London: Robert Hale, 1961) in northern South Australia, including the opal fields; it features the efforts of J. Earle Dixon, Adelaide insurance investigator, to locate a missing geologist. The NSW writer, **Tom Howard**, sets *Howard's Price* (Sydney: Rastar Press, 1987), in a lightly disguised University of Adelaide, where the eponymous hero, ex-cop turned thriller writer, is writer-in-residence: the campus is shattered by rape, murder and possible suicide (a combination by no means so far-fetched as it sounds). **William Hatfield**, the pseudonym of Ernest Chapman (1892–1969), who was born in Nottingham, came to Australia in 1911 and spent ten years on cattle stations in the north, wrote *Ginger Murdoch* (Sydney: Angus & Robertson, 1932), which is set in northern South Australia and south-west Queensland (the Birdsville region), and includes castle-rustling. **Ralph Hayes**, an American writer born in 1927, sets his *Opal Ridge* (New York: Nordon, 1980), in the South Australian opal fields. **André Jute** is, or has been, an Adelaide resident who was born in South Africa in 1945. His output includes *Festival* (Melbourne: Hyland House, 1982), about a Hungarian conductor who decides to defect at the Adelaide Festival of Arts. **Louis Kaye**, the pseudonym of **Noel Wilson Norman**, who was born near Hobart in 1901, did an opal-mining story, *Tightened Belts* (Wright & Brown, 1934), which includes gun-fights over claims; his *Tybal Men* (London: Wright & Brown, [1931]) is described in its foreword by **A.G. Hales** as 'the strongest, grimmest novel . . . on Australian backblock life since Marcus Clarke': it involves crooked property dealing. **Conrad H. Sayce**'s *Golden Buckles* (Melbourne: A. McCubbin, 1920), has part of its action in Adelaide and Oodnadatta; it presents a murder within a love story; **Kylie Tennant**'s *Ma Jones and the Little White Cannibals* (London: Macmillan, 1967), is an unlikely collection of interlinked stories featuring as detective a large middle-aged lady; Adelaide is amongst the various Australian settings; **Crawford Vaughan**'s *Golden Wattle Time* (Sydney: Frank Johnson, 1942), 'The Dramatic Story of Adam Lindsay Gordon' is set partly in South Australia; **Edward G. Wollaston**'s *'Ulipa': A South Australian Story* (Ballarat: E.E. Campbell, 1896) includes murder in a South Australian setting (the author perhaps hailed from Victoria); **Dick Wordley**'s *Murder Got Married* (Sydney: Invincible, ca. 1950), is set partly in Adelaide: an insurance investigator deals with the case of a middle-aged playboy who died soon after marriage to a beautiful redhead.

Unavoidably, this article has the shape of a series of lists rather than of a discussion of links between writers. South Australia seems never to have generated a 'school' of crime writers comparable to the 'Friendly Street' poets. The McGuires, for instance, are listed apart: Frances is known not to have a high opinion of the fiction of her more famous husband. I suspect that the case is similar throughout Australia, with the exception of Sydney at the present day, where South Australian Stuart Coupe is one of the integrative factors (partly through his journal *Mean Streets*).

NOTES

1. Paul Depasquale, bookseller, has written *A Critical History of South Australian Literature 1836–1930 with subjectively annotated Bibliographies* (Warradale, South Aust.: Pioneer Books, March 1978). He has also published two specialist studies in 1982, *Guy Boothby* and *Sherlock Holmes and Doctor Nikola*.

2. Paul Depasquale, *Patrick Eiffe* (Warradale: Pioneer Books, 1980).

CONTRIBUTORS

Margaret Allen teaches Women's Studies at the University of Adelaide. Her research interests include nineteenth-century South Australian women writers. She is currently working on British-American Quaker women of the late nineteenth and early twentieth centuries.

Philip Butterss teaches Australian literature and Cultural Studies at the University of Adelaide. He has published on nineteenth- and early twentieth-century Australian literature, and is co-editor (with Elizabeth Webby) of *The Penguin Book of Australian Ballads*.

Kerryn Goldsworthy grew up in rural South Australia, studied at the University of Adelaide, and is now a senior lecturer at the University of Melbourne. She has published a collection of short fiction, *North of the Moonlight Sonata*, is a former editor of *Australian Book Review*, and has edited two anthologies of Australian writing. Her current projects are a book on Helen Garner and a book about nineteenth-century women's diaries and letters.

Rick Hosking teaches English and Australian Studies at the Flinders University of South Australia. He is a fifth-generation South Australian, and is currently researching South Australian contact narratives. He has published widely on Australian and postcolonial literature.

Susan Hosking is a lecturer in the English department at the University of Adelaide. Her particular interests are contemporary Australian fiction, and literature which reflects the interaction of Aboriginal and non-Aboriginal cultures. Her publications include articles on Katharine Susannah Prichard, Mudrooroo and Archie Weller. Recently she co-edited *Hope and Fear: An Anthology of South Australian Women's*

Writing 1894–1994, celebrating the centenary of women's suffrage in this state.

Lyn Jacobs is a senior lecturer in English and Australian Studies at the Flinders University of South Australia where she convenes topics in Australian contemporary fiction, Australian poetry and Australian studies. She is vice-president of the International Australian Studies Association, and has published articles and reviews, and edited essays on Australian writing, and is currently completing a bibliography of Australian literary responses to Asia.

Susan Magarey is director of the Research Centre for Women's Studies at the University of Adelaide, editor of *Australian Feminist Studies*, and author of the prize-winning monograph *Unbridling the Tongues of Women: A Biography of Catherine Helen Spence*.

Brian Matthews holds a personal chair in English at Flinders University, and is currently director of the Menzies Centre for Australian Studies in London. He is the author of fiction and non-fiction including the multi-award winning biography, *Louisa*; *Quickening and Other Stories*; *Oval Dreams: Larrikin Essays on Sport and Low Culture*; and (jointly with Peter Goldsworthy on whom he writes in this volume), a novel, *Magpie*. He has also written extensively for radio and has published widely in academic and popular journals on Australian and British literature, sport and popular culture.

Robert Sellick is a senior lecturer in the English department at the University of Adelaide where he teaches Australian literature. He has published widely on Australian and postcolonial topics, and is currently editing the journals of the explorer, Ludwig Leichhardt.

David Smith teaches English at the University of Adelaide. He has published on left-wing writers, nineteenth-century fiction and modern drama. He is currently exploring the use of space in late nineteenth-century writing.

Andrew Taylor is Professor of English at Edith Cowan University, Western Australia, and previously taught for many years at the University of Adelaide. He is the author of the critical study, *Reading Australian*

Poetry, and also of numerous books of poetry. His most recent collection is *Sandstone* (UQP, 1995). He has also published widely on American and Australian literature.

Michael J. Tolley is an associate professor in the English department at the University of Adelaide. He is a William Blake scholar and editor of Blake's illustrations for Edward Young's *Night Thoughts*. He is also a bibliographer of crime in Australasian fiction (forthcoming from The Borgo Press); publisher-editor of *The Body Dabbler*, a journal on crime fiction; series editor of the Wakefield Crime Classics; and has published many reviews of crime fiction and science fiction.

Barbara Wall completed an MA at the University of Adelaide in 1950, was Senior English Mistress at Woodlands Girls Grammar School until 1981, and was awarded a PhD from Flinders in 1988. Her *The Narrator's Voice: The Dilemma of Children's Fiction* won the book award of the Children's Literature Association (USA) for an outstanding contribution to the history, scholarship and criticism of children's literature. Her latest book, *Our Own Matilda* (Wakefield, 1994), examines the life and work of Matilda Evans.

INDEX OF NAMES

Wakefield Press

Wakefield Press has been publishing good Australian books for over fifty years. For a catalogue of current and forthcoming titles, or to add your name to our mailing list, send your name and address to Wakefield Press, Box 2266, Kent Town, South Australia 5071.

TELEPHONE (08) 362 8800   FAX (08) 362 7592

Wakefield Press thanks Wirra Wirra Vineyards for its support.